NYC STREET VENDORS

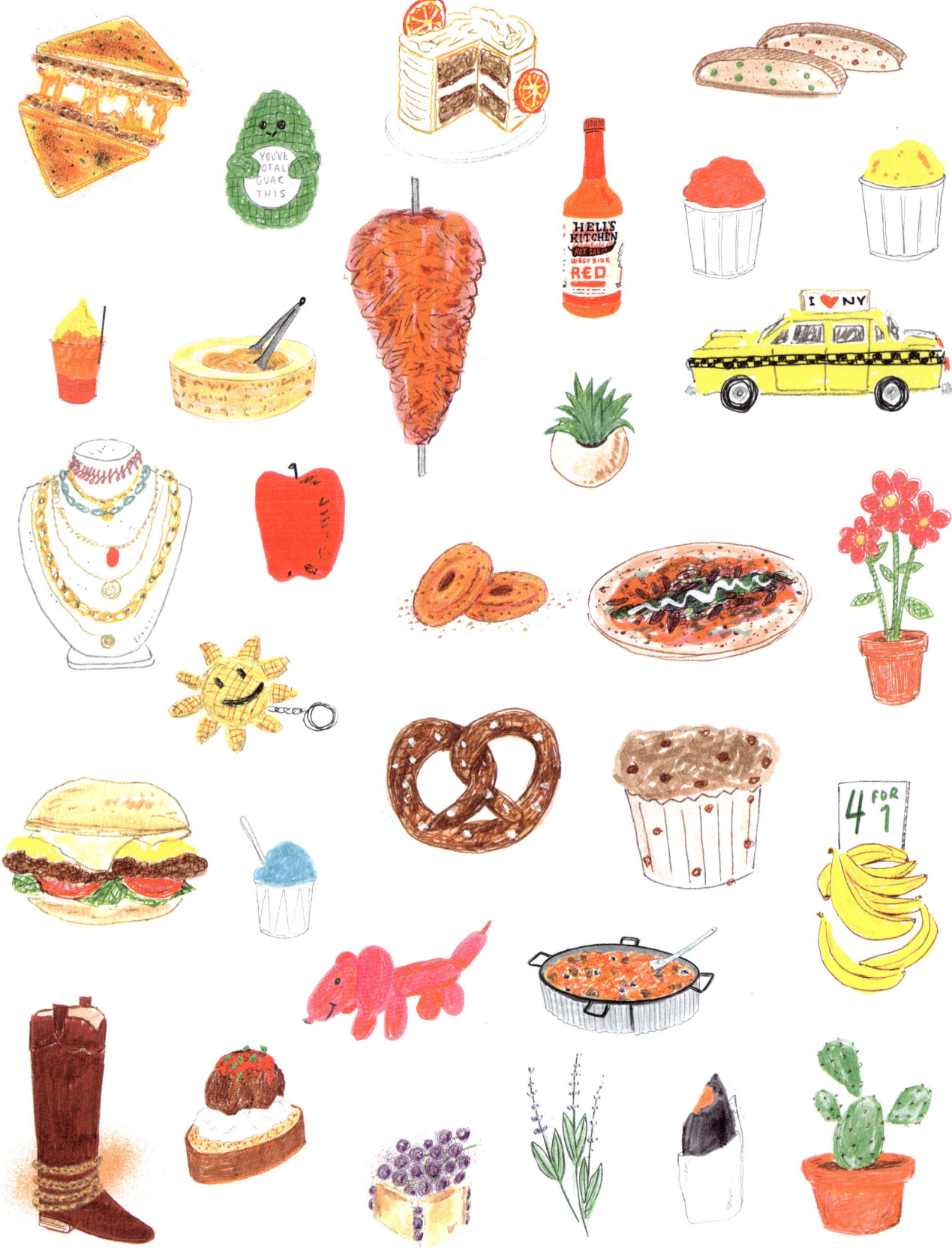

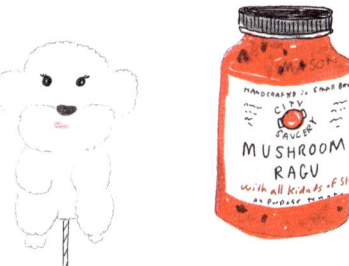

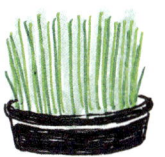
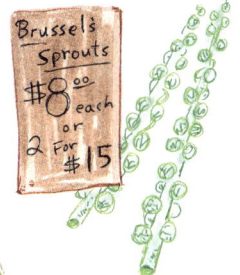
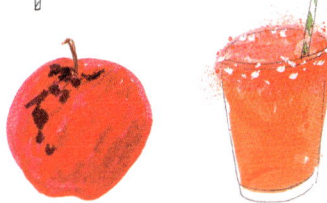
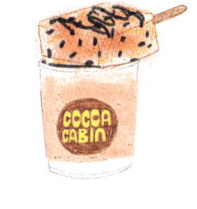
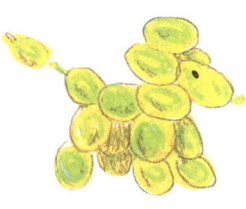
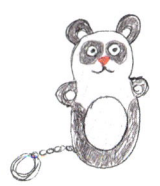
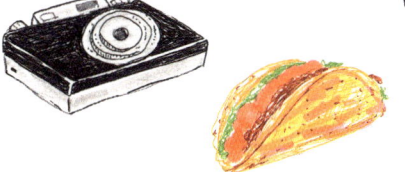
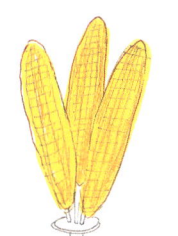
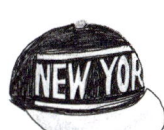
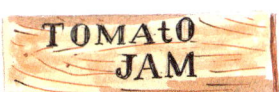
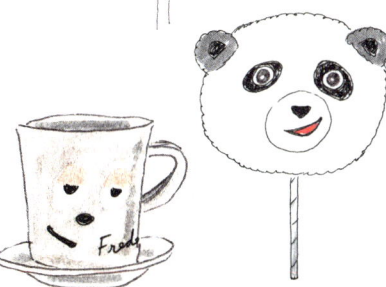
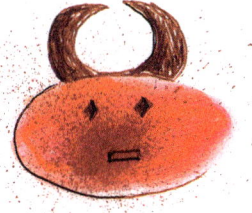
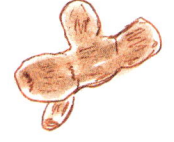
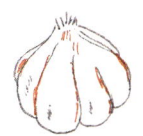
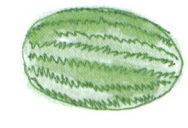
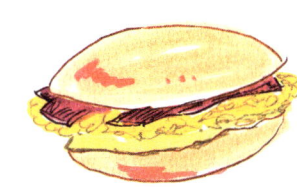
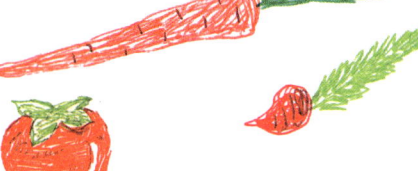

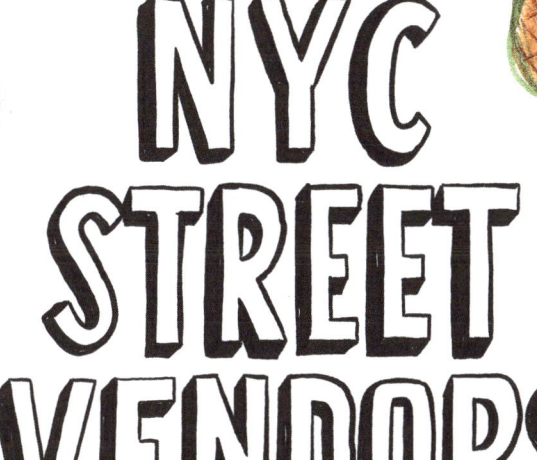

NYC STREET VENDORS

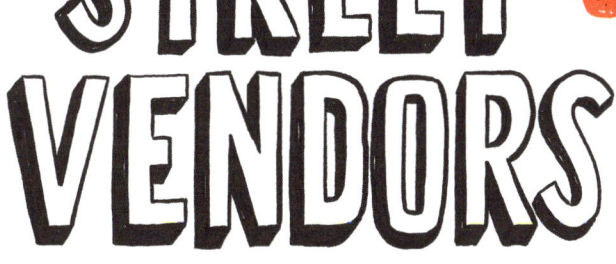

Food Trucks, Coffee Carts, Market Stalls, and More

JOEL HOLLAND

words by

DAVID DODGE

foreword by
JAEKI CHO
of
RIGHTEOUS EATS

PRESTEL
Munich • London • New York

CONTENTS

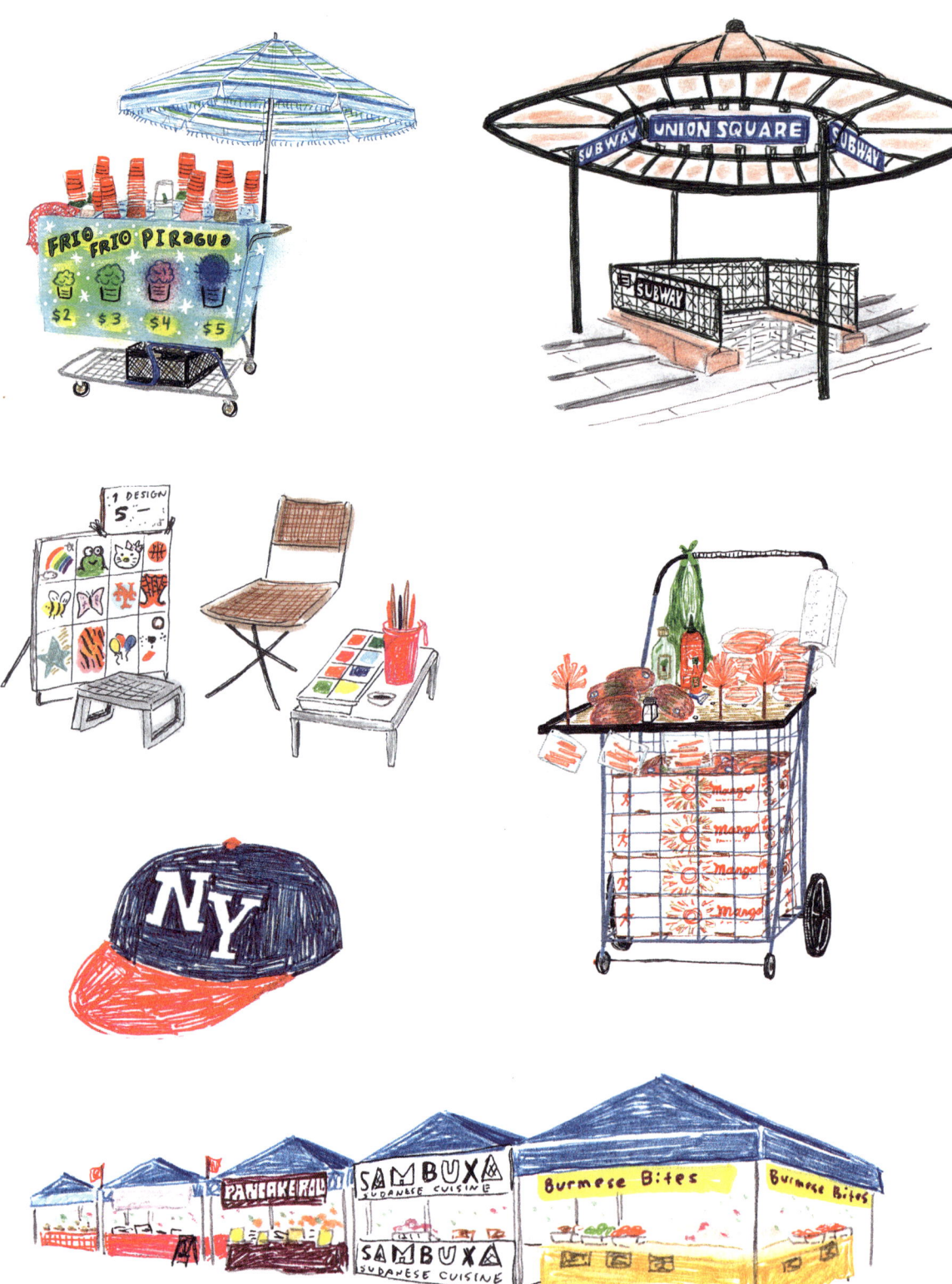

FOREWORD
~

Yo, when did it start, this thing called vending in the streets? Before sushi became omakase, it was Edo-period street food: hand-pressed nigiri, eaten standing up. The hot dog? A German import, reinvented in Coney Island, later a NYC staple slung by Greeks, Eastern Europeans, then Egyptians, Afghans, Bangladeshis. Knishes were hawked on pushcarts by Ashkenazi Jews in the early 1900s. Italian ices, rooted in Sicilian granita, evolved into an essential part of New York summers—first sold by Italians and later remixed by Puerto Rican, Dominican, and now Central American vendors. Lately I've seen arepas and patacón sandwich carts popping up under the 7 train, thanks to Venezuelan migration.

Street vending is older than "branding." Older than social media. It's survival. Proof of concept. A side hustle turned family legacy, a dream on wheels . . . or under a sombrero.

I grew up in Queens—Sunnyside, Elmhurst, Corona, Flushing. This was my tasting menu. Halal carts on Seventy-Third and Broadway, in Jackson Heights, feeding the city's take on chicken and rice before it was famous. Mangoes with Tajín in Ziplocs. Nuts 4 Nuts crackling in winter air. Mister Softee's jingle echoing down my block in '98, my first summer in America. Flushing's lamb-skewer carts, once a portal to Xinjiang, now mostly gone from Main Street.

What I didn't know then—and only learned through running my social media platform Righteous Eats, which champions New York's diverse food scene—is how much heart, hustle, and hardship lives inside each cart. These are the owners of the city's smallest businesses. Many work without safety nets. Still, they show up. Rain, heat, headlines.

The King of Falafel & Shawarma shimmying on the corner. Dosa Man slinging Pondicherry crepes in Washington Square. Evelia's Tamales rising from a shopping cart to a brick and mortar. Nansense flipping Afghan smash burgers from a mail truck.

Mike's Hot Honey launched from a red trike. Birria-Landia turning Jackson Heights into a Coatzingo side street after dark. Arepa Lady lighting up Roosevelt Ave. Jamrock Jerk blessing NYC with its smoke. A-Pou's dumplings that taste like someone's grandma still approves.

These aren't hobbies. They're full-time, full-soul operations.

But laws haven't caught up. Permits are capped, and many get rented on the gray market for tens of thousands. Vendors are ticketed, harassed, shut down. Corona Plaza—once a grassroots haven of Latin American street food—was dulled by strict new legal constraints in 2023, because the system never built a way to support both vendors and neighbors.

Still, vendors rise. At Queens Night Market. At Bronx Night Market. At Smorgasburg. At Union Square Greenmarket. These aren't just food fairs—they're test kitchens, stages, launchpads.

NYC Street Vendors is a love letter to the sidewalk soul of New York. Joel Holland's illustrations bring the energy, and David Dodge breaks down vendors' tales with respect. From churro sellers in subway stations to NYPL's Bookmobile. From Quick Phone Repair to Common Books. From Tong's fuchkas to the Park Poet. So next time you grab a taco from El Rey del Taco or sambusas from Makina . . . ask the person's name. Tip like you're investing. Because you are.

Street vending is New York. It's tongs on a grill. The sizzle of ambition. The scent of your childhood—even if you just got here yesterday. Support it. Advocate for it. Maybe even bring your dream to the block. Aight, peace and blessings.

Jaeki Cho is the cofounder of Righteous Eats, a media platform turned nonprofit that champions New York's immigrant-run food businesses and advocates for the people behind the plate. When he's not documenting the flavors of the city, he's running off the calories or traveling the globe in search of stories shaped by migration, memory, and the rise of third-culture identities.

INTRODUCTION

~

The work ethic of New Yorkers is an integral part of the city's identity. Yet even in the Big Apple, a place known for its ambitious residents, from aspiring Broadway performers to sleepless Wall Street traders, you will find no harder workers than street vendors.

This book builds upon our first two collaborations, *NYC Storefronts* and *Brooklyn Storefronts*, which explored brick-and-mortar shops in Manhattan and Brooklyn, respectively. For our third book about our home city, we are thrilled to turn our attention to mobile vendors—the smallest of New York's small businesses—throughout all five boroughs.

In these pages, we'll introduce you to the proprietors behind some of the city's famed street vending operations. You'll meet Casee "Amadeo" Falce, a military veteran and founder of Blue Dove Coffee (p. 110), who wakes up every morning at 2:30 to set up his cart in Manhattan's Union Square for the morning rush hour. You'll read about Makayla Wray, who outfitted an old nut-roasting cart with sewing machines to offer curbside tailoring services during the COVID-19 pandemic (p. 94). You'll learn about Andrés Baffigo, a prodemocracy advocate forced to flee his native Venezuela, who now owns Canaima Food Truck, based in Williamsburg, Brooklyn (p. 135).

Mobile vendors have long been a vital part of the area's economy and culture, dating back to when the Lenape and neighboring tribes traded goods on the island they called Manahatta. During the 1600s Dutch and English settlers—the city's original immigrants—began selling food and goods in open-air markets here as well. By the nineteenth and early twentieth centuries, more waves of newcomers from across the world began selling things like knishes, baked potatoes, pretzels, apples, newspapers, peanuts, shoe shines, ice cream, hot dogs, and everything in between on the city's streets.

Today, according to a survey conducted by the Immigration Research Initiative, there are roughly 23,000 street vendors in New York. About 96 percent are immigrants, and they hail from more than 60 different countries. In their daily work they introduce other New Yorkers to their native countries, cultures, and cuisines, and they take joy in doing so—95 percent reported that they love what they do.

While the story of New York's street vendors is primarily one of determination and ingenuity, it is also one of overpolicing, harassment, and regulation. In 1983 the city implemented a permitting system for mobile businesses, capping the total number allowed to operate at just 3,000, which has since been raised to 4,450. The vast majority of the 23,000 New Yorkers making their living as street vendors, then, have been forced to do so in the shadows for decades, often leading to tickets, arrests, and even violence.

Organizations such as the Street Vendor Project (SVP), a community-based group with almost 3,000 members, advocate for more permits and better working conditions to help these vendors attain the legitimacy and dignity that they so rightfully deserve. For example, after the city shut down a popular informal outdoor market in Queens's Corona Plaza (p. 146) in 2023, SVP worked with the vendors to win special permits to continue to operate—though at a much-reduced footprint. Still, it represents a rare concession from the city in the ongoing effort to bring legitimacy to street vendors.

No New Yorker could imagine a city without our street vendors. We stand in long lines for our morning coffee and bagel, flock to outdoor markets, and trek to the city's outskirts to sample the latest in-demand street food. So, next time you find yourself deciding between your favorite halal cart and taco stand for lunch, we hope this book inspires you to appreciate the city's street vendors a bit more, and to thank them for providing something most other places cannot—an ability to globetrot by simply taking a quick stroll down the block.

—David Dodge and Joel Holland

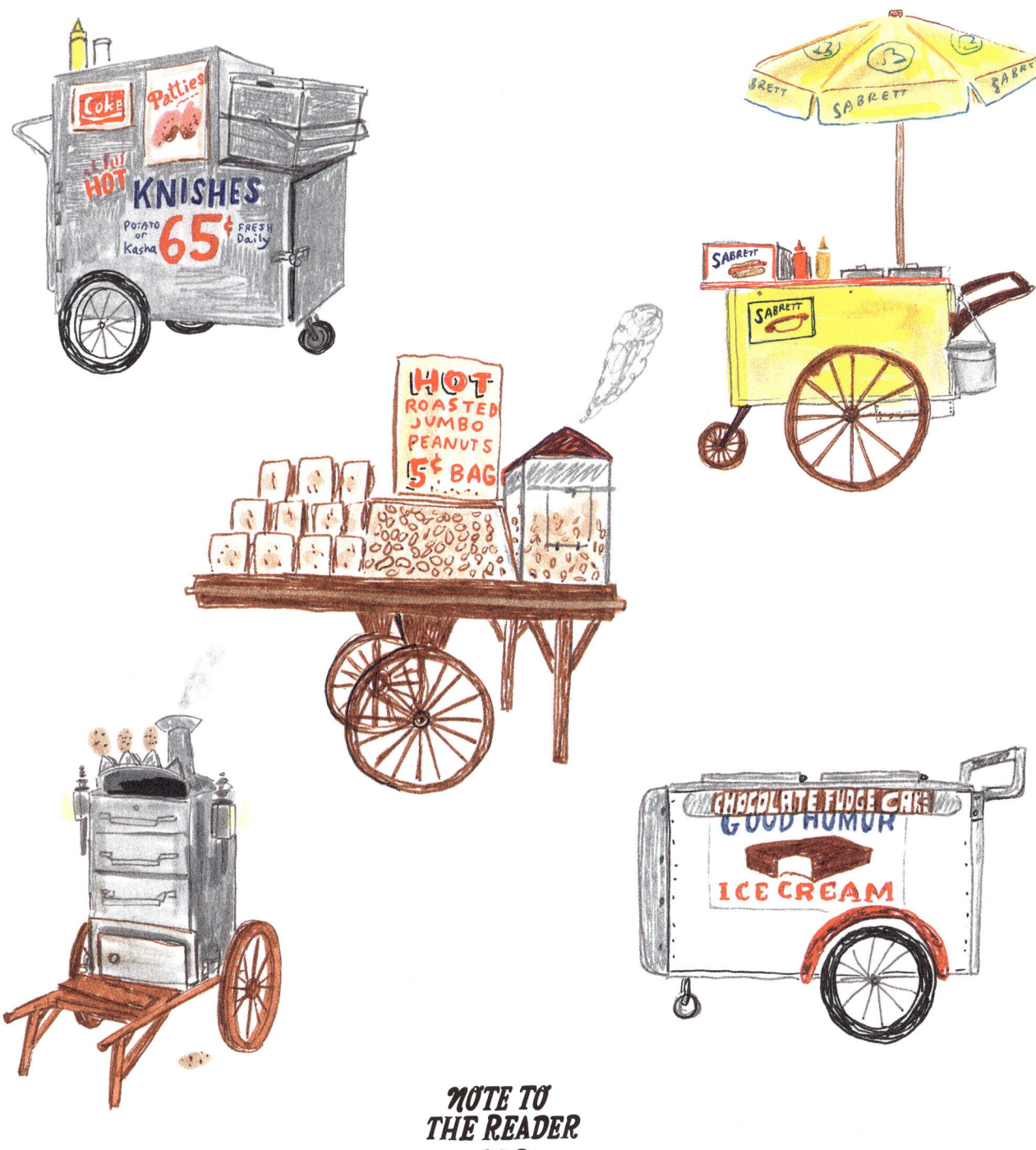

NOTE TO THE READER

New York is known for many things—among them, constant change. Care has been taken to provide current names, locations, and descriptions for the trucks, carts, and people in this book, but by nature these vendors are mobile. Not only are they frequently moving around the city, they're often adapting, expanding, or reimagining what they do. Please check online for up-to-date information (the index at the back of this book lists websites and social media accounts, when available).

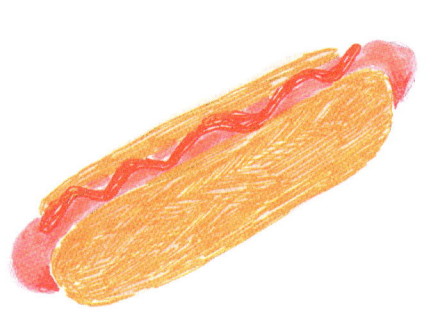

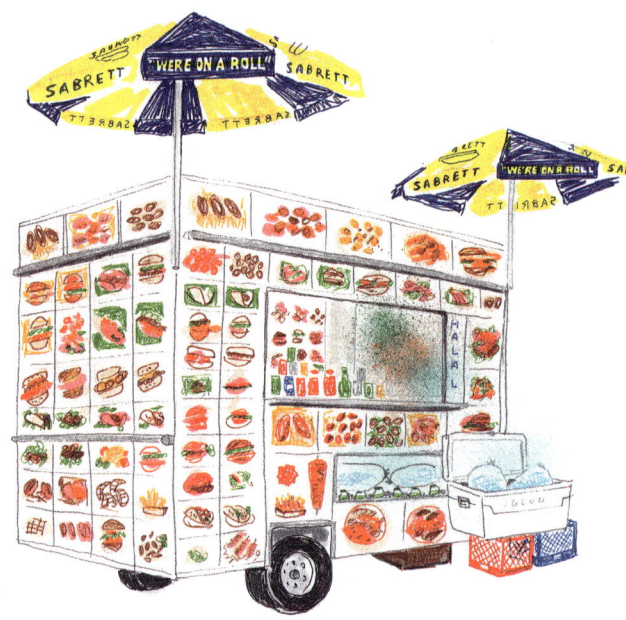

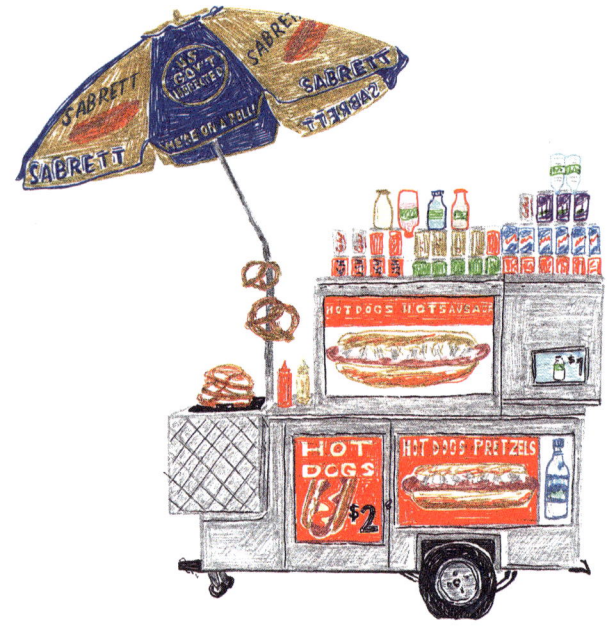

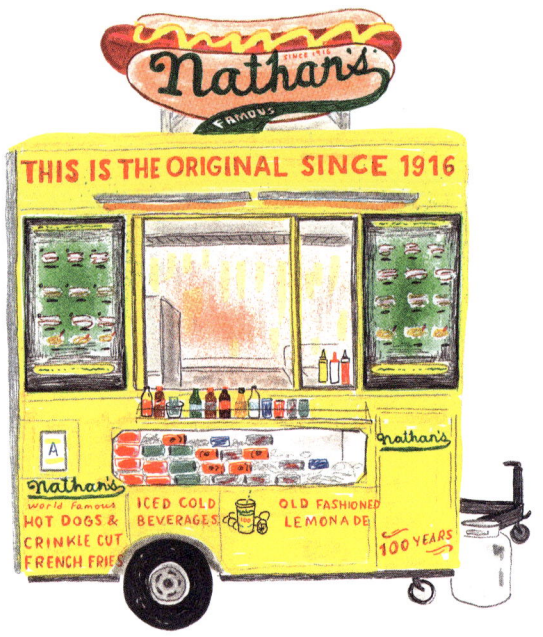

Hot Dog Vendors

In New York City street food offerings come and go over the years—but throughout it all, there's remained at least one constant: the iconic hot dog, traditionally served with spicy mustard, sauerkraut, and onion sauce.

The hot dog's domination of the Big Apple's street food scene has its roots in the 1860s, aided in part by a wave of Central and Eastern European immigrants who brought their beloved schnitzels and wieners along with them. Charles Feltman, a German pushcart vendor in Brooklyn's Coney Island, was arguably the first to turn the hot dog into the street food we know and love today. His innovation? Placing the wiener inside a bun, finally freeing it from the shackles of forks and knives. His dogs were such a hit with Coney Island beachgoers that the business eventually transformed into Feltman's Ocean Pavilion, a now-defunct restaurant that once occupied an entire city block during the 1920s, selling forty thousand hot dogs a day.

Nathan Handwerker, a Polish immigrant who worked as a bread slicer at Feltman's, helped the hot dog reach new heights. In 1916 he and his wife, Ida, left the business to start their own small hot dog stand on Surf and Stillwell Avenues in Coney Island, thus returning the hot dog to its street vending roots. Ida's secret spicy recipe helped make the business a success, as did their price point (while a Feltman dog would set you back a dime, Nathan and Ida sold theirs for a cool nickel). Today Nathan's hot dogs can be found at street carts in every borough of New York City, as well as in grocery stores, restaurants, and stadiums the world over.

The New York hot dog vendor has withstood the test of time, even amid stiff competition from gourmet food trucks that have firmly taken hold of the street food scene.

Hot dog carts, however, are more than just another type of food vendor—like yellow cabs and jaywalkers, they are a permanent and cherished part of the city's fabric.

Birria-Landia

Prior to this food truck venture, brothers José and Jesús Moreno, originally from Coatzingo in Puebla, Mexico, had dabbled mostly in Italian cuisine, working in well-known New York eateries including Lupa, Parm, and Del Posto. While helping to build out the Los Angeles location of Eataly, the popular Italian marketplace that got its start in New York, José fell in love with Tijuana-style birria de res—slow-cooked beef marinated in adobo sauce. Soon after, in 2019, the brothers launched Birria-Landia in Jackson Heights, Queens.

The truck offers four main items: tacos, tostadas, mulitas (melted cheese and birria between two tortillas), and consommé (a flavorful broth made from the birria's cooking juices). While Birria-Landia was originally a neighborhood spot frequented mostly by locals, word quickly got out; some patrons write in online reviews about waiting a half hour in line, or more, for a chance to sample some authentic birria. Soon the brothers began buying additional trucks, parking them in new locations, including in Williamsburg, Brooklyn, and the Lower East Side in Manhattan.

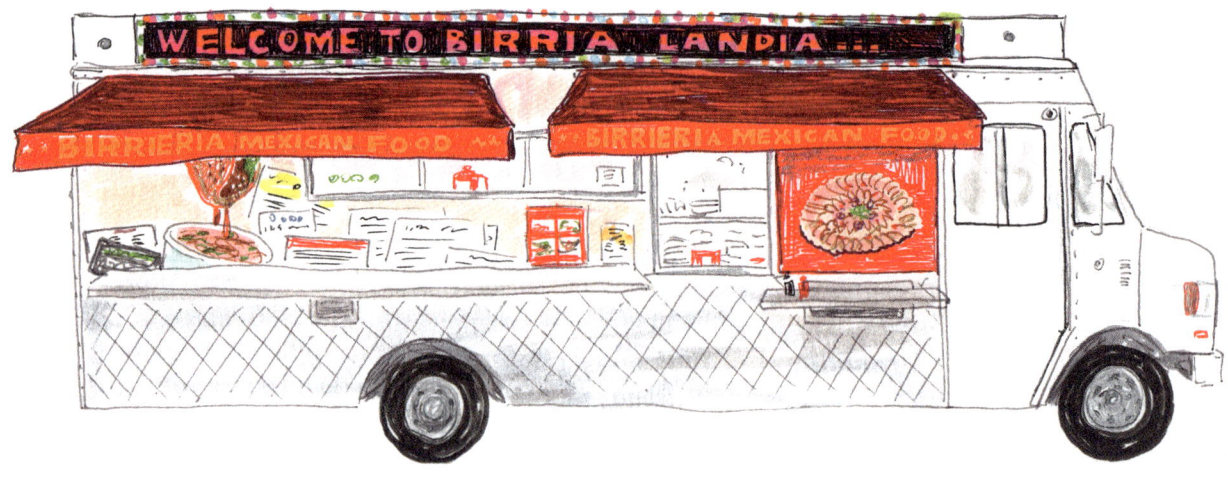

Jamrock Jerk

Magnus and Anthyne McKellar, pioneering street food vendors originally from Jamaica, started this venture in 2016 with an aim to provide customers with an authentic jerk experience. At first both had their sights set on other goals—Magnus was on his way to becoming an assistant train conductor on the Long Island Rail Road, while Anthyne was pursuing a degree to become a registered nurse. When their food cart took off, however, they decided to commit themselves to the jerk business full time.

Notably, Jamrock Jerk has the distinction of being the city's first legally permitted mobile cart equipped with the necessary grills and smokers to produce genuine Jamaican jerk cuisine. Unlike some street vendors who prefer to keep operations to a few recognizable areas, you can also find Jamrock Jerk's carts all over the city—from the Bronx's Little Italy to Forest Hills in Queens.

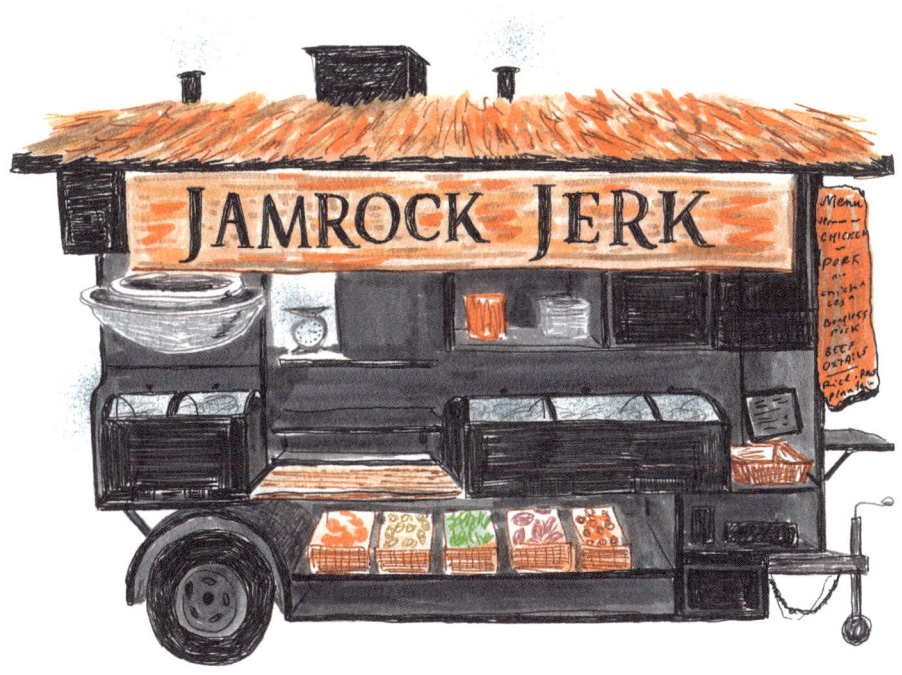

NY Dosas

Known as the Dosa Man, Thiru Kumar, a native of Jaffna, Sri Lanka, owns and operates this food cart—which for his many regulars is as synonymous with Manhattan's Washington Square Park as the iconic arch or fountain. Spurred by his home country's civil war, Thiru first immigrated to New York with his family in 1995 after winning the Green Card Lottery. When he first arrived, he took on construction jobs, pumped gas, and worked in an iron factory.

Thiru was inspired to start his cart while helping a friend at a dosa restaurant in Flushing, Queens. He set up shop at his now-trademark spot at 50 Washington Square South in 2001 and has served South Indian vegan food to hungry Greenwich Village residents, NYU students, and the park's typical cast of kooky characters ever since. In 2007 he was honored with the prestigious Vendy Award, organized by the Street Vendor Project.

Thiru's food has always been vegan, putting him well ahead of the current plant-based craze that's taken hold in the city.

His menu, inspired by his grandmother's cooking, includes a variety of dosas—fermented crepes made from rice and lentils and stuffed with various fillings—which he always serves with a dollop of chutney and a side of lentil stew. He's best known for the Special Pondicherry, a dosa filled with spiced potatoes and a mixture of fresh vegetables. Though it was his invention, word of the dish spread, and now Pondicherry appears on menus back in Sri Lanka.

Thiru's cart has gained fame far beyond Greenwich Village, with daily visitors from around the globe standing in line for a chance to sample his food. After ordering, it's not uncommon to see tourists ask for selfies with the famous Dosa Man—a request he's happy to oblige. When cooking, "my grandmother told me you have to put a lot of love into it," he told *VICE*'s YouTube channel, Munchies, in 2020—which is what he plans to do for "as long as I have energy."

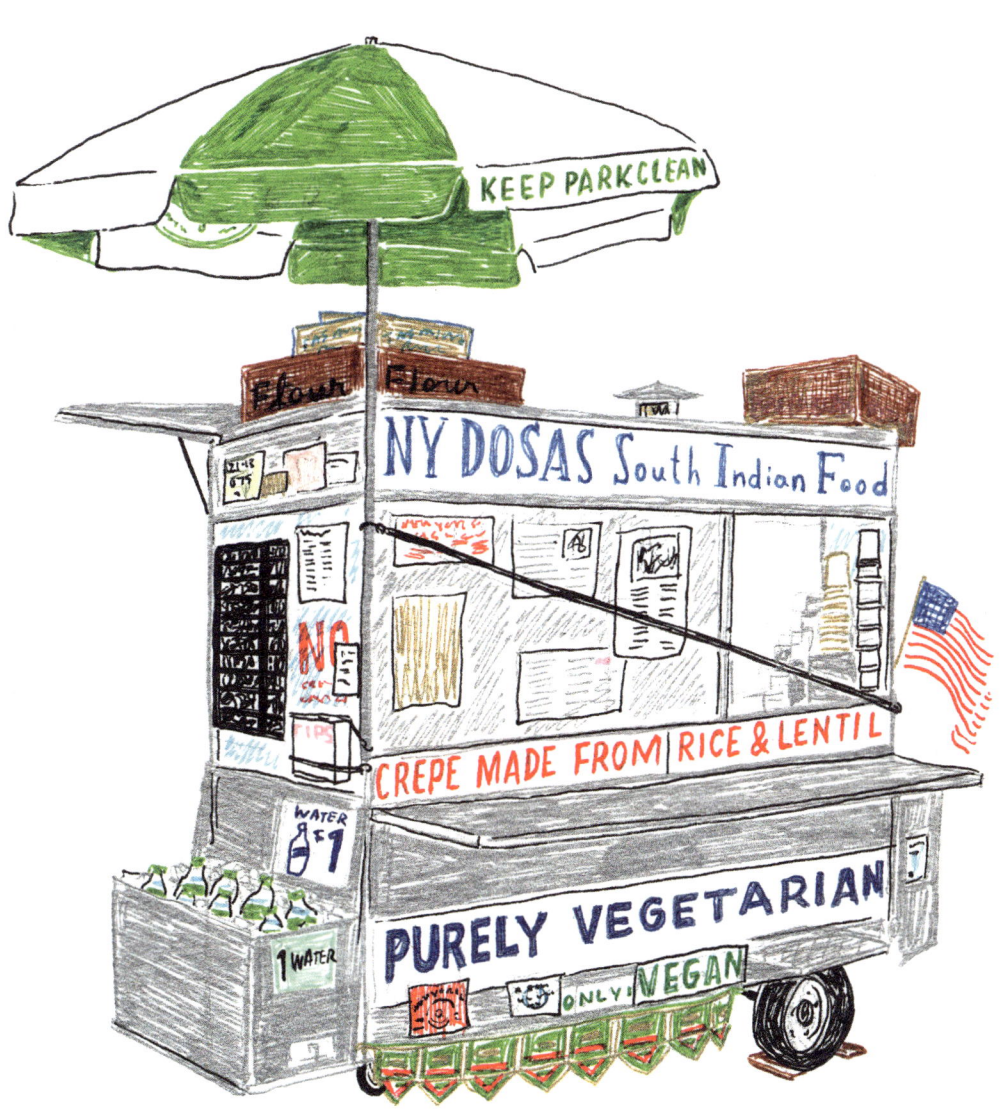

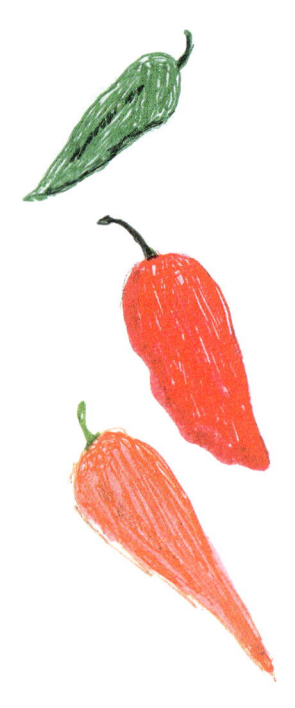

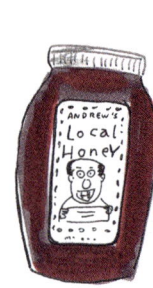

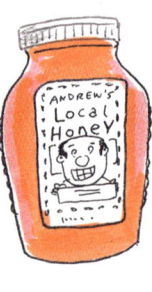

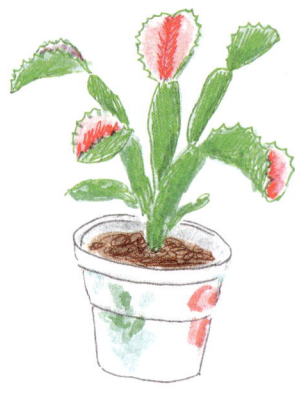

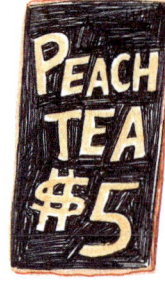

PEACH
TEA
$5

Union Square
Greenmarket

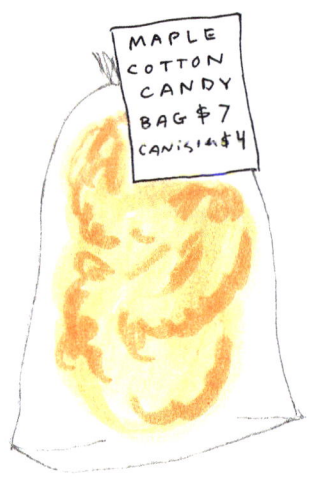

MAPLE
COTTON
CANDY
BAG $7
CANISTER $4

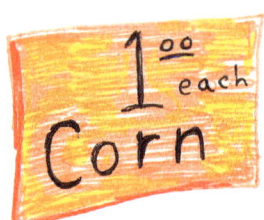

1⁰⁰ each
Corn

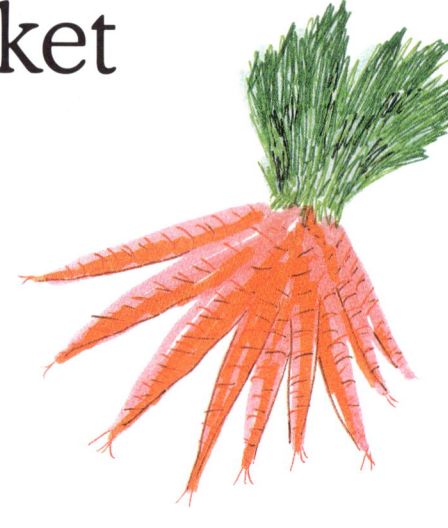

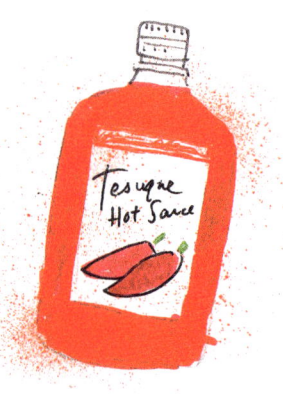

Tesuque
Hot Sauce

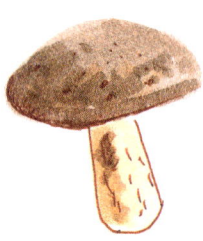

Need some kohlrabi for your winter stew, or a carnivorous plant to protect your apartment from pesky insects? Since 1976 New Yorkers have flocked to the Union Square Greenmarket for these rare finds, along with more common offerings, including other local vegetables, fruit, bread, flowers, cheese, honey, and more. At Beth's Farm Kitchen, for example, you can peruse through a colorful selection of jams, chutneys, and pickles. A couple stalls away, pick up some freshly foraged fungi at Bulich Mushroom Farm. Before you leave, be sure to treat yourself to a cup of apple cider (and maybe a donut?) from Red Jacket Orchards.

When the Union Square Greenmarket first opened as part of a visionary project by the nonprofit organization GrowNYC, it was one of the only places for New Yorkers to buy produce directly from local farmers and bakers. Ideally, founder Barry Benepe would like this type of collaboration to become the norm, rather than the exception. "I would like to see all the stores sell food directly from the farmers," he told GrowNYC in 2016 for an article in their series Greenmarket 40 for 40 on Medium. "I want to see the Greenmarket go out of business because all the stores go local."

Until then GrowNYC (true to its name!) will continue to grow—rapidly; today the organization operates forty-eight greenmarkets spread throughout all five boroughs. Still, the one at Union Square, located in the heart of Lower Manhattan, remains the biggest and most popular in the city.

Over one hundred forty farmers, fishers, bakers, artisans, and others set up shop there every week during one of the four days it's open year-round, and more than sixty thousand people visit each day.

Restaurateur Danny Meyer has even credited the market with his decision to open two of his best-known eateries, Gramercy Tavern and Union Square Cafe, nearby. "If the Union Square farmers' market were to close, I may as well not even have restaurants," he told *New York* magazine in a 2003 interview.

Lani's Farm

Lani's Farm, a family-owned enterprise based in New Jersey, is a beloved fixture at the Union Square Greenmarket and known for its impressive variety of produce. You will certainly find your traditional potatoes, tomatoes, and herbs here, all grown using organic and sustainable practices. But even the most seasoned chef will be introduced to something new at this stall—that is, unless you regularly cook with ingredients like baby tatsoi, ruby streaks mustard, or red veined sorrel.

Among its most unique offerings are an impressive variety of carnivorous plants. Eugenia, who works at the farm, got the idea to begin selling the insect-eaters at the stall from her son, who has been growing them for decades. The business offers eight different varieties, including temperate sundew, Mexican butterwort, the tropical pitcher plant, as well as the classic venus flytrap. Not sure which is the best flesh-eating flora for you? Stop by to explore your options with Eugenia. As she promised in a social media post, there's a "carnivorous plant for everybody."

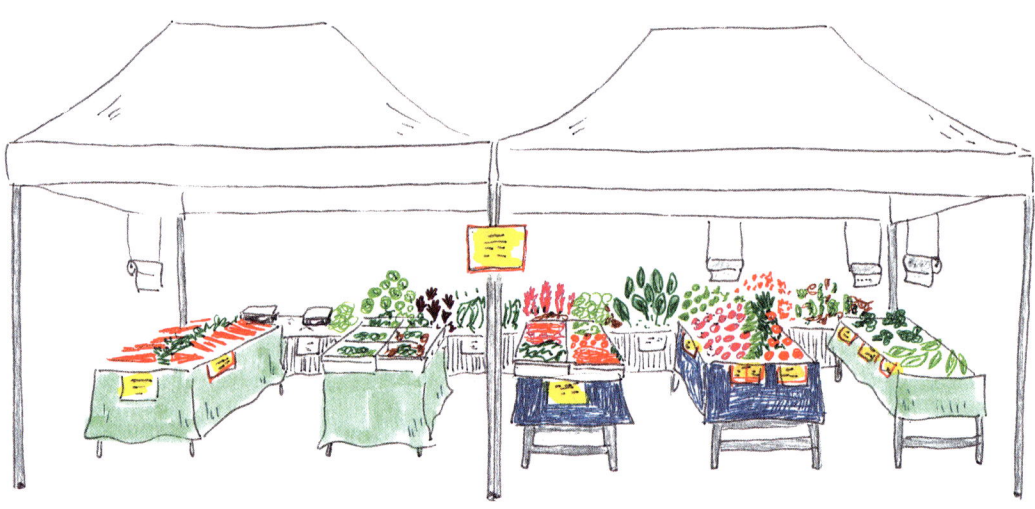

Springs Fireplace

———

Greg Kessler and Lauren Jarvis were inspired to start this hot pepper and salsa company in 2022 following their extensive travels around the globe. "We want to teach people about where these foods come from," they explain on their website. "Food can transport us through taste."

The couple started growing peppers on their East Hampton farm, sourcing them from all over the world. Most of their offerings are difficult to find in the northeastern United States. They make Tesuque, their most popular hot sauce, with peppers from an area outside of Santa Fe, New Mexico; locals have cultivated the pepper there for over three centuries. For fire-breathing enthusiasts, their hottest sauce is Aji Peach, which is made from Aleppo peppers from Syria and ají límon peppers from Peru. A relatively new addition to the Union Square Greenmarket, Springs Fireplace products can also be found in dozens of other markets and independent stores across New York and even some spots outside the region, like Minneapolis and Los Angeles.

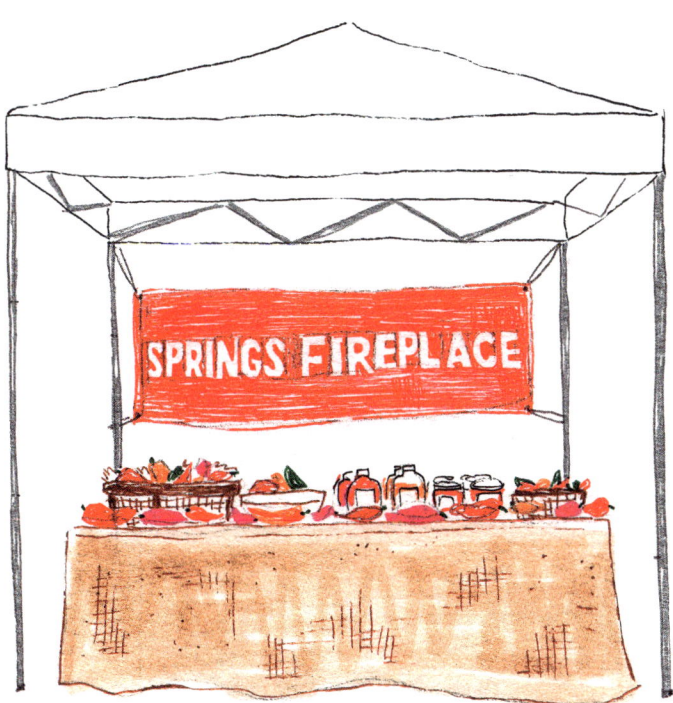

Andrew's Honey

It's hard to miss this colorful honey vendor when they set up in Union Square—which is for the best, since they have an active beehive on-site. The family-run business stretches back to the 1800s and is run today by Andrew Coté, a fourth-generation apiarist. At his stall customers can pick up a basic jar of honey or opt for one of his more unusual blends, which include flavors like orange blossom, turmeric, and matcha.

Andrew has a passion for urban beekeeping and maintains hives in every borough in the city, allowing patrons to source their honey as hyperlocally as they'd like. Upper East Side socialites can purchase a pot for their next charcuterie board from the prestigious Central Park apiary, for instance, while Brooklyn hipsters may prefer the easy vibes of the Bushwick hives, located just across the street from the White Castle at the Myrtle-Wyckoff subway station. Aspiring beekeepers can get in on the buzz, too, by purchasing Andrew's at-home apiary kits that consist of three pounds of honeybees (with their queen, of course). His mission extends even beyond New York City: Bees Without Borders, a nonprofit he founded, helps train beekeepers in countries across the globe.

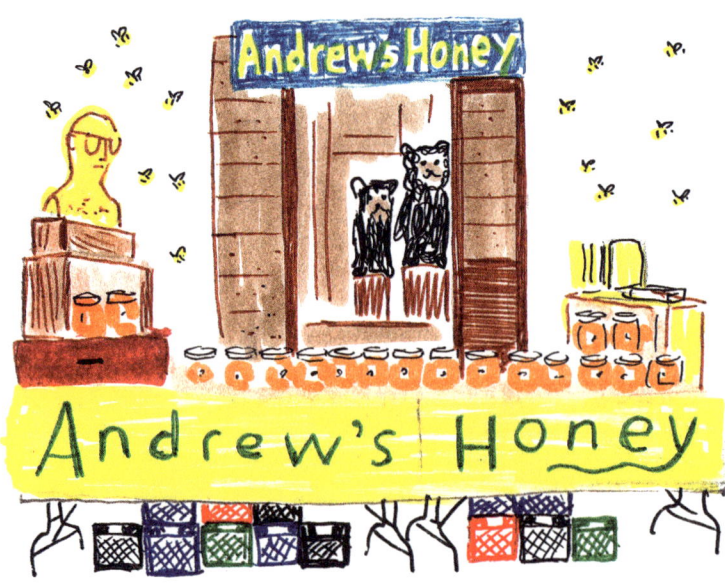

Mushroom Queens

Well before he and his brother, Jeff, started their fungi-focused farm based in Queens' Ozone Park neighborhood, Adam Novzen was growing mushrooms in his apartment, turning his absentee roommate's space into a makeshift factory. In the spring of 2020—when cultivating produce at home took off in a major way due to the COVID-19 pandemic—the brothers decided to assist fellow fanatics interested in growing their own mushrooms. From their newly established farm, these fun guys (get it?) crafted DIY kits to help others, according to their website, "bring the flavors and textures of fresh mushrooms into their homes."

Today Mushroom Queens also reigns supreme with its stalls, selling mushrooms and fungi-based tinctures at farmers markets around the city, including those at Union Square and Tompkins Square Park in Manhattan, and at Forest Hills in Queens. At these markets amateur growers can also choose from different kits that produce lion's mane, oyster, chestnut, and other varietals. Fortunately, according to the brothers, even if you don't have much of a green thumb (or fungi finger?) you can still be successful with these kits—they contain all you'll need to start your own mushroom kingdom.

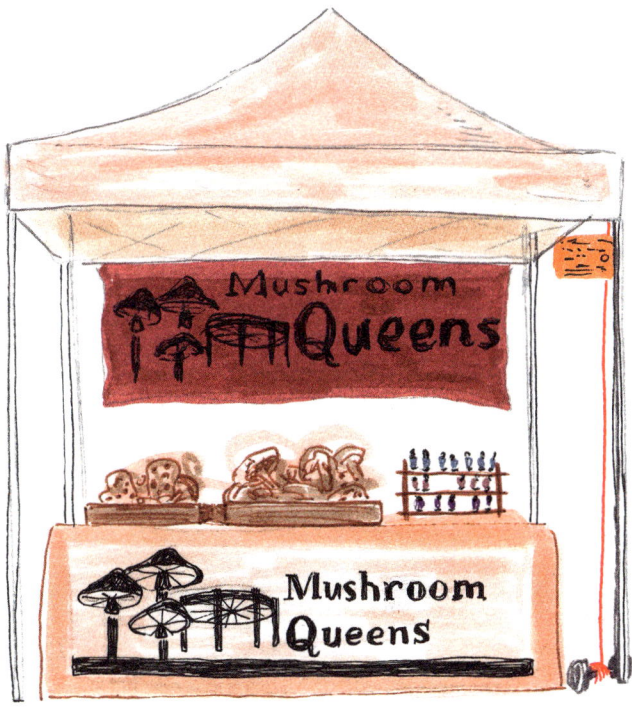

Sigmund's Pretzels

Professional chef Lina Kulchinsky started the iconic Sigmund's Pretzels in 2009, which Martha Stewart once deemed "the very best soft pretzels in the United States." Sigmund's carts have become a regular presence at festivals and outdoor markets like Madison Square Eats and Oktoberfest NYC, plus many other events, public and private. Today Lina's baked goods are on the menu of over fifty bars in the city and sold at Sigmund's sister restaurant, Debbie's Burgers in Bushwick, Brooklyn. You can also find them online and in stores across the country.

The design of Sigmund's pretzel cart is a throwback to an earlier era of street vending—a vintage, old-timey feel that comes in several colors, including white and gray. However, if you spot a pretzel cart at a fancy wedding or private event, you may not even know it comes from Sigmund's: For a few thousand dollars, you can have the cart custom branded however you'd like.

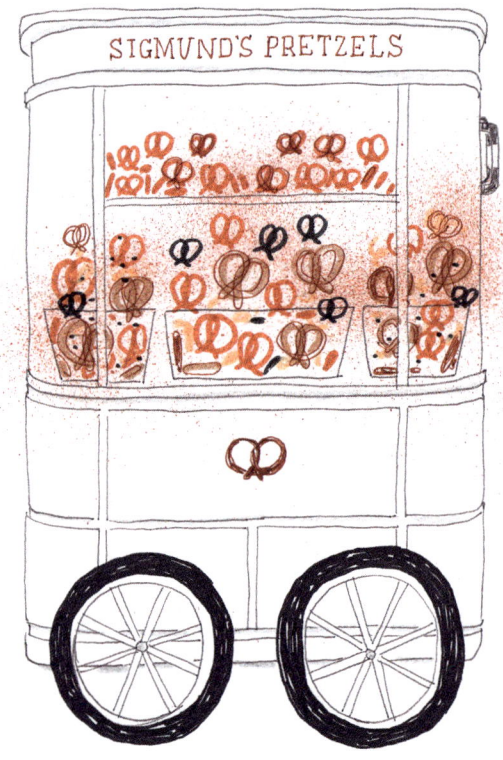

The Mudtruck

MUD has been an integral part of the city's coffee scene since Greg Northrop and Nina Berott founded the business in 2000. The couple helped jumpstart the now-crowded specialty-coffee truck trend by eschewing a traditional brick-and-mortar space and bringing unique and high-end blends straight to New York's streets.

For years the company's bright orange truck was just as much of a landmark in Manhattan's Astor Place as artist Tony Rosenthal's *Alamo* (better known to locals as "that spinning black cube sculpture thing"). In 2015 Greg and Nina shut down the truck—preferring instead to focus on their East Village café, Mudspot, which they had opened in 2003. But their website still includes a page where they "keep on truckin,'" featuring photos of their mobile beginnings. MUD also now has a strong retail presence online, selling its coffee and merchandise (most of which, yes, is bright orange) to its devoted regulars.

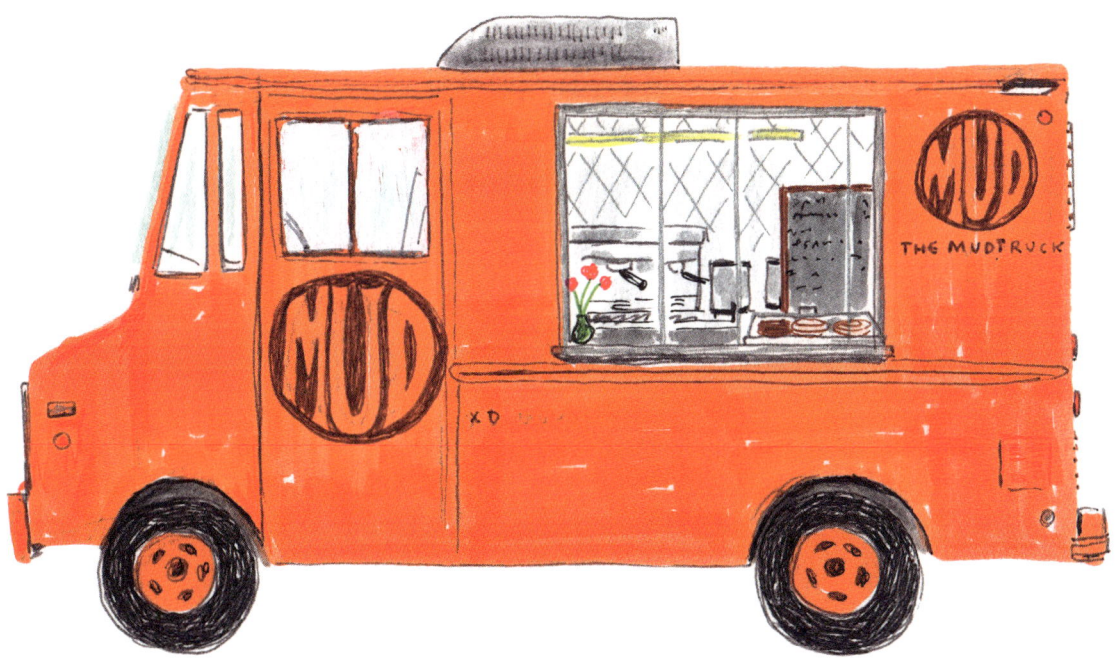

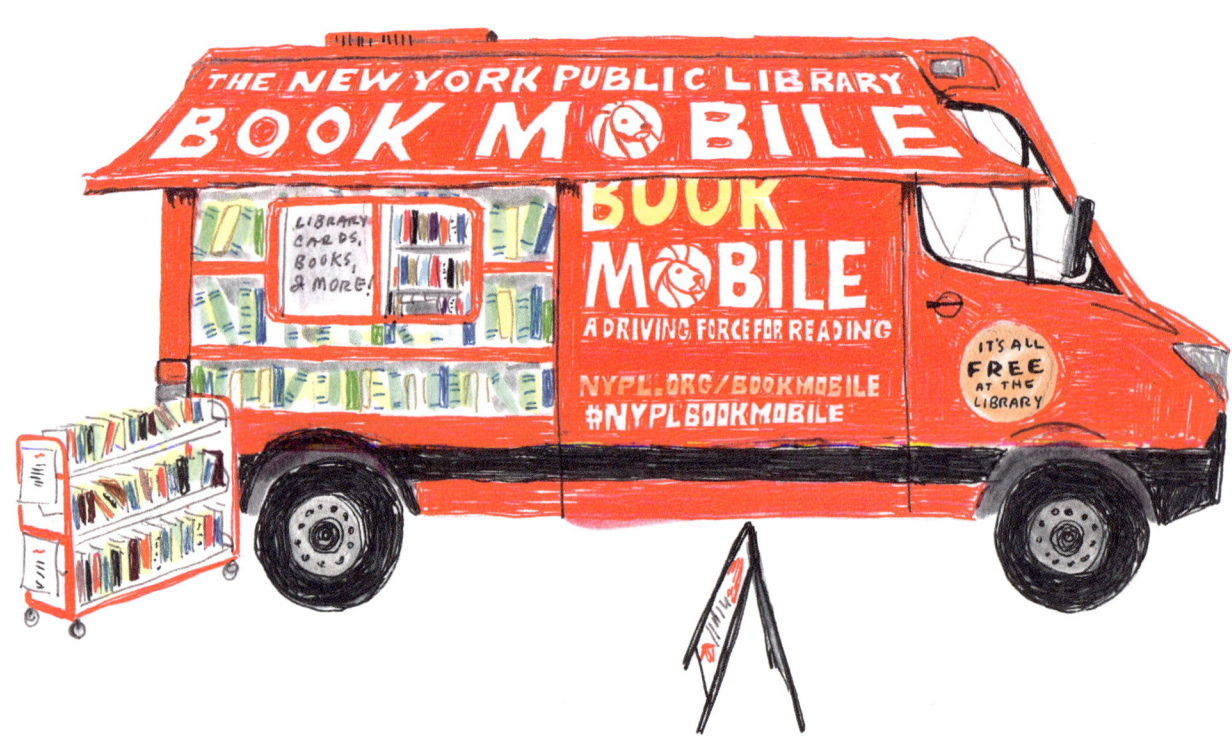

NYPL Bookmobile

For much of the last century, the New York Public Library (NYPL) has brought literature directly to the people thanks to its bookmobiles, which are more or less what they sound like: libraries on wheels. One of the first iterations, the Bronx Traveling Library, debuted in 1928, focusing on parts of the borough that lacked permanent library facilities—and was soon a familiar, welcome sight in many underserved areas. A similar version roamed the streets of Staten Island in the early 1920s. Photographs from the era depict children eagerly lining up to access books from these mobile units. Though discontinued by NYPL for a time, the Bookmobile returned in 2019 and once again serves Manhattan, the Bronx, and Staten Island (Queens and Brooklyn have separate library systems—both of which also offer mobile services).

The NYPL Bookmobile is part of a long tradition of mobile libraries and bookstores in the United States.

The American School Library, a traveling bookstore started in the late 1830s by publisher Harper and Brothers, is among the earliest on record. Vendors traveled the country offering the same fifty books for sale, a biography of George Washington and *The Swiss Family Robinson* among them. The set cost twenty dollars at the time and came complete with a wooden carrying case.

In 1904 one of the US's first known lending libraries on wheels debuted in Washington County, Maryland. It was the brainchild of the librarian Mary Lemist Titcomb, who called her horse-drawn buggy, the outsides of which were outfitted with shelves of books, the "library wagon." (In 2018 Sharlee Glenn turned Mary's story into a children's book.) The advent of the automobile helped the idea of libraries on wheels take hold, as did the Library Services Act of 1956, which helped fund the creation of two hundred new bookmobiles across the country.

By the 1960s and 1970s, there were over two thousand mobile libraries roaming the US. Those numbers have dwindled since, but, according to the 2019 Public Library Survey, there are still well over six hundred mobile libraries active today. Want to find out where Gotham's Bookmobile will be next? No need to look to the night sky for a glowing symbol—just check online.

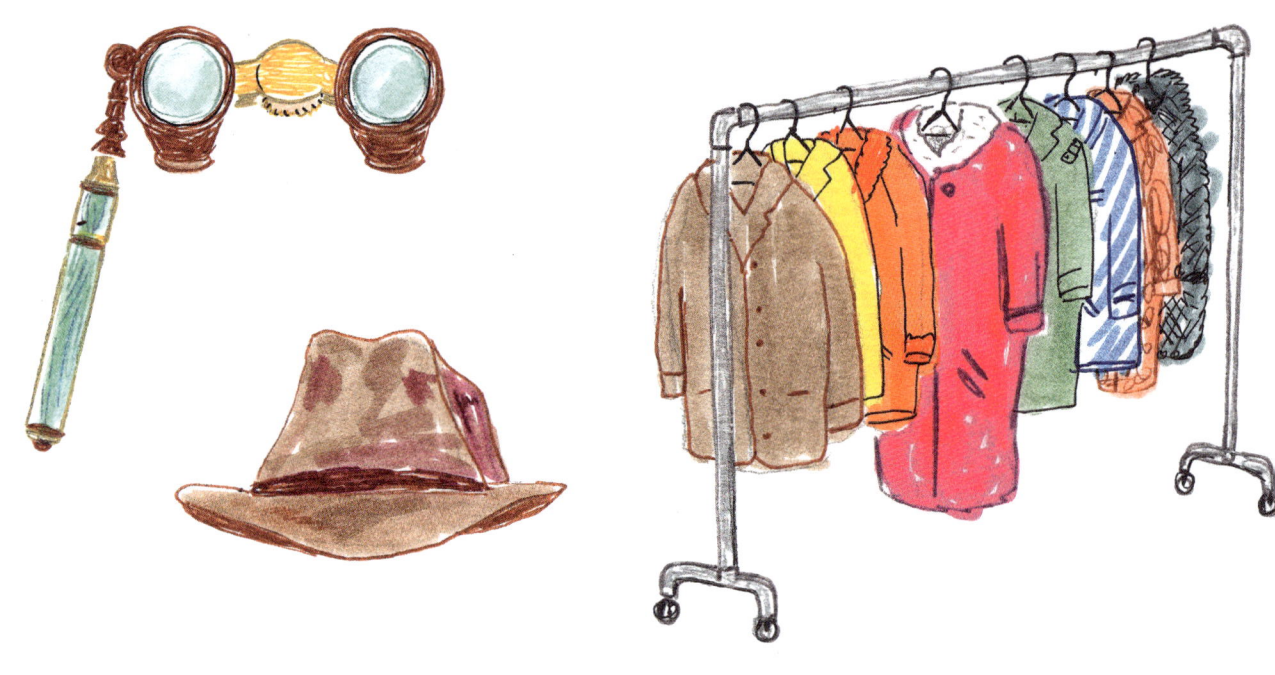

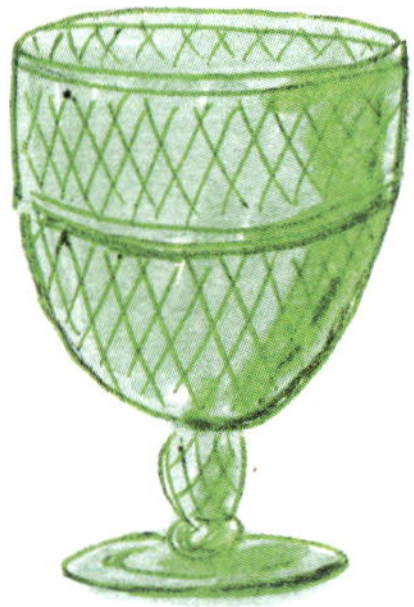

Brooklyn Flea

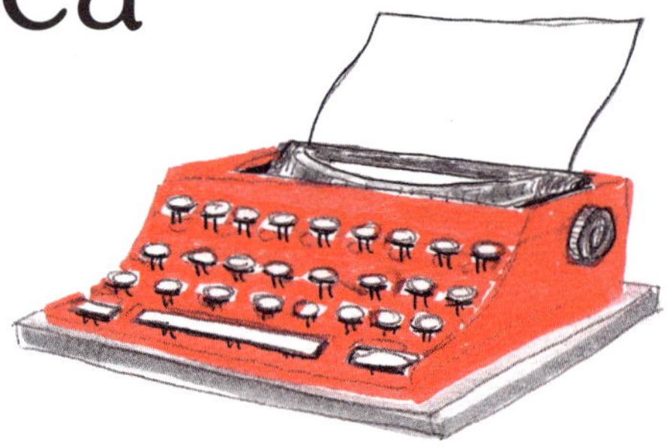

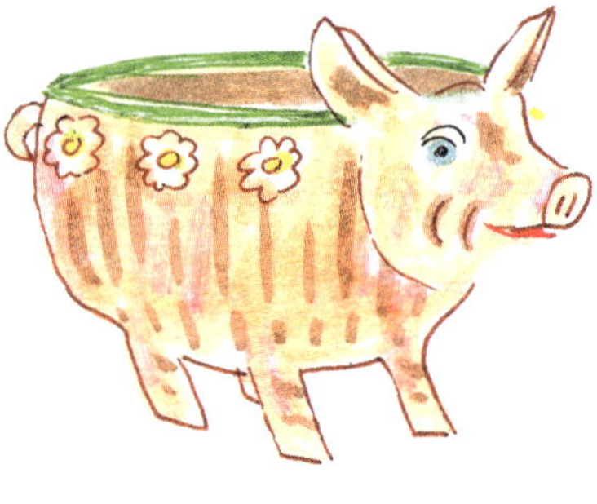

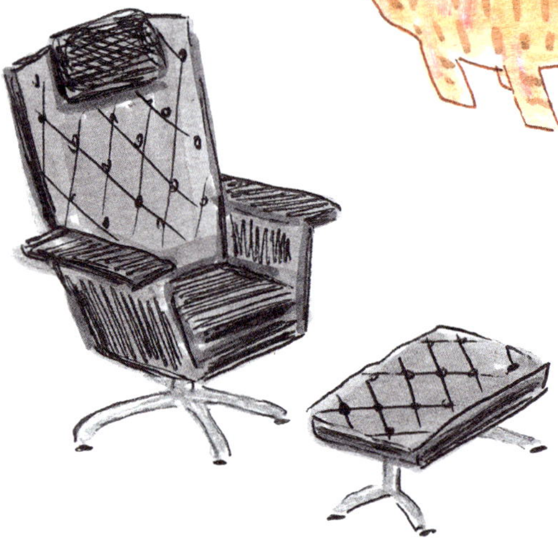

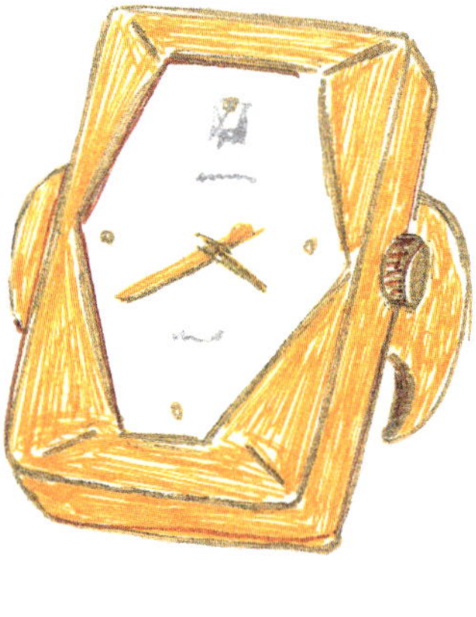

While there's a time and place for a market selling taxidermic goat heads, or VHS tapes from the early 1990s capturing a random family's vacation, these are not the types of items you will find at the Brooklyn Flea.

From its inception in 2008 at a schoolyard in Fort Greene, Jonathan Butler and Eric Demby sought to differentiate their market by carefully vetting vendors with an eye for high-quality, unique items. This move away from the traditional tchotchke-filled fleas quickly put the market on the map and led the duo to expand to other locations, including DUMBO, and to take over the historic flea in Chelsea in 2019 (p. 86). At their markets, you can find hundreds of hand-selected vendors selling antiques, furniture, vintage clothing, jewelry, art, and more.

At Van der Most Modern, for instance, you can pick up a piece of midcentury Dutch furniture. Louise Goods has got you covered for all your handcrafted leather needs. Twice the Fiyah is a great stall to visit if you're in the market (literally) for vintage watches, jewelry, and clothes—its owner, Elma Blint, even sells some of her own designs. Other vendors include food stalls and various artisans who make and sell their own goods.

The Brooklyn Flea has helped launch several careers too. Dan's Parents' House, founded by Dan Treiber and Reina Mia, originally started selling items from Dan's old family home in 2008 to generate extra income. Initially founded "as a goof," as the couple told the *Bronx Times* in 2016, the venture has evolved into a successful business—which today includes 239 Play!, their brick-and-mortar store on City Island Avenue in the Bronx. Though it might not be what they'd first intended for their careers, they have the Brooklyn Flea to thank for letting them "sell joy for a living," as they write on their website.

Nuts 4 Nuts

You can't wander too far into Midtown Manhattan without catching a whiff of the sweet, familiar aroma of roasted nuts. Originally from Mendoza, Argentina, Alejandro Rad started selling candied peanuts, known as maní garrapiñada, in 1989, along with variations made with cashews, almonds, and more. Several years later, in 1993, he forged a partnership with Cliff Stanton to create Nuts 4 Nuts—a seed that has since sprouted into a business that includes dozens of pushcarts around the city.

Alejandro and Cliff didn't become New York's preeminent nut kings easily, however: The two had to fight strict city regulations and turf battles with other would-be vendors to claim that title. In a 2018 video for the *VICE* YouTube channel Munchies, Alejandro alluded to an advantage he held over his competitors. "Let's put it this way," he said. "I was able to hold in my hand a big weapon: hot, caramelized nuts." Today, fortunately, Alejandro no longer needs to use his nuts as ammunition to protect his business—the company is a success, selling their products online and in all fifty states.

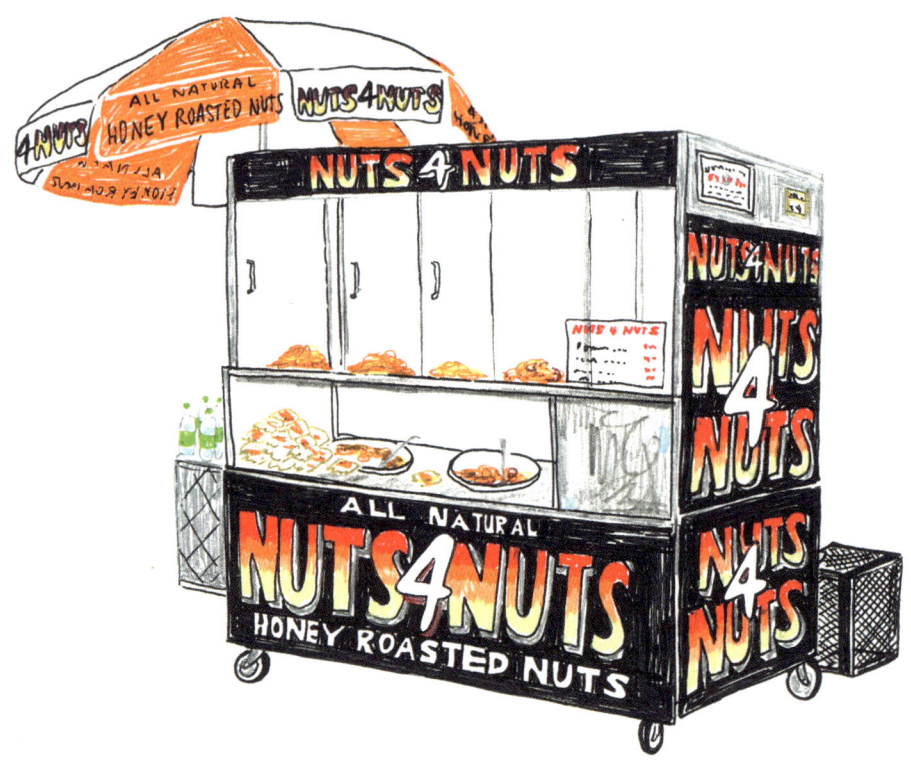

The Cheong Fun Cart

Located on the corner of Hester and Elizabeth Streets in Manhattan's Chinatown, this popular street food vendor specializes in cheong fun—a traditional Cantonese rice noodle typically rolled around roast pork, shrimp, or vegetables. Each order also comes with scallions and sauces (soy and hot), as well as an optional egg (one online reviewer recommends: "Always add an egg"). The result is a delicious concoction you can smell "50 paces away," as *Condé Nast Traveler* wrote in a review, "especially when the wind carries notes of sesame, soy, and pork."

In a 2022 article, *The Infatuation* doled out a helpful pro tip for foodies who decide to seek out the business: "The cart is parked right in front of Hong Kong Supermarket, so pick up some frozen scallion pancakes, chocolate Pocky, and a jar of chili crisp while you're there."

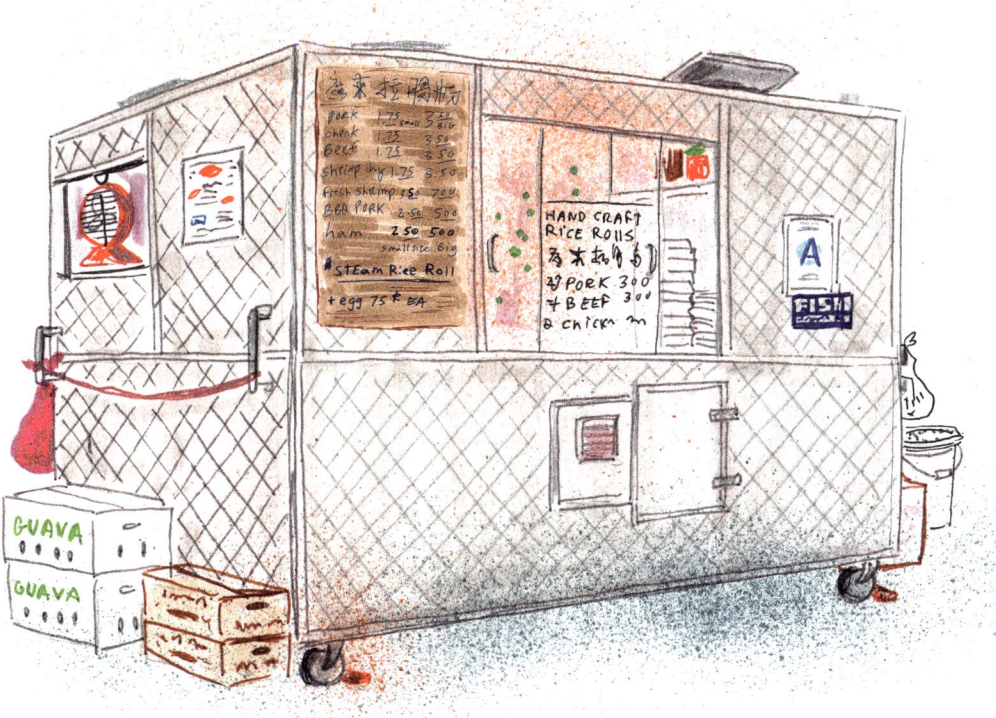

Churro Vendors

There are few better scents in this world than freshly made churros—it's an aroma many New Yorkers are fortunate to encounter daily as they pass by vendors in the subway system or on busy street corners.

The doughy treat, typically fried in hot oil and coated with a generous dusting of sugar and cinnamon, originated in Spain and became popular throughout Latin America. As New York's population of Latin American immigrants has increased in recent decades, so, too, has the presence of this beloved snack.

In a 2013 interview with the website *Welcome to Harlem*, Julio, a churro maker originally from Mexico City, said he whips up between two to three thousand of the sweet treats a day; he then resells them to vendors who operate across the city. One such vendor, Lorena, told the food site *Edible Brooklyn* in 2019 that she typically buys a hundred churros from a person like Julio for about thirty-five dollars, and then resells them for two dollars for a set of three. On a good day, she'll net about fifty dollars by selling all the churros, as well as some other items she offers.

Like a lot of street vendors, however, a high number of churro sellers work without permits, given the extremely limited number provided by the city—leaving them vulnerable to ongoing police harassment, arrests, and fines. Most churro vendors, in fact, are used to being ticketed or arrested multiple times over, a cost they have come to see as the price of doing business.

For years many New Yorkers were unaware that some of their favorite vendors were operating in the shadows and subject to ongoing policing. In 2019, however, images went viral following the arrest of a Brooklyn-based churro vendor, Elsa Morochoduchi, who is originally from Ecuador. She told *The New York Times* she hadn't even tried to seek out a permit from the city, due to anti-immigrant bias. Even those who do get permits, however, are often subjected to harassment. A vendor named Carmita told ABC News that, despite her license, "every time I try to sell, I get a ticket." At the time of her interview in 2019, she was on the hook for twelve thousand dollars, even though she had the necessary paperwork. (The NYPD, for their part, claimed the citations were due to "lack of cooperation.")

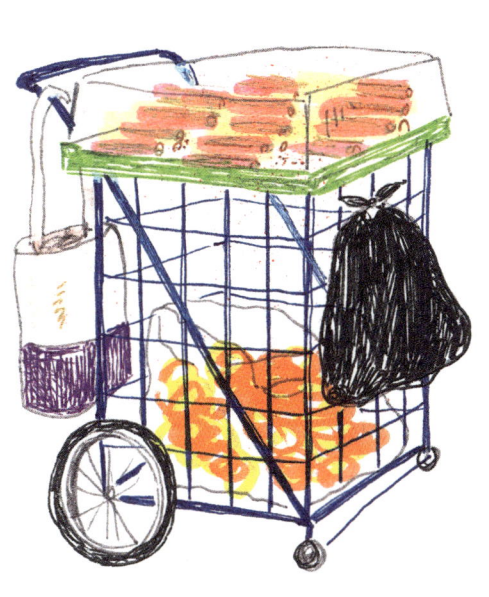

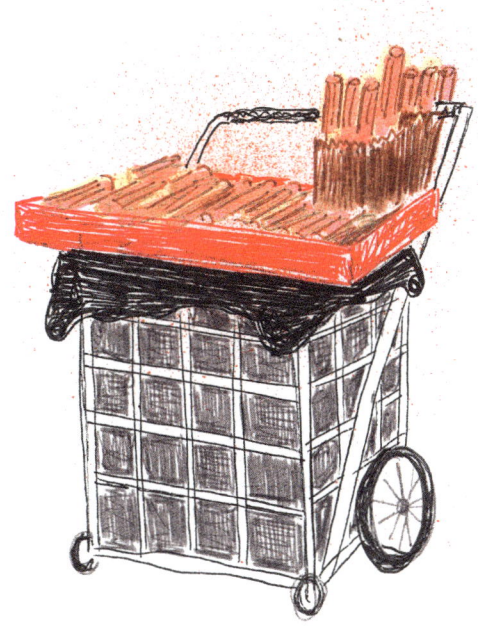

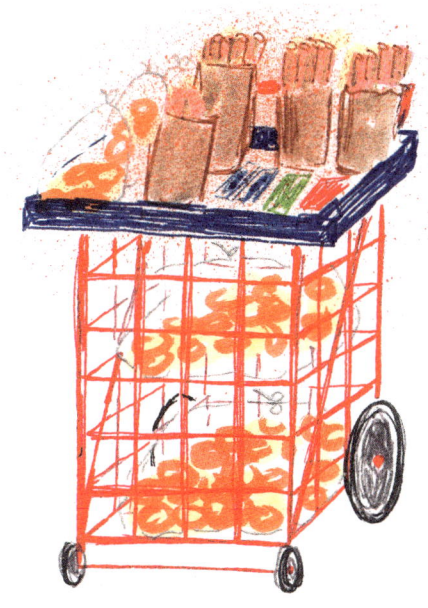

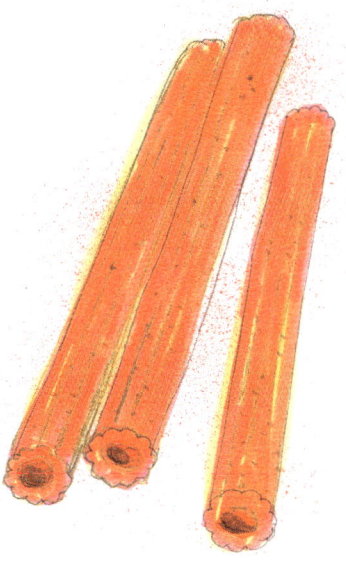

Graffitery

You can usually find this popular food truck, which first opened in 2023, on Richmond Avenue in Staten Island. As the name might suggest, its exterior—and interior—is decorated with graffiti art. The truck's logo features its name tagged using 1980s-inspired blocked lettering painted in neon colors against a yellow background.

Graffitery is known for fusing traditional halal food with some unexpected twists. The jerk chicken taco, topped with mango salsa, is a crowd pleaser, as is the Nashville hot chicken sandwich. The King's Meal is a platter with both items, plus a quesadilla and chopped cheese sandwich. According to one online review, Graffitery has the "best chop cheese on sesame bread, doesn't get better than this!" Another said, "Certainly the best food truck on the island!"

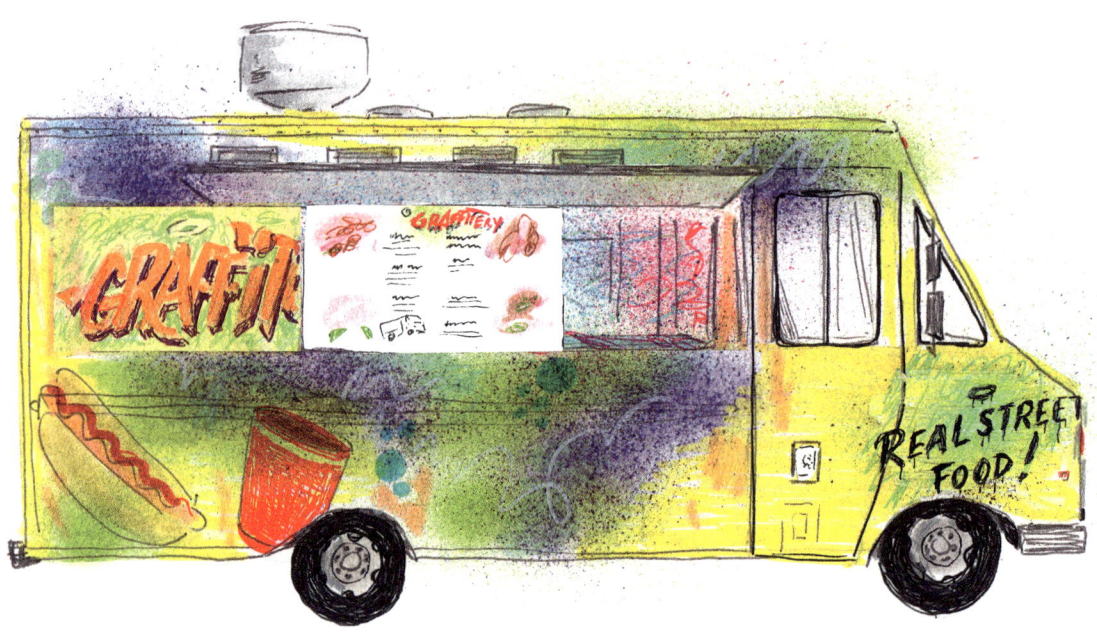

Quick Phone Repair

This Williamsburg, Brooklyn–based business affirms, "Electronics have a long life; we believe in repair," according to a message scrawled, at times, on a dry-erase board propped against their renovated truck trailer. The proprietors claim to be able to fix your phone, laptop, or gaming console "no matter the damage." While customers wait for their cracked screen to be replaced or water damage to be inspected, they can also peruse items for sale inside the trailer, which include cases, cords, and other typical electronic ephemera.

In July 2024 a disgruntled Threads user (and likely car owner) posted a photo of the mobile electronics-repair shop with the caption, "Someone dropped an entire phone repair shop into a parking space in Williamsburg. Should this be car parking instead?" According to dozens of responses from locals, the answer was a resounding "no, thank you."

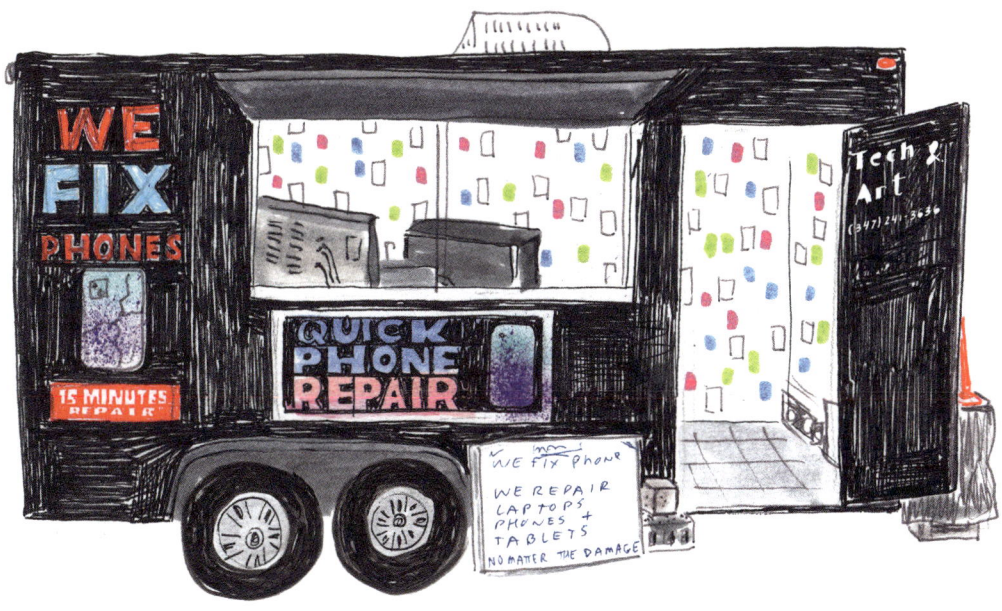

El Rey del Taco

This family-run Mexican food truck has been a staple on the streets of Queens since 2006. Over the years the business has expanded to include four locations, with three in Astoria (two trucks, including the original at Thirtieth Avenue and Thirty-Third Street, and a brick and mortar) and one in Bayside (a truck on Northern Boulevard). The vehicles are painted in green, red, and white—the colors of the Mexican flag—and a miniature truck, stuffed with tacos, is incorporated into their logo.

At El Rey you'll find traditional Mexican tacos filled with spicy chicken, pork, or beef tongue, as well as tortas, burritos, quesadillas, and more. A Vendy Award finalist in 2014, the business manages to please even the pickiest enthusiasts of Mexican cuisine. The trucks are also a common stopover for late night revelers. "Drinky drink drunk," one such online reviewer eloquently stated. "These tacos hit the spot after a long night of destroying my liver."

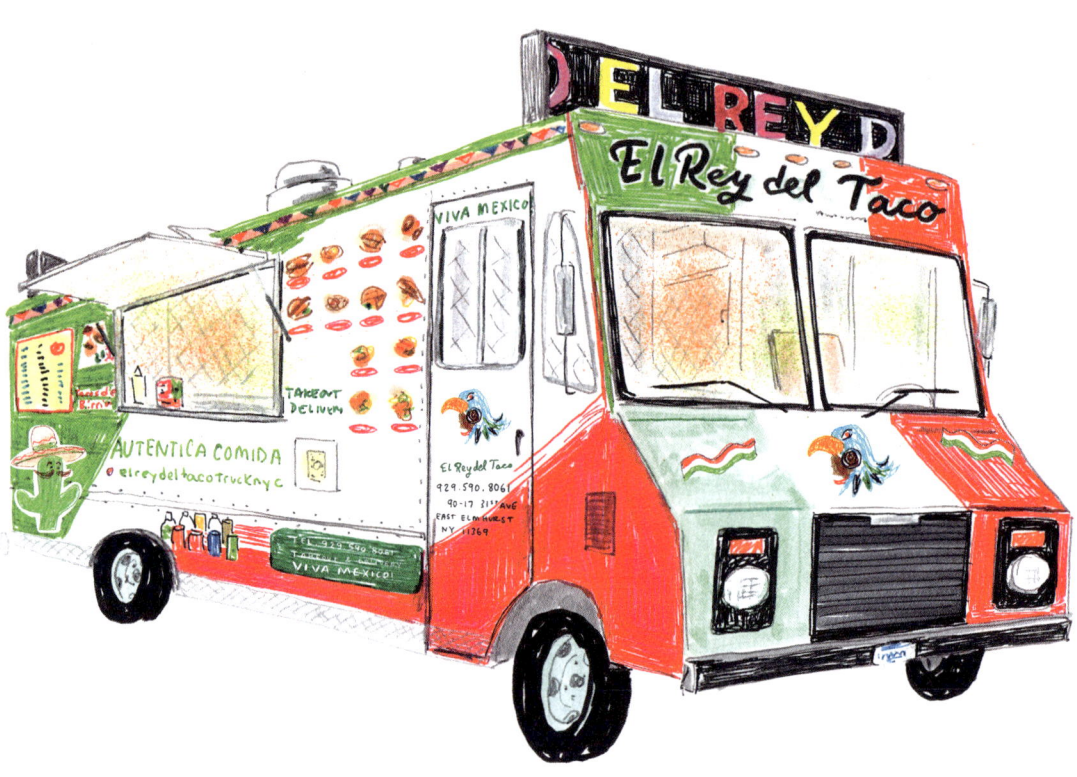

Divine Flavored Catering

Godshelter Abodunrin, who operates several Nigerian food trucks and carts (and who is known to most of his regulars as Divine), founded his business as a catering company in 2005. A graduate of the New York School of Culinary Arts, he started the venture after recognizing a gap of "accessible Nigerian dishes" in New York's food landscape. As he writes on his website, "Our mission is to provide an unforgettable culinary experience that transports you straight to the streets of Nigeria."

Favorites include several varieties of egusi soup, a West African dish thickened with seeds from a vine native to the region, and amala, a paste made from yam, cassava, and plantain flour. Today you no longer need to hire Divine to cater your events to sample his food—simply stop by his food cart, parked daily in front of the Nigerian Embassy at Forty-Fourth Street and Second Avenue in Manhattan, or his additional locations in Brooklyn and Philadelphia.

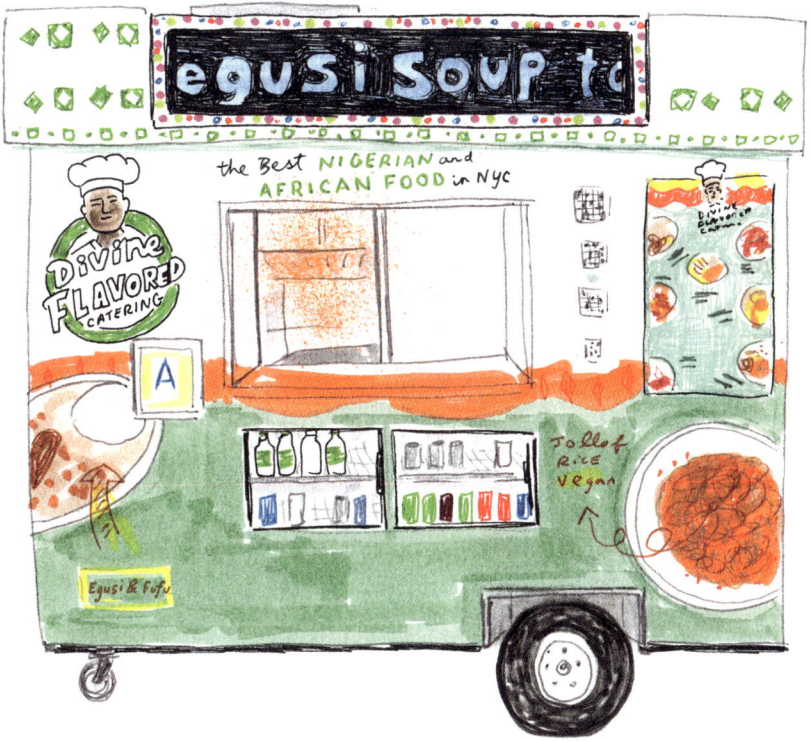

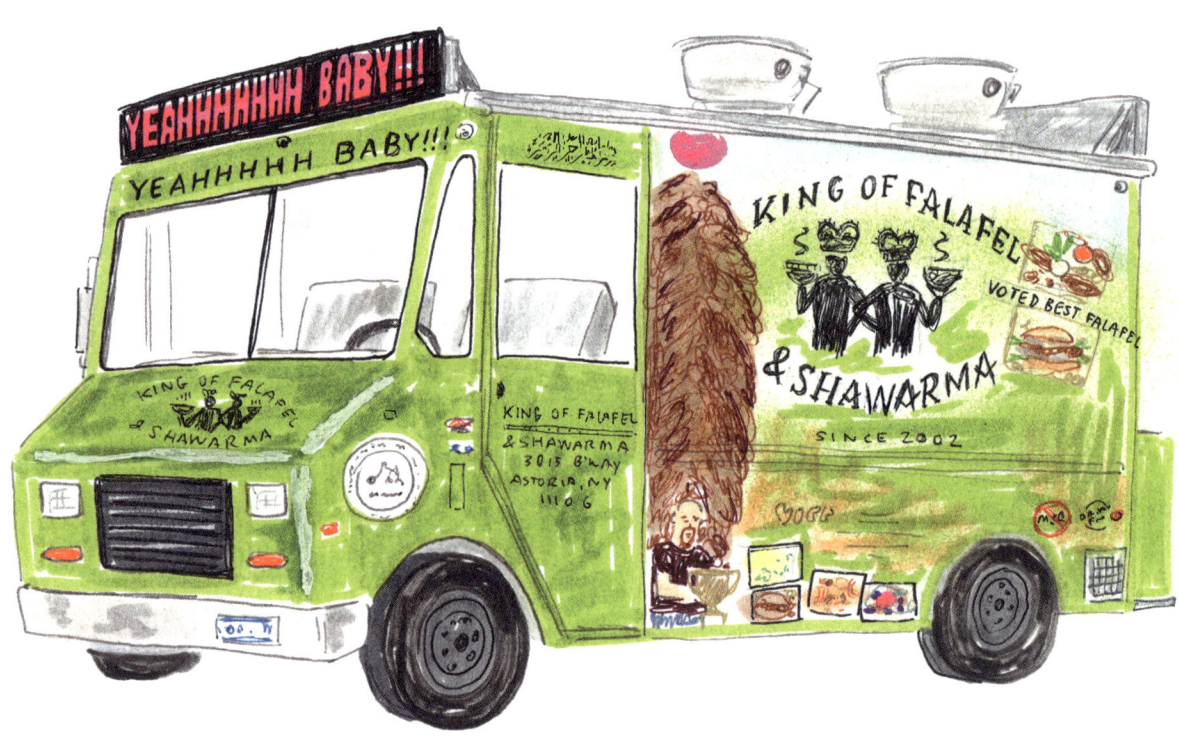

King of Falafel & Shawarma

Fares "Freddy" Zeideia's renowned
street food business offers passersby
authentic Palestinian cuisine.

Originally from Ramallah, Freddy founded the venture in 2002, starting with a single location on the corner of Broadway and Thirtieth Street in Astoria, Queens. "I didn't want to open it in the city," he said in an interview for the *VICE* YouTube channel, Munchies. "I wanted to stay locally."

That decision was motivated, in part, by his preexisting popularity in Astoria. "I knew everyone in the area, so people would say, 'Freddy, you're the king of the neighborhood.'" He took the nickname and applied it to his new business, where customers quickly grew to appreciate his offerings, like homemade tahini sauce and pita bread. "You have to sell yourself, along with your food," he told *The New York Times* in a 2016 article.

He put this belief to practice at the 2010 Vendy Awards, when he surprised the gathered guests, following his win, with a celebratory belly dance. Anyone already familiar with Freddy, however, would be no stranger to his trademark moves, which are often on display while he works.

Since those early days, this neighborhood-anointed royal has expanded his kingdom to include trucks in Manhattan and the Bronx and a brick-and-mortar restaurant in Astoria—which has allowed Freddy to cook his food, for the first time, in a full-sized kitchen. ("This grill is the size of my entire cart," he told the *Times*.) In 2024 he went even farther afield, opening a restaurant in Chicago, which is home to the largest Palestinian community in the United States.

Despite all his growth, his humble food trucks are as popular today as ever. During the lunchtime rush hour, it's not uncommon to see a line of hungry workers stretching down the block, waiting their turn to order his chicken shawarma, lamb gyro, and falafel. As a token of his appreciation, Freddy will often pass out samples of falafel to customers as they wait.

Beignet Café

Los Angeles native Dave Leach has been bringing the "Big Easy to the Big Apple," as he writes on his website, with his beignet cart since 2020. He got his start as a street vendor during the COVID-19 pandemic, simply selling cups of coffee from Café du Monde, the famed beignet spot in New Orleans, to his neighbors. While appreciative, these customers noticed a fatal flaw in his business plan: You can't very well serve Café du Monde coffee without offering up what the NOLA institution is best known for, its beignets.

Soon after, Dave booked a flight to New Orleans to learn the secret to making a beignet—a deep-fried pastry with a generous dusting of powdered sugar—straight from the pros at Café du Monde. Today you can catch his charming green-and-white stand on the west side of Union Square.

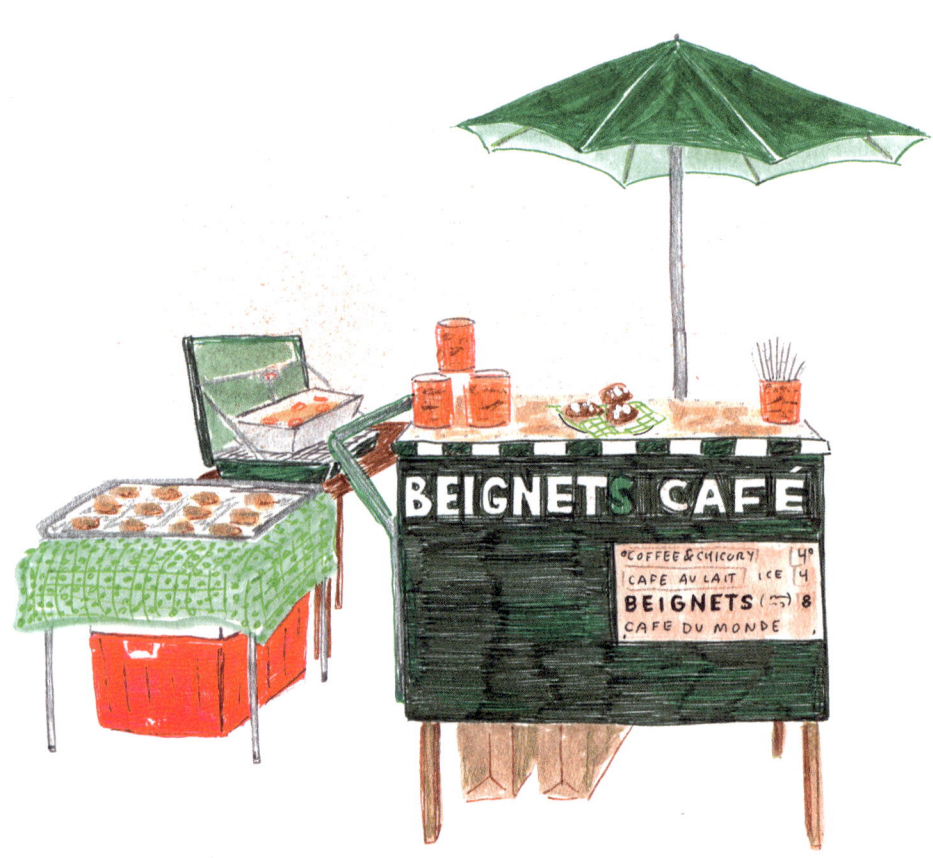

Los Tacos City Habanero

This street food vendor is stationed at the corner of Vernon Boulevard and Forty-Eighth Avenue in Long Island City, Queens. Here, you can find all the trappings of a Mexican restaurant bundled inside a small truck. The menu includes typical Mexican dishes like tacos, burritos, quesadillas, tortas, and tostadas. Customer favorites include the al pastor tacos—featuring well-seasoned pork, pineapple, onions, cilantro, and guacamole, all wrapped in fresh corn tortillas—as well as the shrimp quesadilla and goat tacos.

While the tacos here are "solid," according to one online reviewer, the nachos are "next level." Another reviewer agreed, noting that the steak nachos here come "loaded with good steak on almost every nacho. Not like a pile of nachos with a couple pieces of rubber steak. I get this every time I come and you should too!"

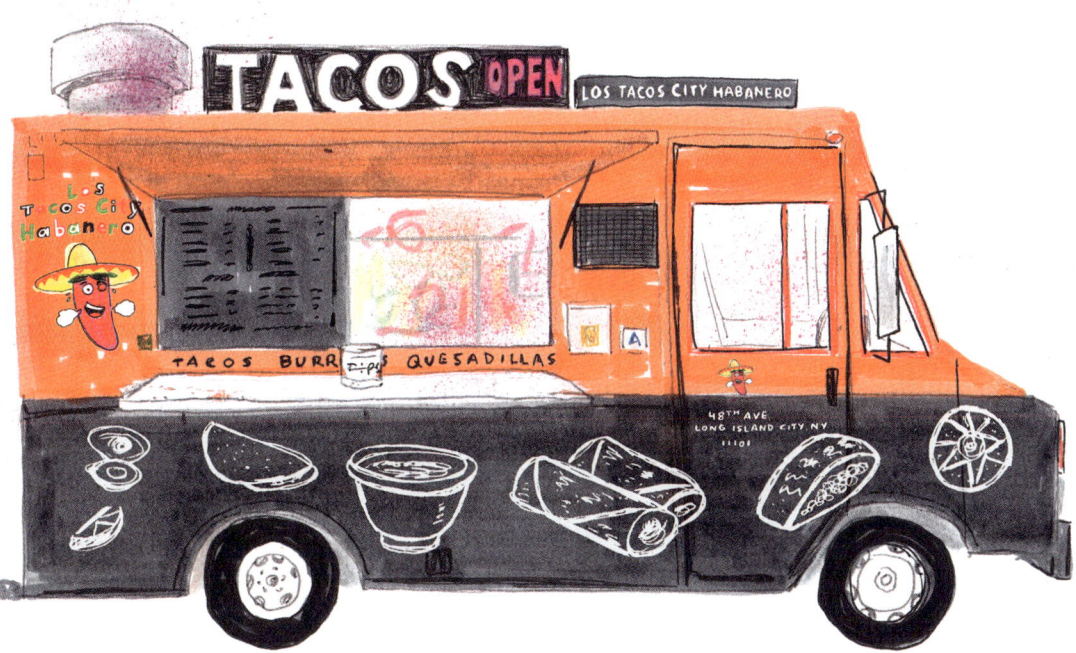

Common Books

Brittany Bond loves books so much, she's spent a lot of her adult life looking for jobs she could "just sit and read at," she told the site *Lit Hub* in 2019. After her daughter was born, however, she also started searching for work she could do with a newborn by her side. In 2018 she had begun posting rare books for sale on her Instagram page. After learning that New York's street vending policy would allow her to sell her collection outdoors without a permit, she asked her brother and sister-in-law to build a bookstore on wheels, complete with a seat for her daughter.

Brittany exclusively stocks books by women, with titles by authors such as Elizabeth Bishop, Jamaica Kincaid, and Doris Lessing. Her only other criterion is that her wares must be paperback, a format that's better for busy New Yorkers who are "commuting on the subways, waiting in laundromats, or sitting in the park," as she told *Untapped New York* in a 2020 interview. You can usually find her near Seward or East River Park in downtown Manhattan.

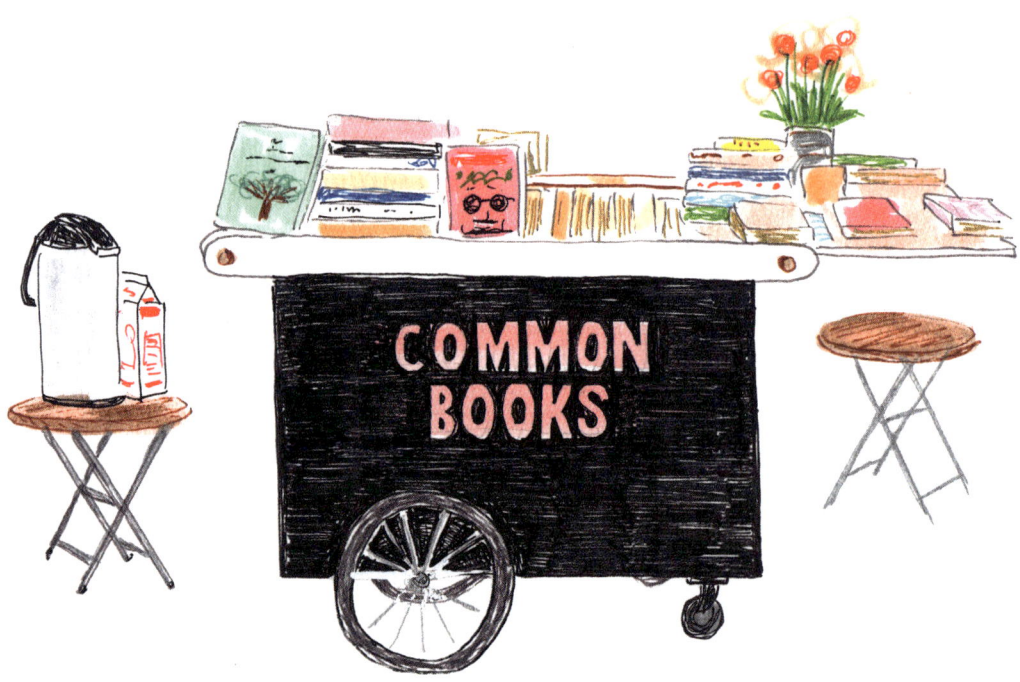

Uncle Gussy's

In 1971 Kostas Karagiorgos (nicknamed Gussy), originally from Greece, started a small food cart on the corner Fifty-First Street and Park Avenue in Manhattan, where he mostly sold hot dogs and pretzels to lunchtime crowds. In 2009, however, his nephews Nick and Franky took over the family business. They began introducing souvlaki, braised beef, and other traditional Greek items to the menu. Then they updated the business's logo to resemble the Parthenon, but with forks as columns.

The rebranding and refocus helped the venture take off—so much so that the Greek Prime Minister Kyriakos Mitsotakis prioritized a visit to the truck during his 2024 trip to New York for the United Nations General Assembly. You can find Uncle Gussy's Monday through Friday in Midtown, on the same corner where Kostas first set up his cart in the early 1970s.

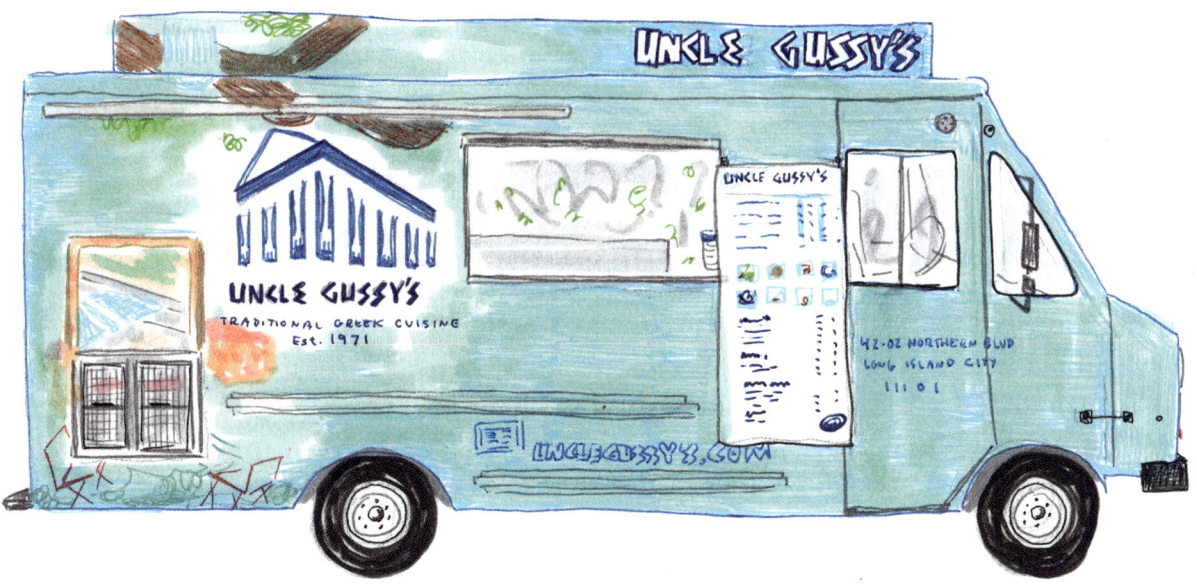

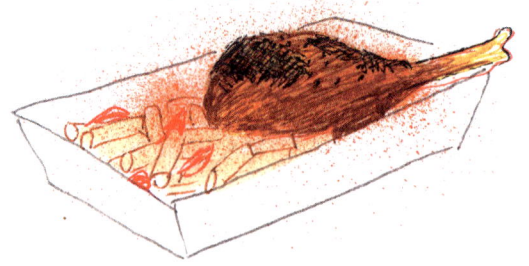
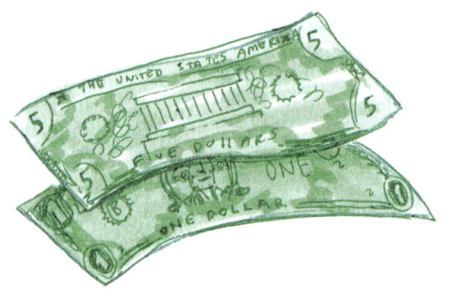
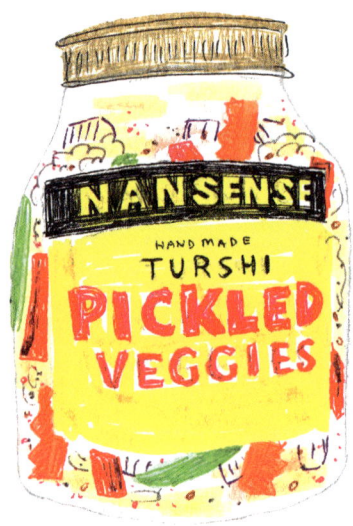
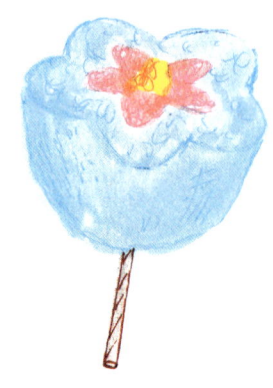

Queens Night Market

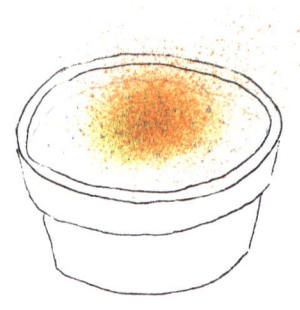
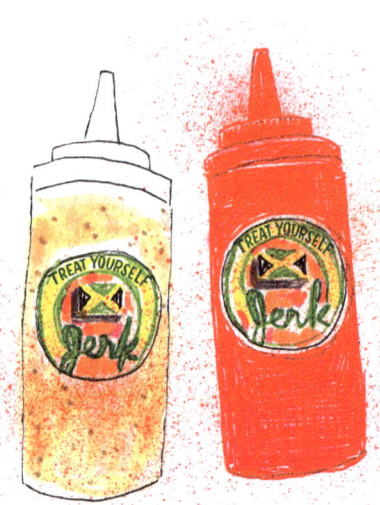
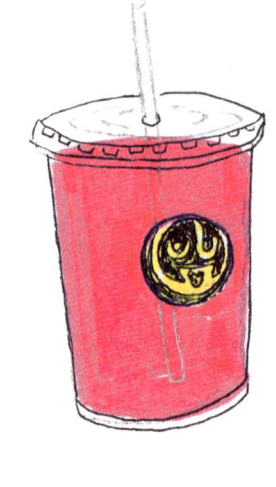
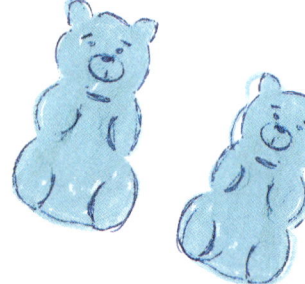
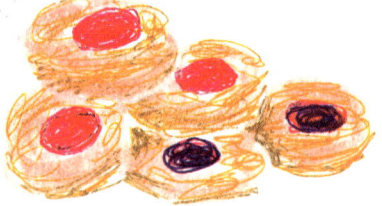

Texas native John Wang fell in love with night markets in Taiwan, where he spent his childhood summers. In 2015 he set out to prove New Yorkers would also flock to food bazaars if one were to exist in the city. His hunch was right. The Queens Night Market, which opened in Flushing Meadows–Corona Park, was an immediate success.

Today the market welcomes twenty thousand visitors on typical Saturday nights from April through October. More than a hundred independent vendors offer international cuisines, art, and products. The unpretentious vibe—what *Condé Nast Traveler* once lovingly characterized as "a chaotic melting pot"—is part of the appeal. It's a spot favored by foodies more interested in leaving with a full belly than a curated Instagram post, though you can go and get your snaps too; no one will notice amid all the hubbub.

One of the things that makes the market so popular is its commitment to affordability.

All food items were initially capped at five dollars (now it's six). As John told *Eater* in 2024, the market celebrates the city's diversity while also pushing back "against the skyrocketing cost of living here."

Many aspiring chefs, especially those from immigrant backgrounds, have used the market as a launching pad to establish themselves in New York's cutthroat culinary world (almost four hundred food businesses have been started at the event, according to John). Karl Palma launched his business, Karl's Balls, at the market in 2015, selling takoyaki—a Japanese street food stuffed with grilled octopus, green onions, ginger, and crispy tempura bits. He now caters at events across the city.

Radu Sirbu, founder of Twister Cake Bakery, started out at small festivals in New Jersey and Manhattan before debuting at the Queens Night Market in 2016. Radu is known for his Transylvanian twister (or chimney) cakes that he makes according to a two-hundred-year-old family recipe. The process involves wrapping dough around a wooden cylinder, baking it over hot cinders, and topping the resulting cake with cocoa powder, cinnamon, sugar, or ground walnuts. Today Radu sells over twenty different products online, including his signature cakes.

Treat Yourself Jerk

———

At this Queens Night Market favorite, jerks are warmly welcomed! Treat Yourself Jerk is on a mission, as its website explains, to "bring the rich, succulent island flavor" of authentic Jamaican jerk chicken, slow cooked and grilled, to the New York masses. The stall's meat is paired with one of three blended sauces: sweet, barbeque, and disrespectful (translation: this is the hot one!). Owned and operated by married couple Alberto and Ria Richardson, the business first debuted at the market in 2016—and the duo were promptly overwhelmed by the response. "We weren't really prepared for the volume of people who wanted to try our food," Alberto told Citizens Bank in a video geared toward prospective entrepreneurs. "Within the first hour and a half, we were just completely wiped out."

Today the Richardsons have learned to better manage the long lines. They've even expanded their footprint to additional pop-ups in and around the city, including at the New York Botanical Garden in the Bronx and Mohegan Sun, a casino in Connecticut.

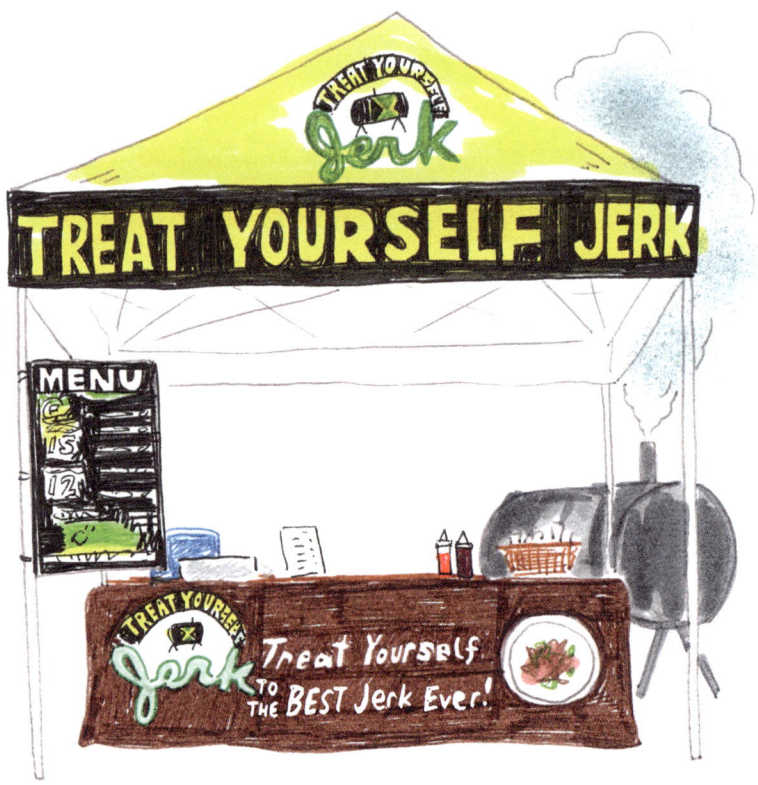

Art Cotton Candy

This vendor is among the most eye-catching at the Queens Night Market thanks to its surprisingly intricate and colorful cotton candy creations, though "sculptures" might be a better word for them. At the Art Cotton Candy stall, customers look on, often hypnotized, as spools of colorful sugar are spun and then carefully shaped into elaborate designs like pieces of fluffy pottery.

Make sure you come with your sweet tooth intact, as these are not small pieces of art. The resulting creations—which include cotton candy flowers, animal heads, and cartoon characters—are as noteworthy for their intricacy as they are for their size. In a picture posted to the business's Instagram page, a young girl happily holds a sugary rabbit head, nearly twice the size of her own, up to the camera. Others proudly display panda bears, poodles, and ducks. One online reviewer even recommended visitors bring a Ziploc bag to savor some of the treat later. "Didn't realize how huge the cotton candy was going to be," they reasoned.

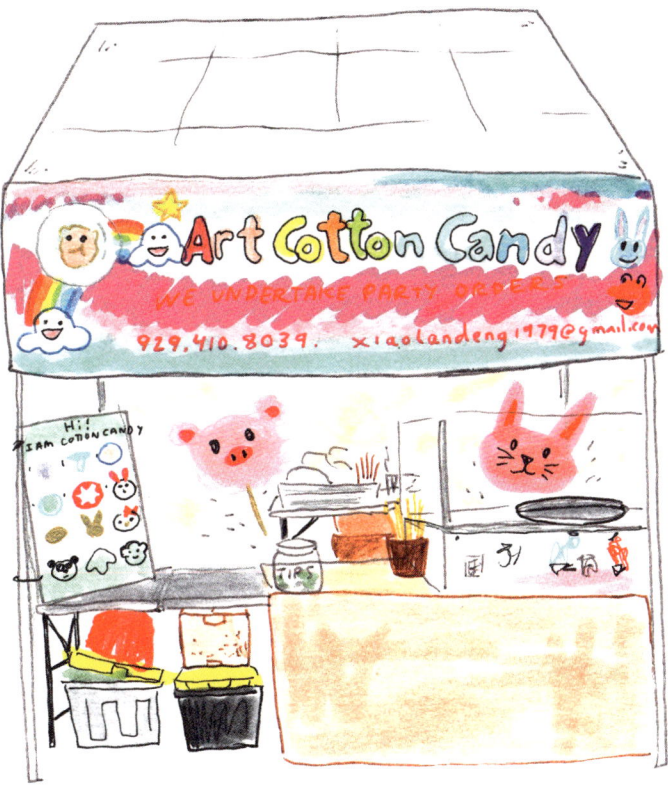

Di Lena's Dolcini

Inspired by their grandmother's cherished cookie recipes—and aided, no doubt, with a degree from the French Culinary Institute—Nicole Di Lena and her sister Carly opened this mobile Italian bakery business in 2010. Among their signature offerings, as suggested by their name, is the round dolcini—a cakelike cookie with anisette glaze and chocolate chips, topped with a healthy sprinkling of rainbow nonpareils.

The sisters also have a taste for the nontraditional, however, with menu items including gummy bears infused with limoncello, amaretto, and prosecco. (They have non-Italian alcohol flavors, too, like piña colada and rum punch.) A mainstay of the Queens Night Market, their treats can also be found at pop-ups across the city, including at the Tribeca Film Festival and Foodtown in East Harlem. The sisters' main location is now a brick-and-mortar store in Ridgefield Park, New Jersey.

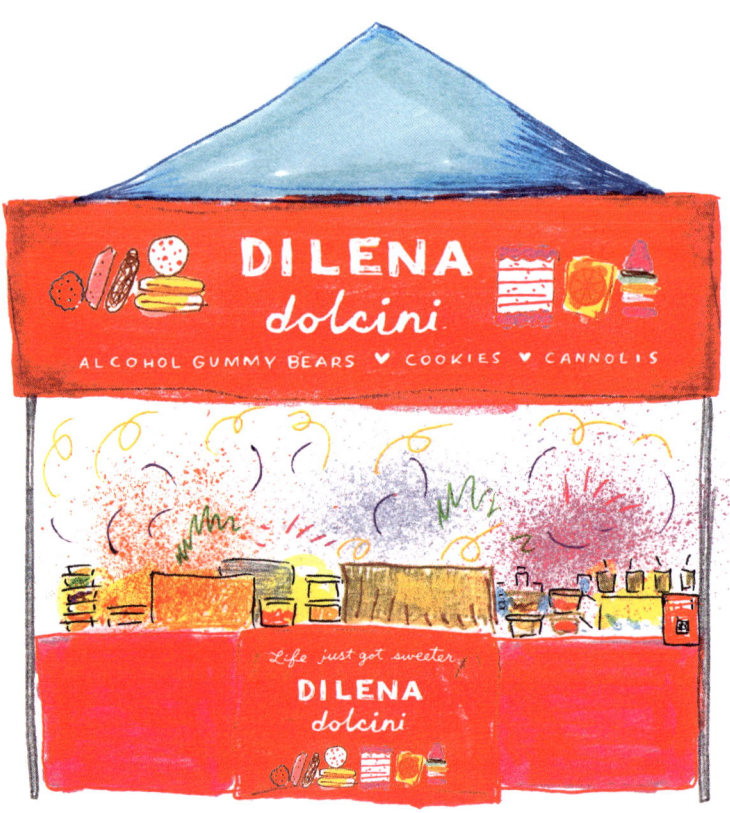

Nansense

———

Mohibullah "Mo" Rahmati started this business in 2018 from a retrofitted mail truck adorned with bright yellow smiling faces that contrast with the dark paint job. (Hidden in the drawings is the business's name in Dari: The eyes spell "nan," and "sense" is written on the tongue.) After debuting his truck in the Chelsea neighborhood of Manhattan, he later expanded his footprint to include the Queens Night Market and Smorgasburg (p. 154) in Williamsburg, Brooklyn.

As one online reviewer said, eating here is "like being transported straight to Kabul through the flavors." Standouts include mantu, dumplings filled with ground beef and topped with garlicky yogurt and split-chickpea korma, and the smashburger, made with Kabuli bread from Kabul Bakery, run by Mo's brothers. These innovations helped Nansense become a *New York Times* Critic's Pick soon after the business opened in 2018—and propelled Mo, in summer 2024, to open his first brick-and-mortar location in Beacon, New York.

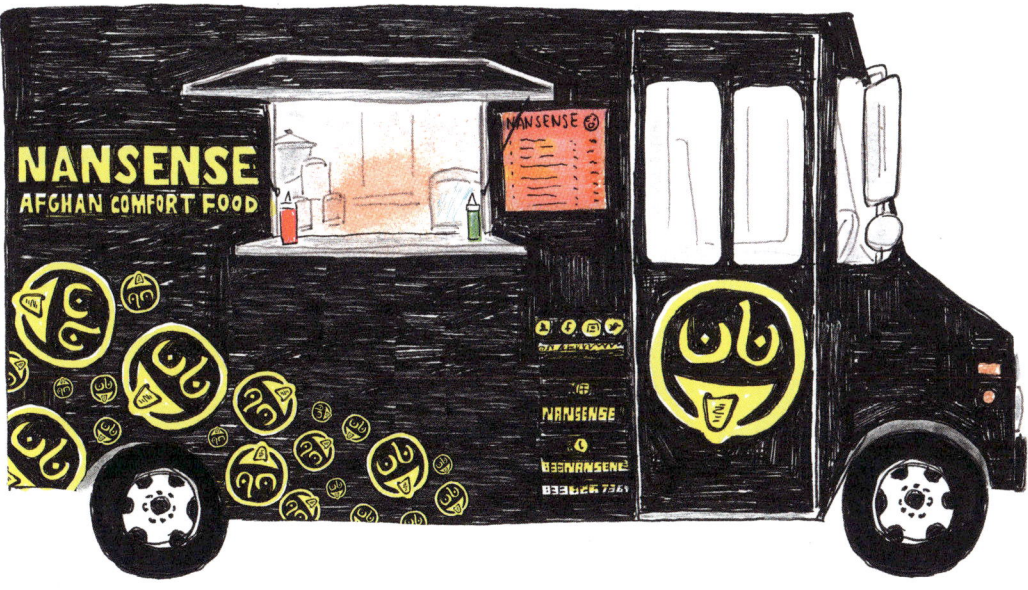

Mike's Hot Honey

Mike Kurtz's nectar-focused journey dates
back to 2003, when, while studying abroad in
Brazil, he tried some chili-infused honey
at a local pizzeria.

The condiment was not, as it turns out, common there (the pizza shop was owned by a Swiss guy)—but Mike was captivated by the unique flavor profile. Inspired, he experimented with recipes when he returned home and eventually developed his very own chili-infused honey.

Initially his habit was just a hobby, the fruits of which he shared with friends and family as holiday gifts. In 2010, however, while apprenticing at Paulie Gee's, a lauded pizzeria in Greenpoint, Brooklyn, Mike introduced his hot honey to Paulie himself. Impressed by the flavor, Paulie began drizzling it over pizzas, leading to the creation of the popular Hellboy pie. After repeated requests from customers, Mike started bottling and selling his hot honey directly from the restaurant. In 2018 he began pedaling (and peddling) his wares around the city in a bright red tricycle dubbed "Mike's Trike," complete with an umbrella and a compartment attached to hold his jars. He'd take his trike to events across the city, where he'd pass out free samples to help create more buzz.

It wouldn't take long for Mike's Hot Honey to become the bee's knees, and today you can find his products in restaurants and retail locations all over the United States and Canada. He's teamed up with local and national chains, too—like Dough Doughnuts, Lou Malnati's, Cold Stone Creamery, and Insomnia Cookies—to spice up their menus. Mike even collaborated with Ewing Athletics in April 2023 on a line of branded sneakers.

The hot honey craze has "gone from novel to trendy," *The New York Times* declared in a 2024 article, "like pumpkin spice and ranch dressing before it." While plenty of competitors now make their own versions—Momofuku even released one in 2023—Mike's is still queen bee.

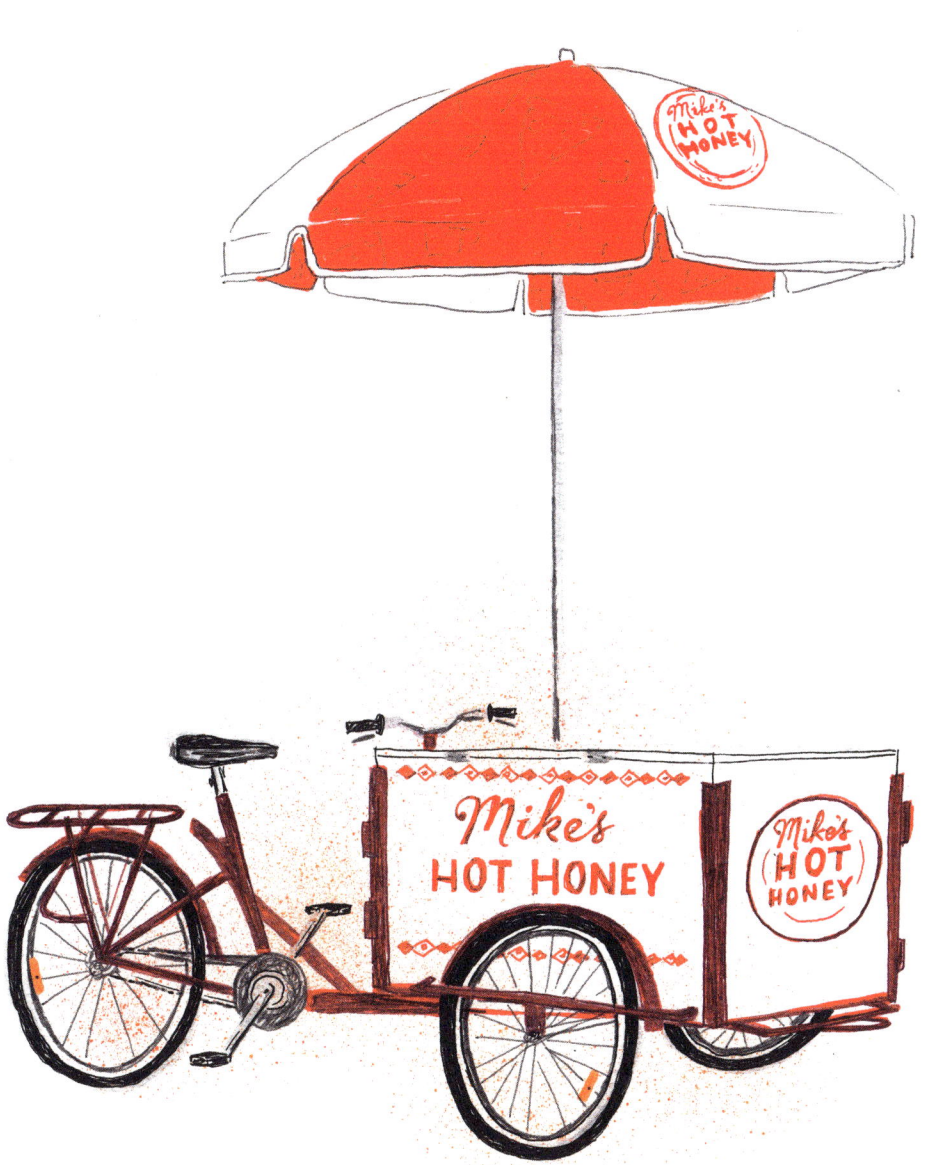

Rollin' Bagels

Quentin Guntur (or "Q" to friends) was just twenty-three years old when he started his own food cart in 2023, but he had already been making bagels at other shops for years. You can catch him most days selling his fresh, hand-rolled wares from the window of his distinctive green cart, which is often parked outside the Court Square subway station in Long Island City, Queens.

Though he's only been in business a few short years, Quentin has already endeared himself to the Long Island City community, with many claiming his are not just the best bagels in the neighborhood but the whole city. He's also committed to doing whatever he can to keep his offerings affordable. "We know eggs are stupid expensive right now," he wrote in an Instagram post in early 2025, amid a bird flu outbreak, but "supporting small businesses shouldn't break the bank." As long as customers "keep showing up," he continued, "we're not raising our prices."

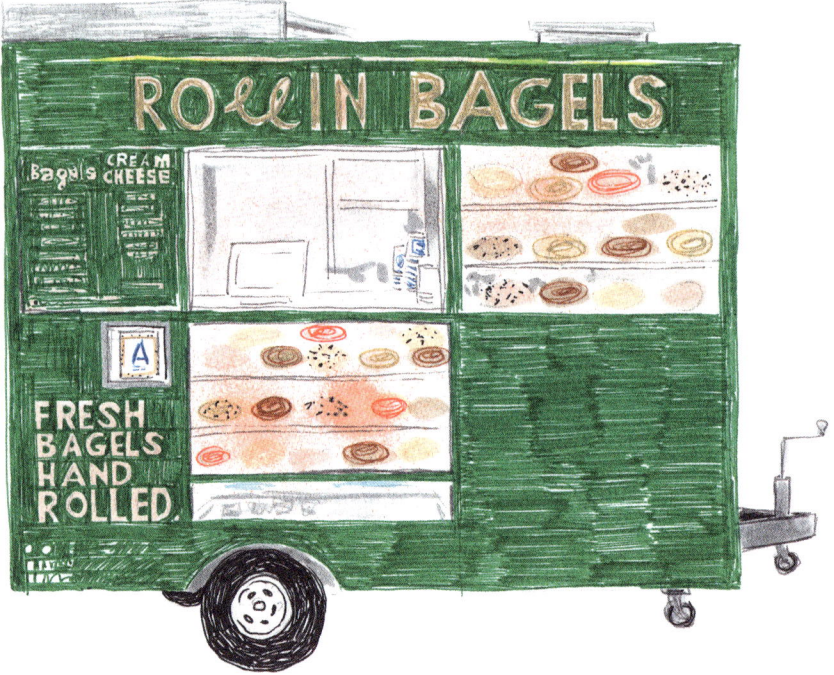

Souvlaki Lady

For a while Elpida Vasiliadis didn't get around to naming her food cart—but since her legions of dedicated customers started calling her the "Souvlaki Lady," she figured it was as good a name as any other. Elpida has run her cherished street food business in Astoria, Queens, since 1990. Stationed at the intersection of Thirty-Third Street and Ditmars Boulevard, her cart has become a culinary landmark, drawing both locals and visitors seeking authentic Greek home cooking.

Her food is inspired by recipes handed down to her by her parents, who owned a restaurant called Psilokastro in Thessaloniki, Greece's second-largest city. At her cart, Elpida cooks up marinated pork and chicken, the aroma carrying down the street and attracting customers. Her secret (or, one of them) to serving perfectly cooked, juicy meat is to grill the skewers evenly on all sides. "Never press them," she told CBS News in a 2018 segment, or else the "juice comes out." Be sure to top whatever you order with her signature Souvlaki Lady Sauce, a tangy aioli—it's "non-negotiable," according to one online reviewer.

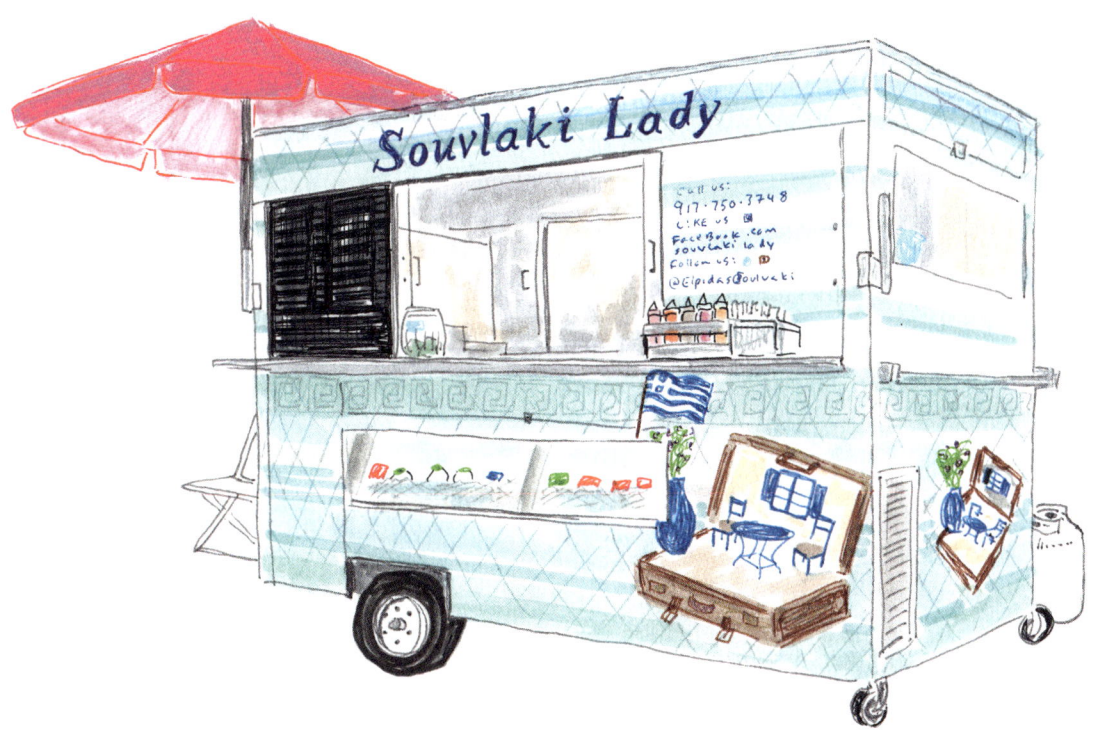

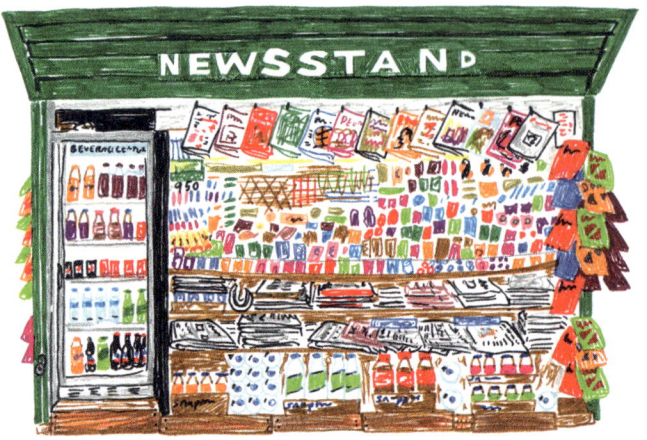

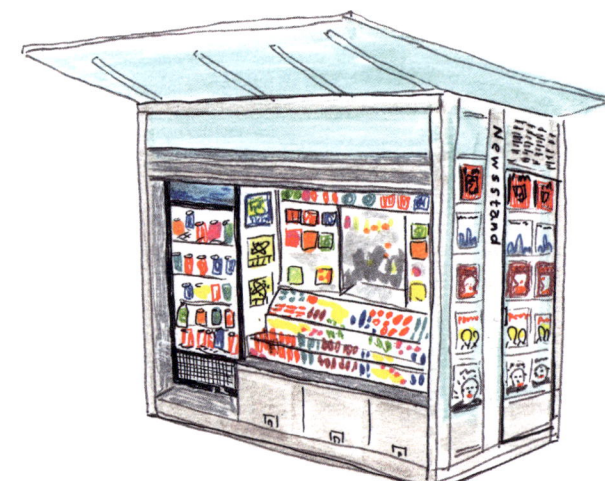

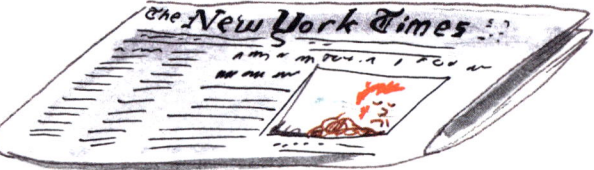

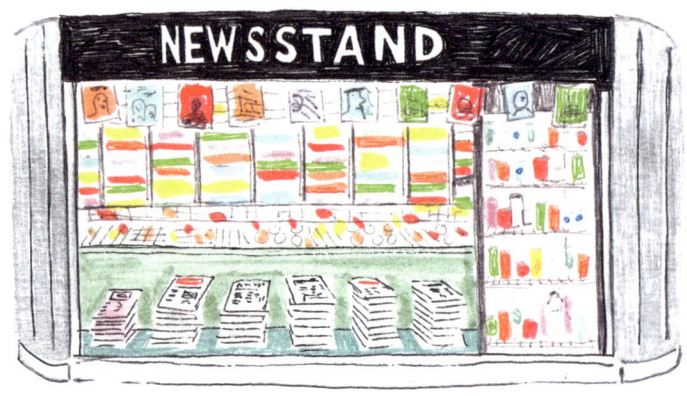

Newspaper Vendors

Newspaper vendors have been vital to New York's streetscape since the nineteenth century and were once a main conduit between the press and the public. These sellers typically purchase papers and magazines in bulk from publishers and then resell them to people passing by.

Throughout the 1800s many of these salespeople were children. Though often canonized in pop culture as precocious boys in *Peaky Blinders* hats screaming "Extra, extra!" from street corners, the reality of these jobs was much grimmer. After publishers increased the wholesale prices of newspapers, these newsboys famously went on strike in 1899, which dramatically impacted the two largest news distributors at the time, the *Evening Journal* and the *New York World*. The strike—which Disney popularized in the 1992 movie *Newsies*—lasted two weeks, ultimately ending in a compromise: While the publishers kept the price hike, they also agreed to buy back any of the newsboys' unsold papers.

In the modern era, most of these vendors (adults now, thankfully, following the advent of child labor laws) sell newspapers and magazines from fixed stands on the streets.

At their peak in 1950, there were over thirteen hundred newsstands in the city. However, as more New Yorkers get their "news" online, there are now just over three hundred stands still in operation, leaving many of them vacant.

Today barely more than a quarter of the old newsstands throughout New York's subway system are in use, leading the MTA to announce plans in 2024 to convert the structures into rent-free spaces available to artists and nonprofit organizations. (The Whitney Museum is among those taking the authority up on the offer.)

Under another proposed pilot program, a couple of above-ground newsstands may also gain a new life as respite and charging stations for food-delivery workers. With a $1 million federal grant, the program would "allow app-based delivery workers time to rest and recharge during their hectic days." Two former Manhattan newspaper kiosks—one downtown near City Hall and the other at Seventy-Second Street on the Upper West Side—would be the first to undergo the transformation, each of which will be complete with fifty e-bike battery chargers.

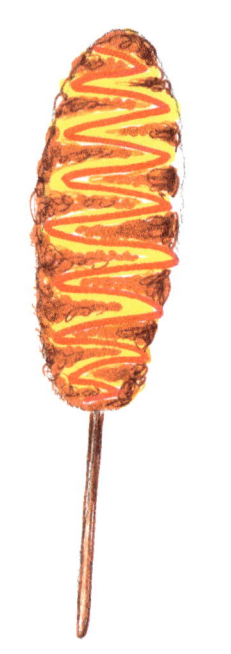
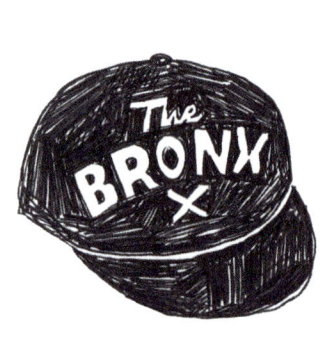
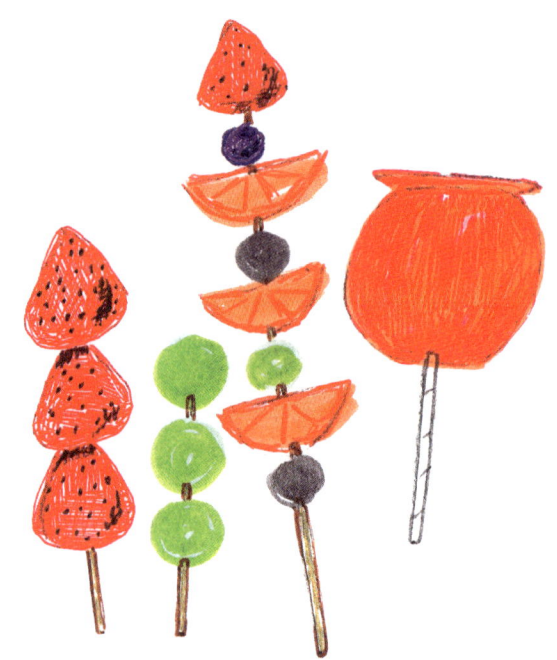

Bronx Night Market

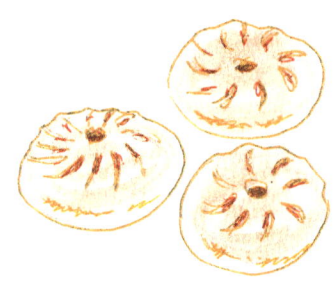
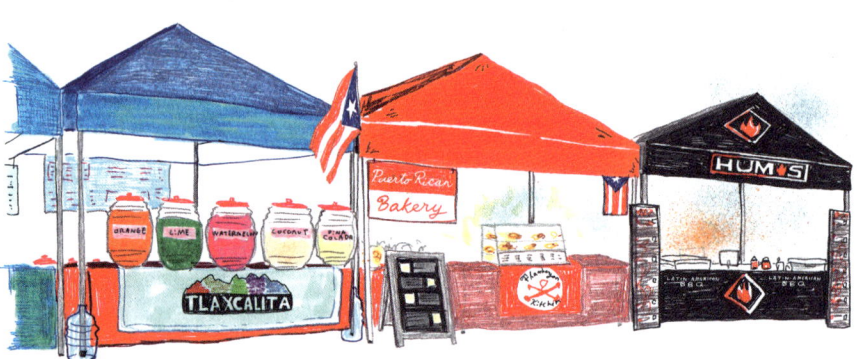
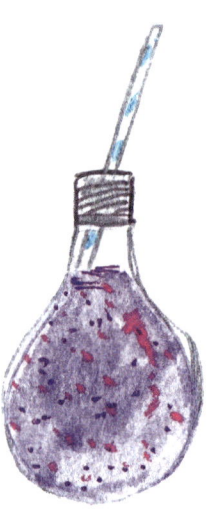

Marco Shalma started this night market in 2017 in the Bronx's Fordham Plaza, where it was open on the first Saturday of each month from April to October, until it closed in 2025. Inspired in part by the famous night markets of Asia, as well as the Queens Night Market (p. 42), which formed in 2015, Marco was eager to create New York's next favorite food destination and to support local vendors in the process. The event included more than 120 rotating small businesses selling food, souvenirs, and art.

Exploring the vendors felt like stepping into a Carmen Sandiego adventure—you never knew where in the world you'd end up.

You would find food representing forty different countries, letting patrons sample Caribbean fare at one stand and West African eats at another. New vendors arrived every year, keeping the experience fresh each time. Some favorites included Paella Party, with a menu boasting traditional paellas made with seafood, meat, and squid ink; and Angie's Delightful Bites, selling empanadas with Caribbean-inspired fillings, including oxtail and jerk chicken.

The success of the Bronx Night Market led Marco, through his larger company, Masc Hospitality Group, to experiment with several ventures all across Manhattan, including the Uptown Market in Harlem, the Vegan Night Market at Columbus Circle, and the Latin Food Fest in Washington Heights (p. 104).

Over the course of eight years, the Bronx Night Market hosted over one million visitors and over twelve hundred small businesses—many of them women- and immigrant-owned. "What we built was never about trend. It was about legacy, love, and a borough that always shows up," Marco said in a statement while announcing the closure. While the Bronx market no longer exists in its original form, the Masc Hospitality Group continues to organize various events in the borough each summer.

Flamboyan Kitchen

———

This family-run bakery, founded in 2022, specializes in Puerto Rican desserts. The women behind the business got the idea to start it after developing a hankering for mallorcas—a traditional Puerto Rican sweet bread. Not finding the treat anywhere in the Bronx near where they lived, they decided to start making and eventually selling mallorcas themselves. "We got in the kitchen and worked on recipes, until they came out just right," according to their website. After successfully re-creating mallorcas, it dawned on these bakers that "there were so many more pastries that we missed and wanted to see. So why not make them ourselves?"

Today they've greatly expanded their menu to include additional Puerto Rican sweets, such as almejas—honey cookies filled with tropical flavors like guava, passion fruit, and pineapple—and dulce de coco, a sugary coconut square. The mobile business regularly can be found at markets and festivals throughout the city, including the Bronx Night Market.

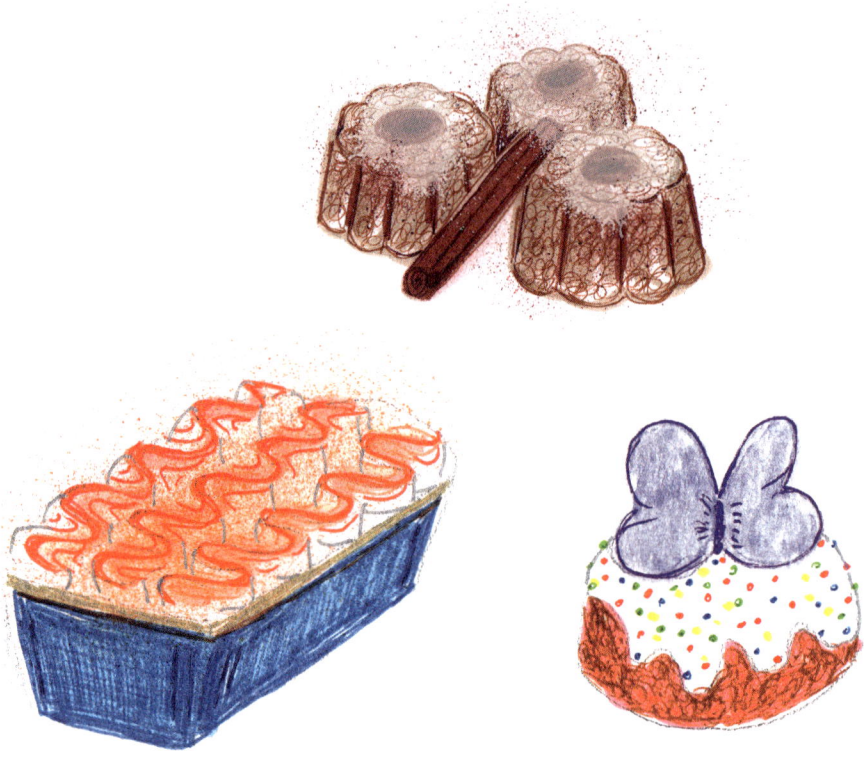

Humos NY

Playing with fire, for the two brothers behind this popular food vendor, is an art form and passion. Named after the Spanish word for "smoke," the venture was born in March 2023 "from a smoke dream," they wrote in an Instagram post. They have an active presence at the Bronx Night Market and other events and festivals across the city.

Ask for the mix grill and you'll be treated to heaps of meat of every cut and type. Sandwiches include the Empire, which comes with a smoked meat of your choice, provolone cheese, and pico de gallo, and the Choripan, filled with chorizo and chimichurri sauce. Humos NY will also be happy to wheel up to your private event, where they "put on a true meat show," according to the website *Untapped New York*, as they cook up orders on "a grill with avant-garde designs." Their success has led the brothers to branch out into other ventures, including dabbling with a seafood pop-up.

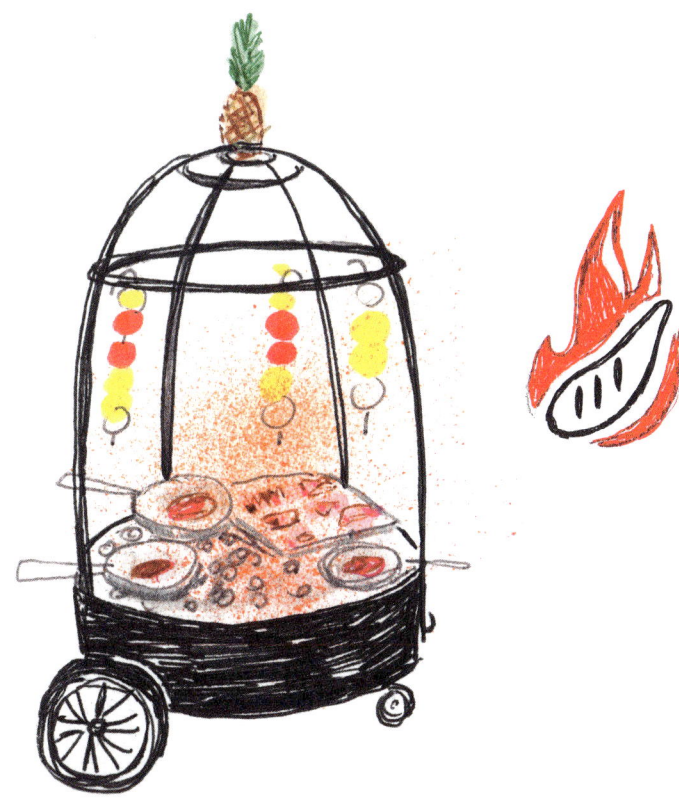

Lei's Litty Kitchen

In 2020 Elisha "Little Lei" Lyew started her Harlem-based business specializing in Southern and seafood dishes. Known to customers as the "spice gal" (she in return refers to them as the "Litty Gang"), Elisha grew up in New York but is originally from North Carolina, with roots in Barbados and Panama—all of which influence her cooking. Favorites include her famous seven-cheese Litty Mac n' Cheese Smacked Bowls, Big Mama's Seafood Fries, and Big Daddy's Cabbage Slaw Pulled Pork Sandwich.

Thanks to the success of her mobile venture, which has been part of the Bronx Night Market, in 2022 Elisha was cast on the first and only season of *Rat in the Kitchen*, a show on TBS hosted by Ludo Lefebvre and Natasha Leggero. The premise centered on six chefs who must collaborate on cooking challenges to earn money, all the while one is secretly trying to sabotage their efforts (think *Top Chef* meets *The Mole*).

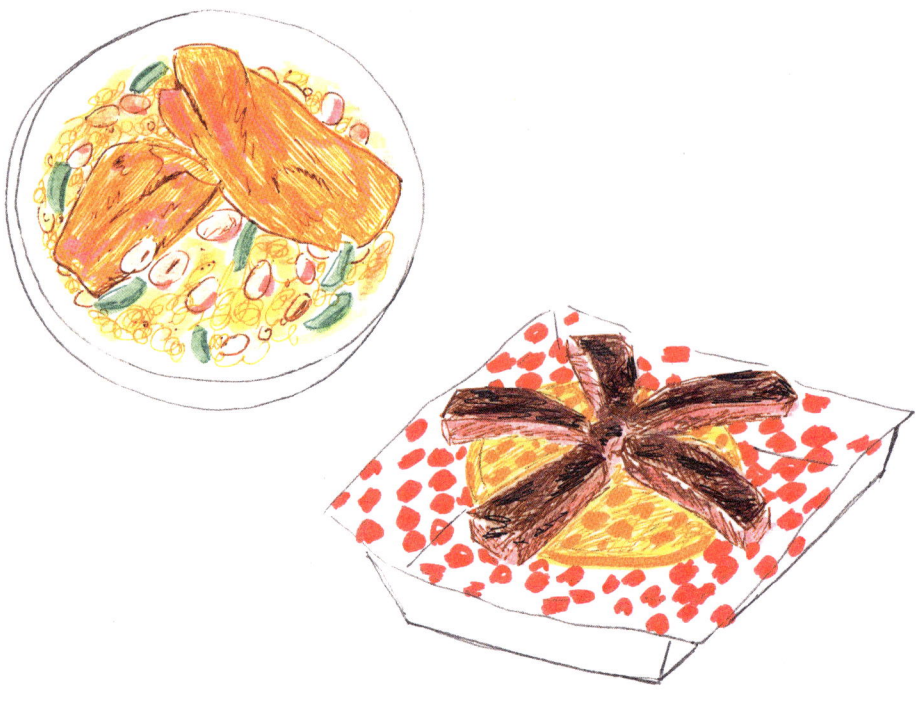

Brazen Flavas

Founded in 2020, this mobile business has set out to elevate a sweet, boozy treat you might not have had since college: the classic Jell-O shot. But don't worry, the Brazen Flavas team promises they've ridded their versions of the "infamous vodka burn." As they write on their site, "Each shot is an invitation to share a special moment with the lit ones, the shy ones, the ready to fly high ones." These brazen entrepreneurs also have created packaging for their shots, with indentations on two sides, that allow "true party animals to stay sexy" (at long last!) by "eliminating the need to stick their fingers or tongues into the cups." All you have to do, they say, is squeeze.

Their menu includes "classic fruit" options, like pineapple and watermelon, as well as shots made to taste like a tiny cocktail, such as a cosmopolitan or sangria. The business has been a presence at the Bronx Night Market, among other festivals, but is also available for delivery, so you can relive your Greek years within the privacy of your own home.

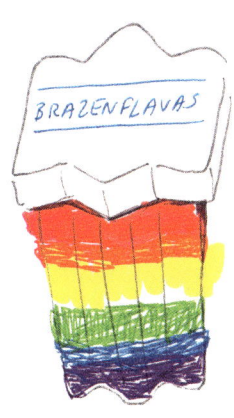
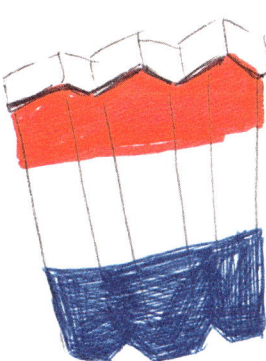
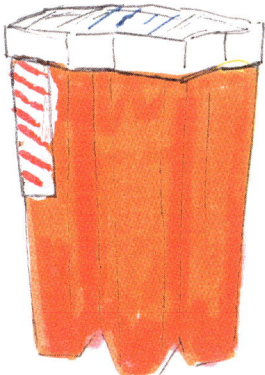

Five Boro Popcorn

The bio on the Instagram page of this mobile business perhaps says it best, proclaiming, simply, "We love popcorn." The food truck, founded in 2023, shows its love by offering a wide variety of sweet and savory flavors, including caramel, chocolate, kettle corn, jalapeño ranch, and white cheddar. During the Christmas season, stop by for a bag of the red-and-green-colored Xmas Kettle Mix. As the truck's name implies, you can find it in every borough throughout the city; some frequent spots in Manhattan include Columbia University and Bryant Park.

The Five Boro Popcorn truck itself is dripping in yellow, with different varieties of the snack painted along the bottom—the overall effect making it looks like a giant popcorn bucket on wheels. And the business's social media pages are awash in popcorn puns. One TikTok post reads, "Join us on our crunchy journey through the diverse tastes of New York City's favorite popcorn truck!" It's followed by an equally (ahem) corny one, "Let's pop it up with unique flavors, one kernel at a time!"

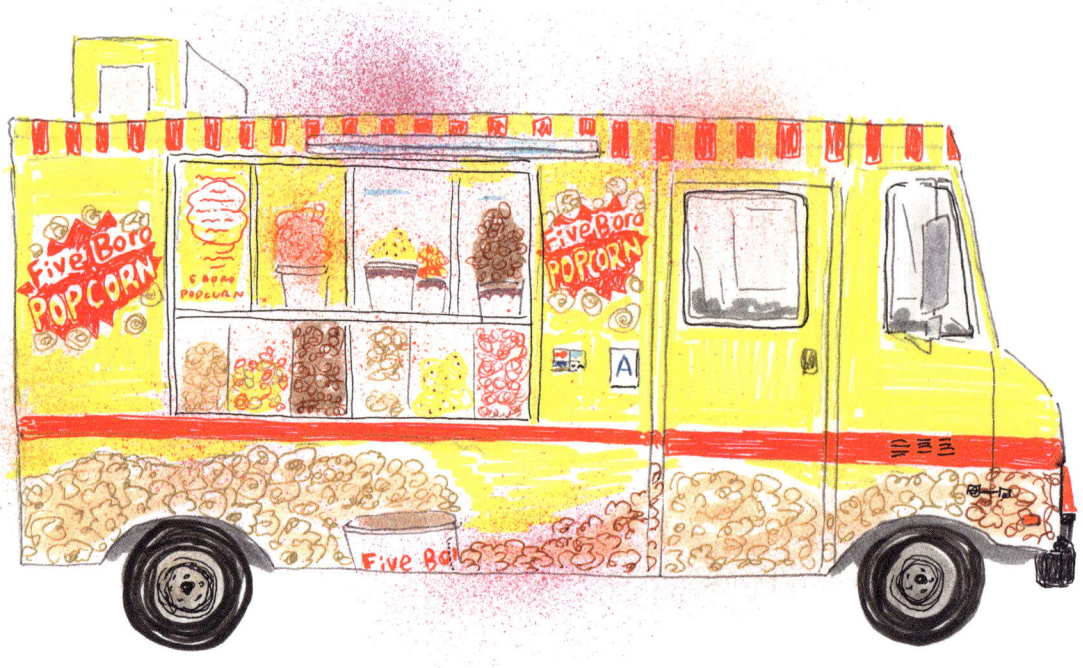

Michael Chen Watch Repair

Many clients of Michael Chen's, a streetside horologist often stationed with his watch-repair cart at 70 Bayard Street in Manhattan's Chinatown, trust no one but him with their timepieces. "Don't waste your time anywhere else. This guy is legit," said one reviewer. He's not just talented, explained another, he's "truly entertaining to watch. He'll change a battery in record time." Other customers noted that you're likely to pay much less with your watches in Michael's care than at a storefront location.

As timepieces became more popular (and affordable) to the public throughout the twentieth century, watch-repair services grew along with the trend. Many of these workers were skilled artisans, often immigrants, who met the growing demand with small kiosks set up on busy street corners throughout the city. Smartphones and the internet have largely killed the practice, but vendors like Michael are helping keep the tradition alive and well.

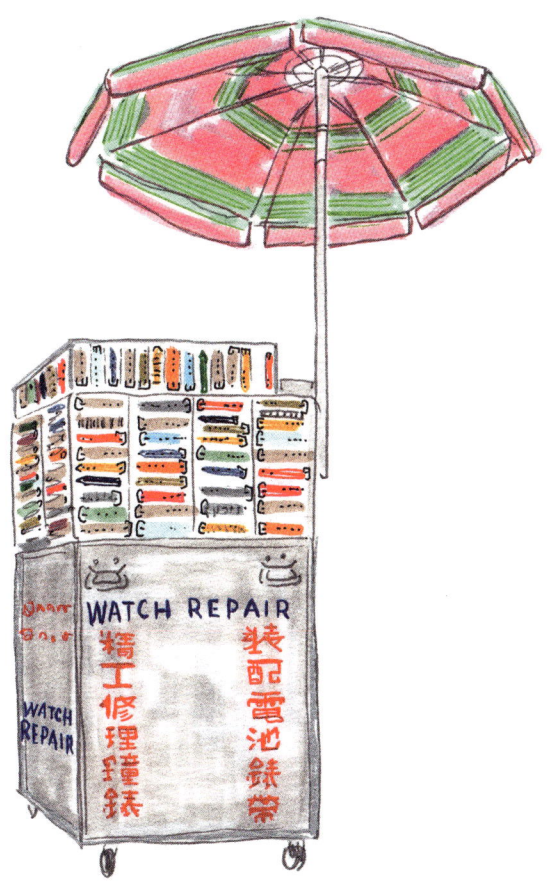

Fruit Stands

Every day at four in the morning, Liton, originally from Bangladesh, wakes and gets ready to go to work—in the dark, so as to not disturb his sleeping wife and son. He takes two subway trains from his home in the Bronx to the west side of Manhattan, where he picks up his fruit stand from a garage on Ninth Avenue. He then rolls the cart three avenues over to his spot at Thirty-Sixth Street and Sixth Avenue, near Herald Square.

A bit past 6 a.m., the fruit suppliers arrive. Liton's offerings are sourced, like those of most other fruit stands—as well as grocery stores and restaurants in the city—from Hunts Point Produce Market in the Bronx, the largest public market of its kind in the world. Even though their wares all come from the same spot, vendors like Liton are known for selling fruit that is often fresher and riper than what you'll find in most supermarkets. (Grocery stores tend to prefer produce that can last on the shelves for several days, but the bananas, apples, and oranges you buy from Liton will be ready to eat on the spot.)

These fruit vendors are scattered all throughout New York's five boroughs, carrying on a tradition dating back a long time. In nineteenth-century London, street produce vendors known as costermongers (or costers) sold fruit and vegetables from stalls and wheeled carts that could travel around the city.

These sorts of vendors were, and continue to be, an important resource in parts of urban areas that otherwise lack access to fresh produce.

Like most New York City street vendors, many produce sellers are immigrants, some of whom work without permits (given the limited number the city provides). Often this has led to police harassment. In April 2022 a fruit vendor was arrested at the Broadway Junction subway station in Brooklyn for operating without a permit, prompting outrage from the public and advocates who argued that the police's handling of the arrest was excessive. It's a good lesson for the powers that be in the city: Don't mess with a New Yorker's "fruit guy."

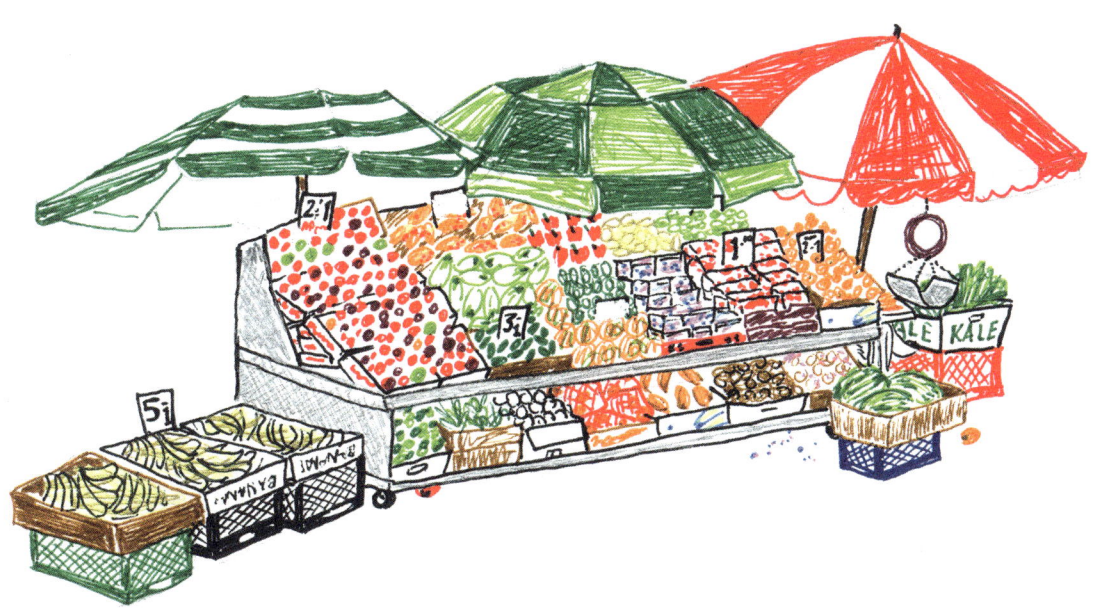

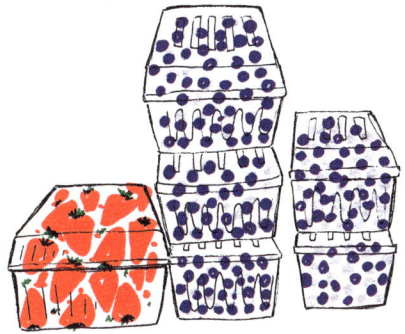

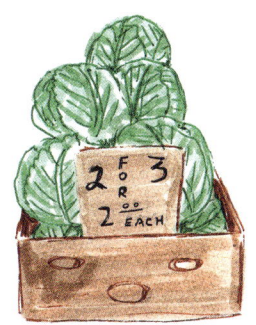

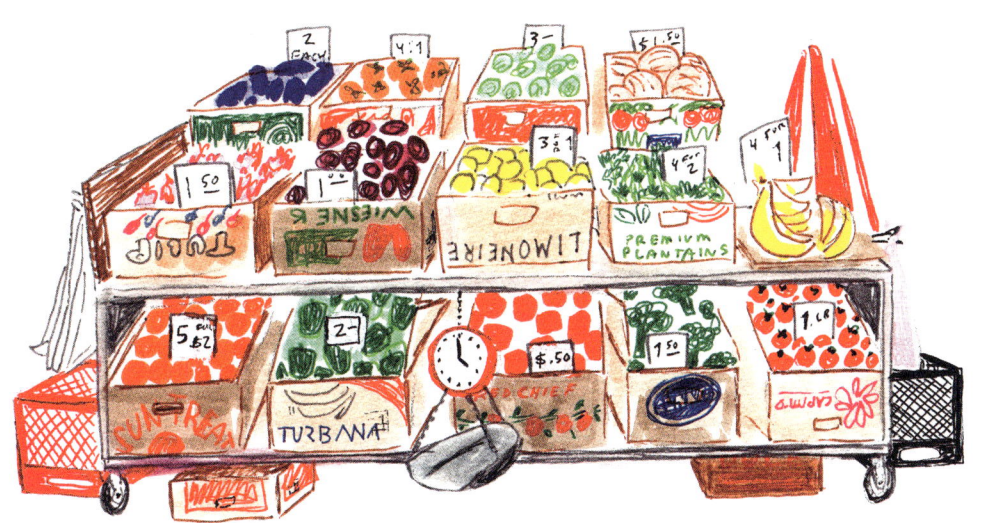

Dominick's Famous Hot Dogs

This family-run street vending business has roots dating back to the late 1950s, with a stall at the annual Feast of San Gennaro, an eleven-day Italian American festival festival in Manhattan's Little Italy. Angelina and Gary D'Angelo own the enterprise today, operating two food trucks—the other is D'Angelo's Sausages—located within walking distance of one another. This one, focused on hot dogs, is parked at Woodhaven Boulevard near Sixty-Fifth Drive, alongside Rego Park in Queens, where it's been stationed since 1959.

Hot dogs from Dominick's are best known for their size—so large they tend to fall out of both sides of the bun. Otherwise, they're served the classic New York way: topped with sautéed onions, sauerkraut, and mustard. In a city full of wieners, these dogs are widely considered to be among the very best—so much so that they were the focus of a 2009 episode of *Top Chef*. During the challenge, contestants had to try their hand at creating a hot dog that could rival the ones Angelina and Gary's family have been making for decades.

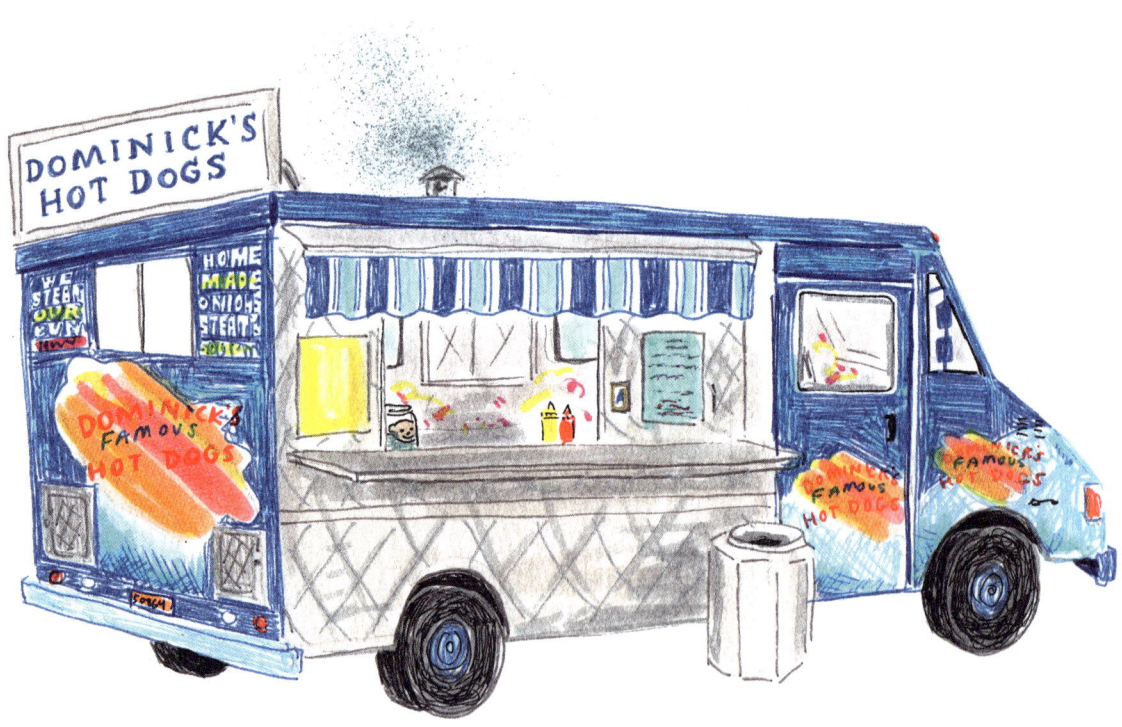

D'Angelo's Sausages

D'Angelo's is the sausage-focused cousin of Dominick's Famous Hot Dogs. It's located a few blocks away along the same stretch of Woodhaven Boulevard, near Sixty-Seventh Drive and was started by the family in 1968, a decade after Dominick's first opened. Though best known for their sausages (which are served in Italian heroes, topped with sautéed peppers and onions), D'Angelo's sells chicken or meatball heroes as well. When asked about their flavorful offerings, Angelina and Gary said they buy their meat from a local butcher but declined to elaborate any further; the exact recipe, they say, is a family secret.

While regulars debate which truck is better—Dominick's or D'Angelo's— at least one online reviewer posed a compromise: "The move," he wrote, is to get "two chili dogs with a Dr. Brown's cream soda" from Dominick's then head down the street to D'Angelo's for a sausage and peppers. "You'll be good for the day. The absolute best."

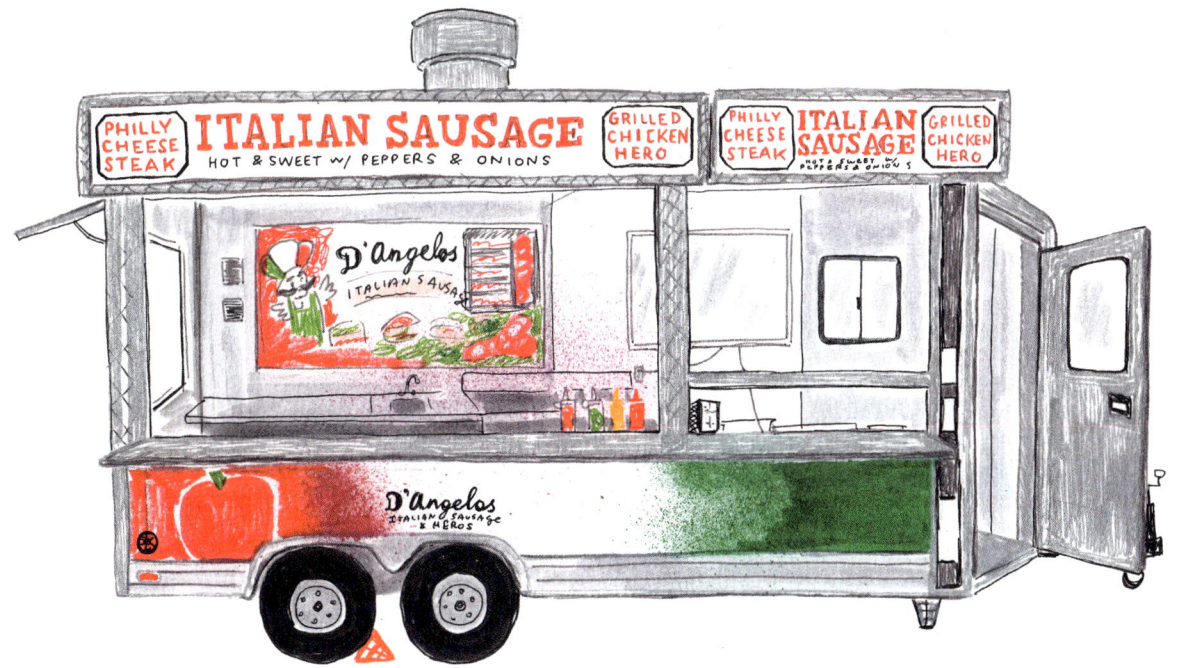

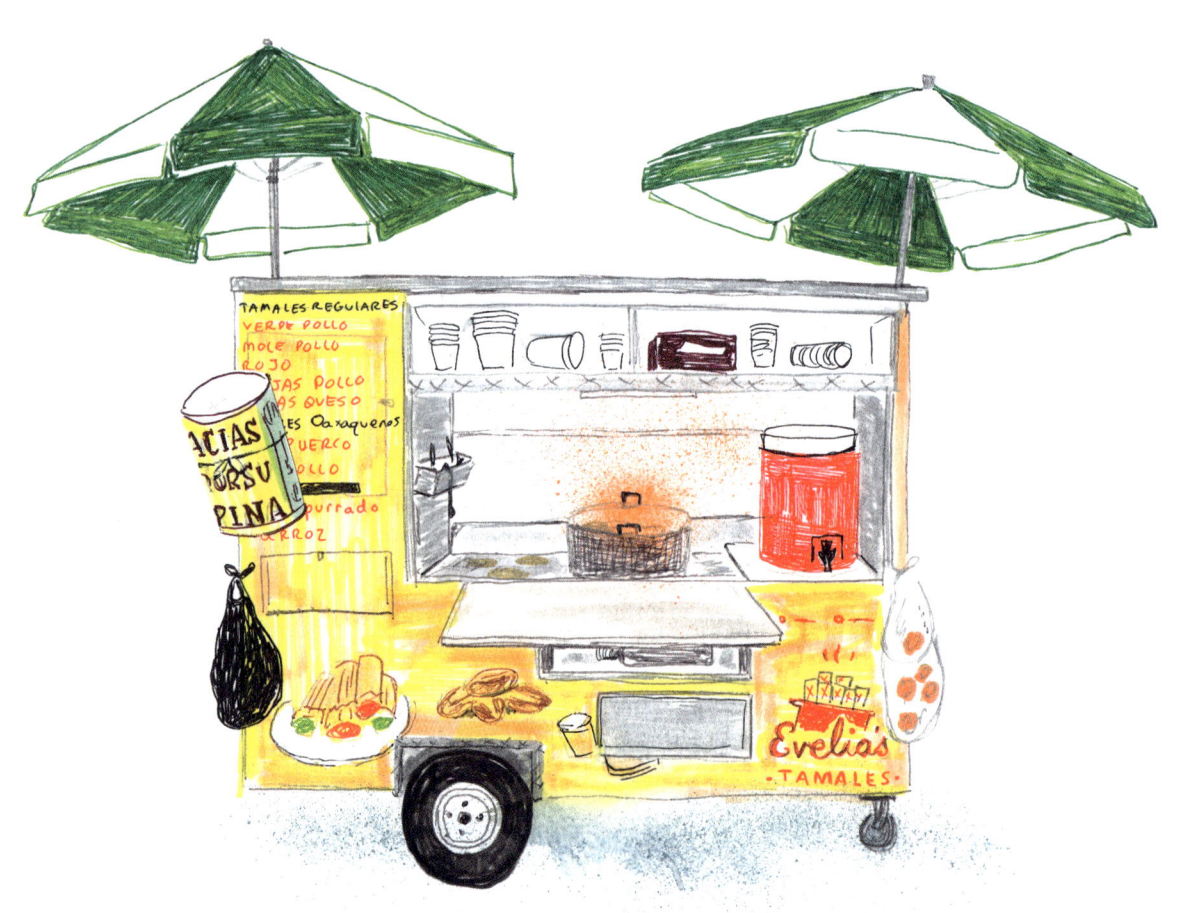

Evelia's Tamales

This spot—which *The New York Times* proclaimed in a 2022 review to be the "most celebrated tamale outlet" in the city—has been delighting patrons with authentic Mexican tamales for decades. Evelia Coyotzi started the business in 2001, after the McDonald's she was working at near the World Trade Center closed following the September 11th attacks. To make ends meet, she started selling tamales from a shopping cart on a street corner in North Corona, Queens. Her offerings quickly took off; her dedication to traditional recipes and quality garnered a loyal customer base, as did the signature fillings.

Evelia's tamales come with a variety of options, including salsa verde, poblano pepper and cheese, and mole. She sells other authentic Mexican goodies as well, including tortas (with some inventive fillings, like hot dogs and Flamin' Hot Cheetos), quesadillas prepared with handmade tortillas from nixtamalized masa, and champurrado, a piping hot cup of chocolate made with cinnamon that's popular with regulars, even during the hot summer months.

Still, it's the tamales that keep Evelia's customers coming back, many of them construction workers who pass by her cart—which is ready for business each day of the week at 4 a.m.—for a quick but substantial bite before heading to their jobs. Her basic tamales cost just $1.50, though in recent years, she has started offering additional options, like tamales filled with beef birria or impossible burger meat, which cost a bit more, at $2.00 a piece.

In 2022 Evelia opened her first brick-and-mortar restaurant a half mile from her pushcart location, along Northern Boulevard in Flushing, where she hung a neon sign bearing an ancient Mexican proverb: "live, love, eat tamales."

Prices here are no different than at her original cart, and the menus are largely the same—but the full-sized kitchen gives her the chance to experiment with new recipes. Evelia shows no signs of slowing her march toward a total tamale takeover of New York. In 2023 she expanded her empire into Manhattan, opening a second street cart venture near the High Line in Chelsea, which she named Antojitos Evelia.

Halal Food Vendors

In discussions about food, the term "halal" has historically denoted a method of preparing meat that makes it acceptable for practicing Muslims to eat. Rules include ensuring that the animal is treated humanely and that a Muslim person be the slaughterer. Today, however, many New Yorkers use the term "halal food" to refer (improperly, according to some) to the many vendors in the city selling a version of a now-ubiquitous street food: lamb, chicken, or falafel served with greens, wrapped in pita or over rice, and topped with red or white sauce. (Those looking for meat prepared according to Islamic dietary laws typically know where to go for the real deal.)

While many halal carts and trucks look alike from the outside (featuring a grill and similar-looking menus and signage), each tends to put a unique spin on its food. Depending on where the vendors are from, they may prepare their sauces or spices slightly differently, for instance.

Halal street food took off in New York starting in the 1990s, thanks in part to an increase in immigrants from Egypt, Bangladesh, and Pakistan throughout the decade, many of whom initially moved to become cab drivers. According to a 2007 *New York Times* article, the number of food vendors in the city who said they hailed from one of these countries grew from 69 to 563 between 1990 and 2005.

Halal vendors may be a newer entrant to New York than some century-old mainstays, like those selling hot dogs and pretzels, but today they are just as much a part of the fabric of the city's street food scene.

Online forums are filled with passionate debates about which trucks or carts are the best. If you happen to be passing by one and want to know if it's worth grabbing a quick bite, check to see if they have a lot of meat on the griddle, suggested one reviewer. "That means it's fresh and popular enough to have high turnover."

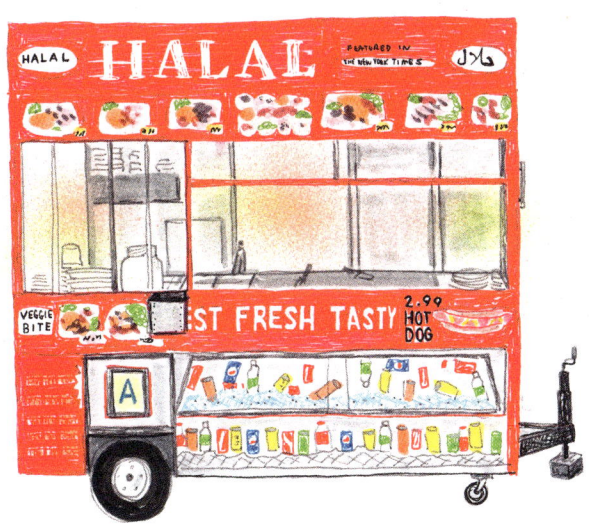

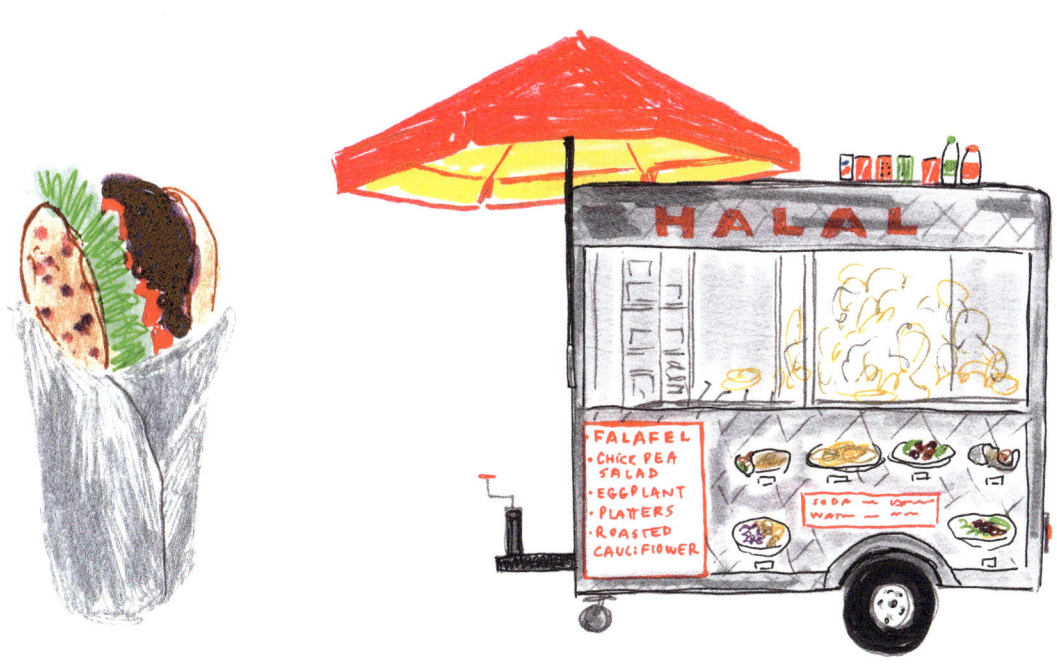

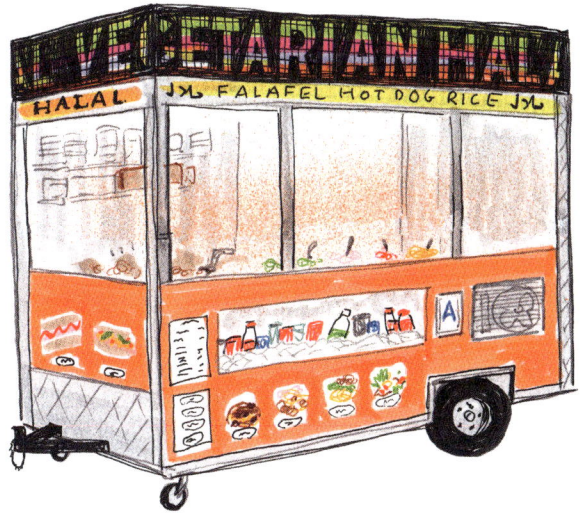

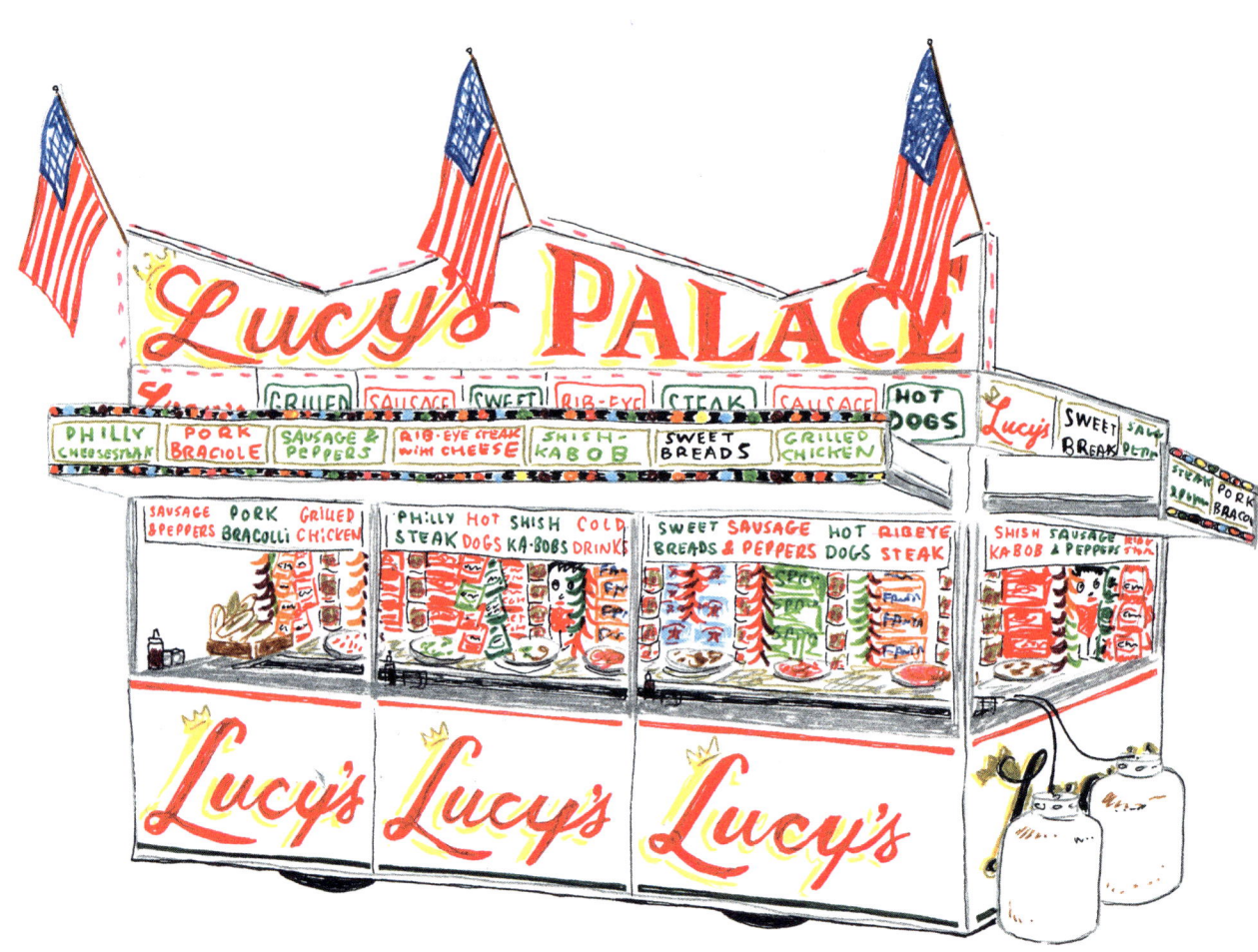

Lucy's Sausage

If there's an Italian festival going on in New York City, "you can be sure to find Lucy's Sausage there," as this street vendor writes on its website. During the annual Feast of San Gennaro in Manhattan's Little Italy the business operates eight separate stands to keep up with the demand, frying around three hundred pounds of homemade ground pork a day. The current proprietor, Lucy Spata, is the third generation of her family to own and operate the venture, which was originally started by her grandmother (also named Lucy) in the late 1920s. Lucy's granddaughter, Lucy—the great-great-granddaughter of the original Lucy—hopes to take over the empire one day. Speaking to the *New York Post* in 2022, the current Lucy noted that, back in her grandmother's day, "San Gennaro was only one block," and the sausage stand consisted of "two metal garbage pails filled with hot coals and topped with a steel plate. The sandwiches were only 25 cents."

Lucy's Sausage features a variety of Italian American favorites, but their sausage and peppers sandwich—made with savory Italian sausage and sautéed with sweet bell peppers and onions—is a favorite. Their menu also includes some of the requisite greatest hits of Italian baked goods and sweets, like braciole, cannoli, zeppole, torrone, and gelato.

Honoring Lucy and her family's decades-long contributions to the Feast of San Gennaro, in 2022 the festival organizers bestowed upon her the royal title of San Gennaro Queen.

In fact, her sausages have become so synonymous with the festival that the business even took part in a two-week-long film shoot for a scene depicting it in *The Godfather Part III*. In the movie, actor Joe Mantegna delivers a lengthy lecture about the importance of Italian immigrants, all while wielding one of Lucy's wieners like a weapon, before finally taking a bite and then proclaiming, "This *salsicce* is wonderful!"

Lucy's stall plays a quirky part in queer art too: It appears in the background on the cover of photographer Gary Lee Boas's book *New York Sex*, which depicts images of gay porn stars, strippers, and sex workers during the early 1980s.

King David Tacos

This food cart cooks up grab-and-go, Austin, Texas–style breakfast tacos each day for busy New Yorkers. Liz Solomon Dwyer, an Austin native, started with just a single Brooklyn-based cart in 2017. Today the business includes a brick-and-mortar spot in Prospect Heights, Brooklyn, and a location in LaGuardia Airport.

The venture is named after Liz's late father, David, who encouraged her to quit her job and start a taco stand when she first moved to New York. "I said, 'That's insane,'" Liz told the website *Edible Manhattan*—only to find herself doing exactly that ten years later. By 2022 she was featured in a *New York Times* write-up titled "New York's Next Great Breakfast Destinations." Customer favorites include the bacon, potato, egg, and cheese taco; a vegetarian option called the Queen Bean, filled with refried beans, scrambled eggs, and cheese; and Mom's Migas, served with scrambled eggs, crispy tortilla strips, and jalapeños.

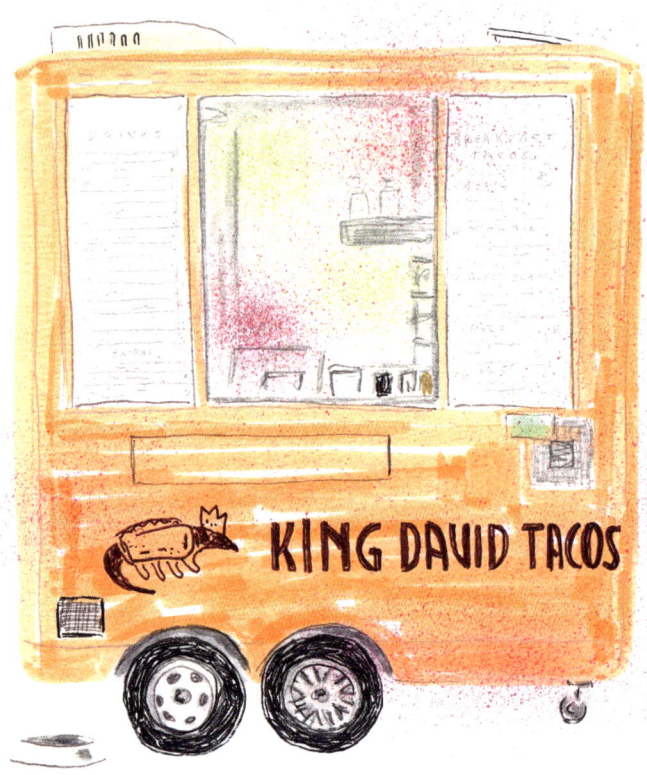

Bodega Truck

Bronx native Jeremy Batista started this mobile business in 2021, thus claiming the mantle of New York's "first and only specialty chopped cheese food truck." Long a super fan of the cheesy sandwich, a staple in bodegas across the city, Jeremy took up experimenting with making his own at home. He began crafting his menu with the O.G., which comes with ground beef, American cheese, salt, pepper, ketchup, mayo, lettuce, and tomato on a roll.

While, today, his mobile venture is only available for private events, in 2025 Jeremy opened two brick-and-mortar locations, both called Bodega City, in Highbridge, the Bronx, and in Williamsburg, Brooklyn. His offerings include nine varieties of chopped cheese, like the Good Mawning, served with bacon, hash browns, and an egg sunny-side up; and the New Yawk, which comes with mozzarella, marinara, and pepperoni. Like Jeremy's truck, his restaurants are an ode to New York's classic bodegas, which would not be complete without the required bodega cat—his are spray-painted on the walls, sitting on loaves of Wonder Bread.

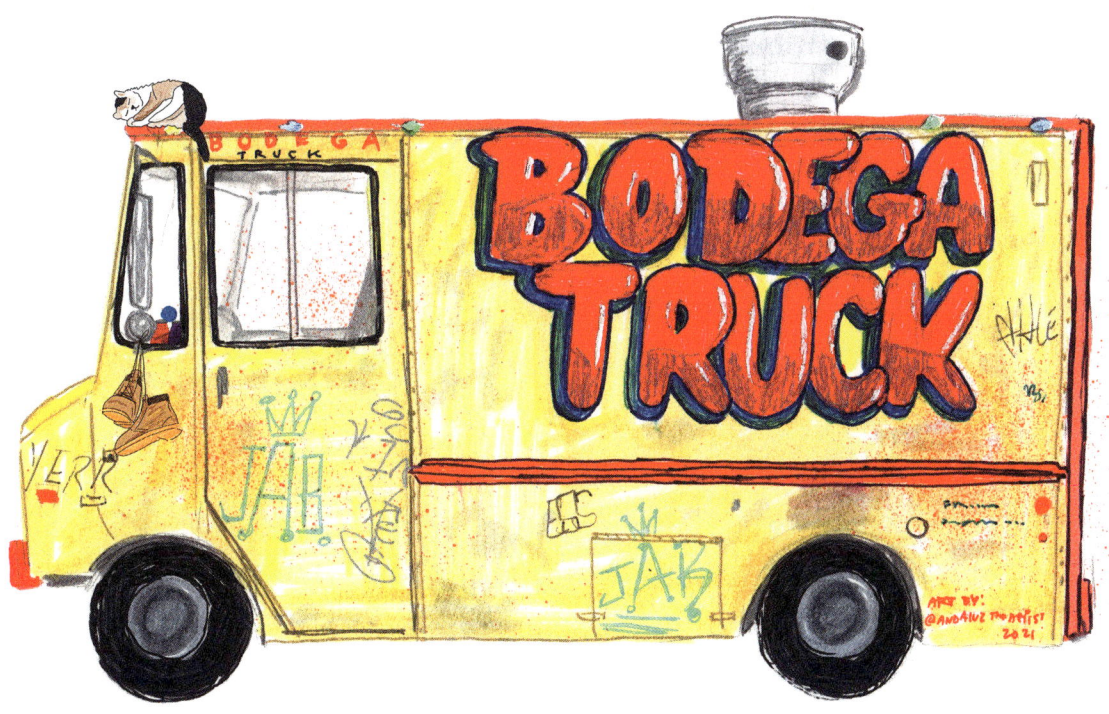

Coffee Carts

Each morning during rush hour, all over the city, students, office workers, and any number of bleary-eyed commuters stand in line at one of the dozens of coffee carts dotting New York's business districts to pick up an impossibly hot cup of joe, a bagel and cream cheese, or maybe a chocolate chip muffin if they're feeling fancy. Lines are long but move quickly. These customers, and the vendors who serve them, have got this daily dance down: Know your order before you're in the front of the line, have your money in hand (exact change, ideally), and then move to the side to let the next person order.

America may run on Dunkin', but these coffee carts fuel New York City—they very well may be the reason it never sleeps.

The boom of coffee carts in New York started, in part, with Greek immigrants who moved here in big numbers during the early 1900s and brought their love of java along with them. According to a 2008 *New York Times* article, at one point there were six hundred Greek-owned coffee shops and carts throughout the city. If you've ever wondered why your coffee is often poured into that iconic blue-and-white paper cup adorned with the classical Greek Anthora design with yellow lettering proclaiming, "We Are Happy to Serve You," this is why; in 1963 the Sherri Cup Company created the vessel to appeal to the hundreds of Greek-owned coffee spots.

Today, thanks to the popularity of these carts and the rise of food trucks, many other coffee vendors have entered the field, from big chains to small, as well as independently owned and operated businesses like the Espresso Guys and Deploy Coffee. This includes venture-capital-backed efforts like Blank Street, which originally started in carts in 2020 but in a few short years quickly exploded to include storefront locations that seemingly cover every last inch of the city. Still, these new enterprises don't seem to have slowed down New York's original coffee carts, thanks to the locals' never-ending need for a quick, cheap caffeine boost.

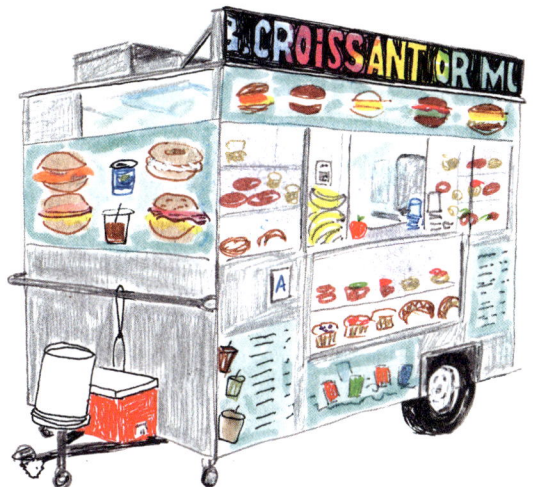

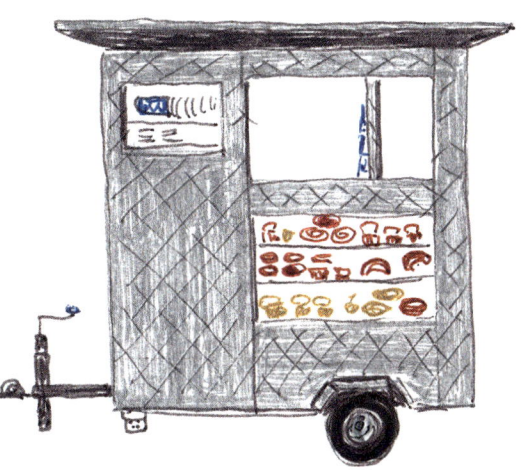

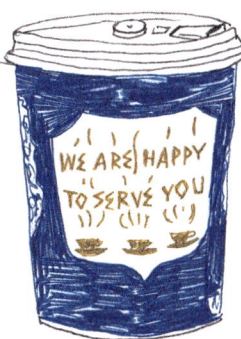

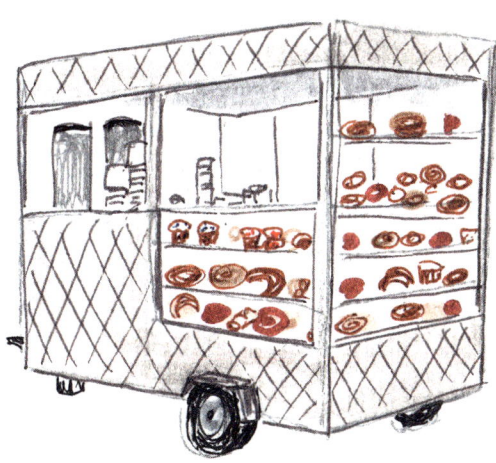

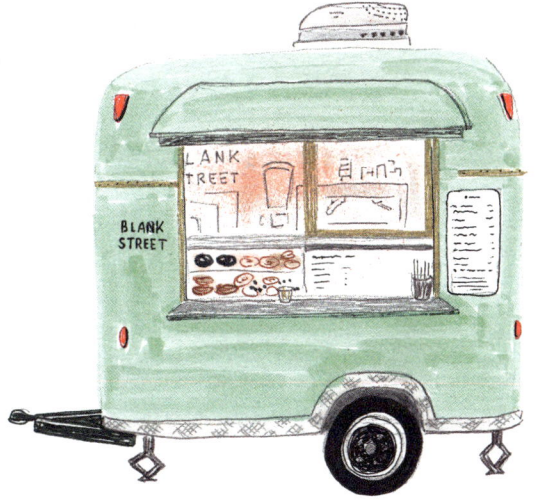

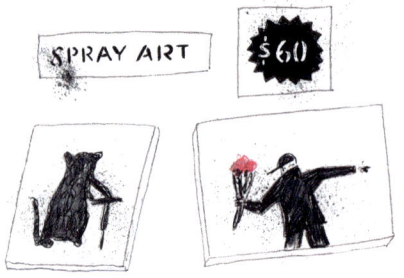

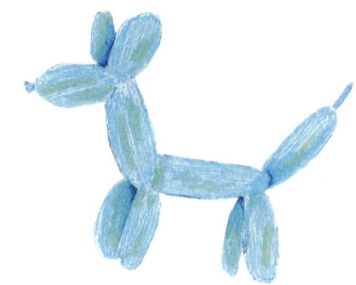

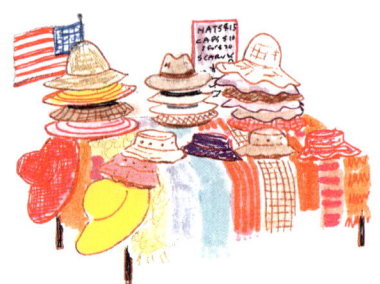

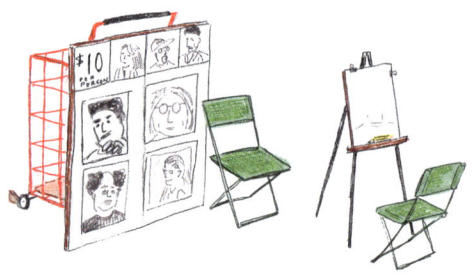

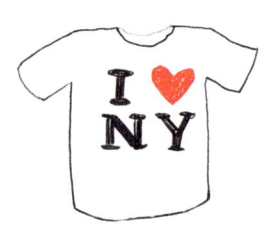

Artists, Writers, and Performers

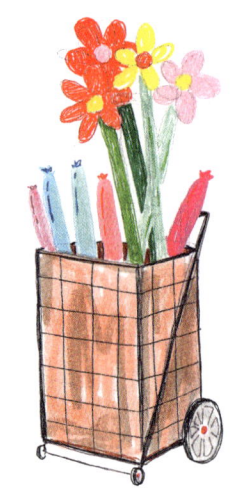

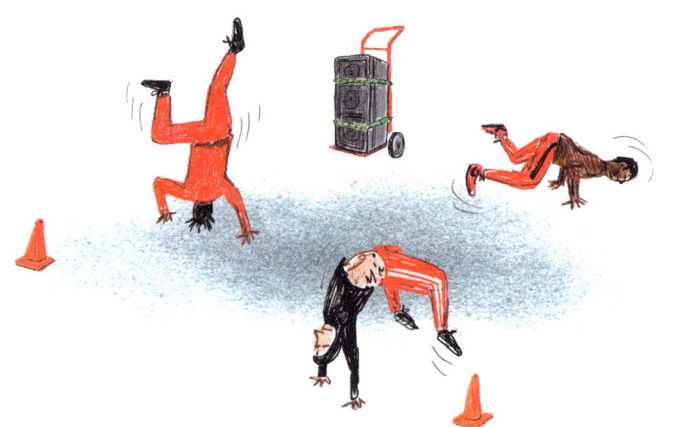

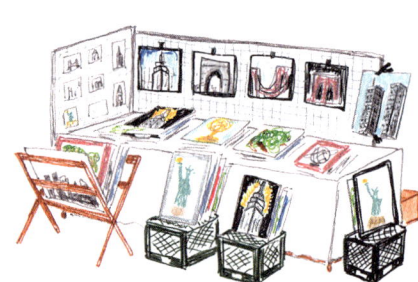

New York has always been an important hub for artists, writers, and performers, and unlike many other types of vendors in the city, these sellers aren't subject to the same strict laws.

Anyone promoting items on the street that can be considered "expressive matter"— including materials that convey personal beliefs, information, or artistic expression— are protected under the First Amendment of the US Constitution.

Whenever you pass by a spray-paint artist, caricaturist, balloon animalist, or anyone else making creations like these on the streets or in parks, they, too, are protected by the First Amendment and don't need special vending permits to sell their art or services. (Though all vendors of expressive matter must still follow some rules, like staying in designated spots in high-traffic pedestrian areas.)

A prominent type of these performers are groups of breakdancers who flip, twirl, and balance on their arms in the city's parks and squares, enticing onlookers to gather around. The crowd mostly consists of tourists, since locals are all too familiar with the ingenious ploy that comes toward the end of the performance. The dancers promise a dazzling final act—a gravity-defying leap over the heads of a half dozen spectators. With volunteers lined up back-to-back, and the crowd's anticipation sufficiently piqued, the performers stop the show to gather donations—only completing the trick (which, admittedly, is very impressive) once they've solicited all they can. Some see it as a shake down of unsuspecting tourists, others see budding entrepreneurs—but either way, it's cheaper than Cirque du Soleil tickets.

Some of the world's most famous artists got their start on the streets of New York. Jean-Michel Basquiat, for instance, began his career selling postcards of his artwork to passersby. In 2013 Banksy, the mischievous British street artist, staged a notorious prank on the art world while selling his work in Central Park. At a simple stall he set up alongside fellow (but far less famous) expressive-matter vendors, he hired an elderly man to sell signed versions of his pieces, which can go for hundreds of thousands of dollars on the fine-art market, for just sixty dollars each.

Felix Morelo

If you've walked through Manhattan's Union Square anytime in the last decade or so, it's likely you've stepped on a "Good Luck Spot." Or maybe a "Bad Luck Spot." Or a "Hugging Spot" or "Kissing Spot." These spots—or rather, chalk circles of various sizes and colors—are the brainchild of artist Felix Morelo, who was born in New York but grew up in Colombia. A graduate of Parsons School of Design, Felix has been drawing these circles with various messages since 2009.

His spots—like the particularly controversial "Suicide Spot"—aren't always ones you want to step on. Two hours after walking through a particularly large "Bad Luck Spot" in Washington Square Park, for example, writer Jaimee Kosanke-Martello and her fiancé learned they had lost their wedding venue, the day before the ceremony. Coincidence? She thinks not. "If we are superstitious about anything," she wrote in a *Huffington Post* article about the experience, "it is Felix Morelo's Bad Luck Spots." Love him or hate him, Felix is accepting solicitations (as well as donations) for your own personal "chalk requests" on his Instagram page.

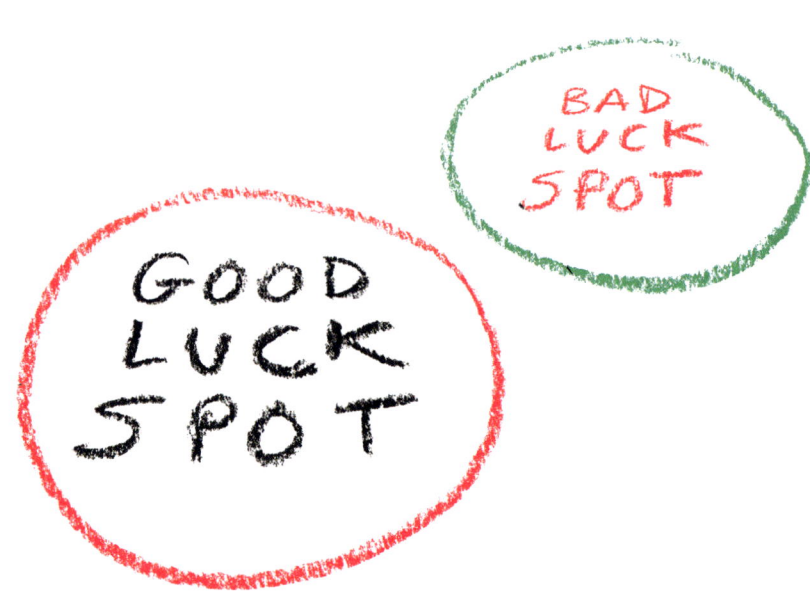

The Park Poet

Peter Chinman, known as the Park Poet, is a New York–based artist who has been crafting personalized poems for pedestrians in Manhattan's Washington Square Park since 2017. After leaving his job, he began hanging out in the park with a sign reading "Ask me for a poem" dangling from his neck or affixed to a small table. Those who do are treated to their very own spontaneous verses, often individualized for each stranger after a brief conversation. One poem from 2019, which the recipient thought was about Peter's ex-lover but was actually about the writer's cat, goes as follows:

> I slink thru your rooms
> I go slack in shafts of light
> It is you who taught me to unwind.

He offers the poems on a "pay-what-you-can" basis, usually between five and twenty dollars. To date he has written over ten thousand poems and has largely made his living by selling them. He's also started amassing his poems into books, which are available for purchase via his website.

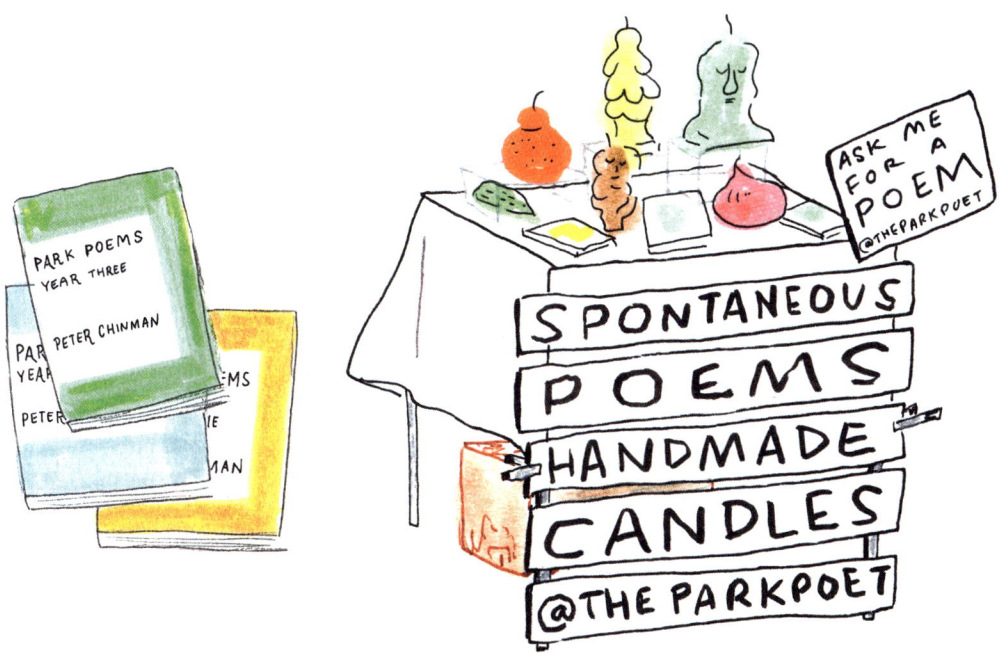

Oriel Ceballos

This successful Panamanian-born, Brooklyn-raised artist, known professionally as OR1EL, got his start selling art on the streets of New York City. His work can veer cartoonish in one moment, as seen in his series of big-eyed animal drawings, and thought-provoking the next (one piece, titled *Family First*, depicts relatives sitting at a dinner table together while money rains down on them). "As a person who has Afro-centric features, I want to make art that speaks to them, to this group," he told *NYCity News Service* in 2023.

Since his start in 2017, Oriel has sold thousands of paintings to people as they've passed by his stand in the subways and streets of New York, helping raise his profile. Today his art is found across the globe in the homes of collectors. In 2023, amid rising commercial success, he finally moved into a studio space—but on occasion, you can still catch him selling his art on the city's streets.

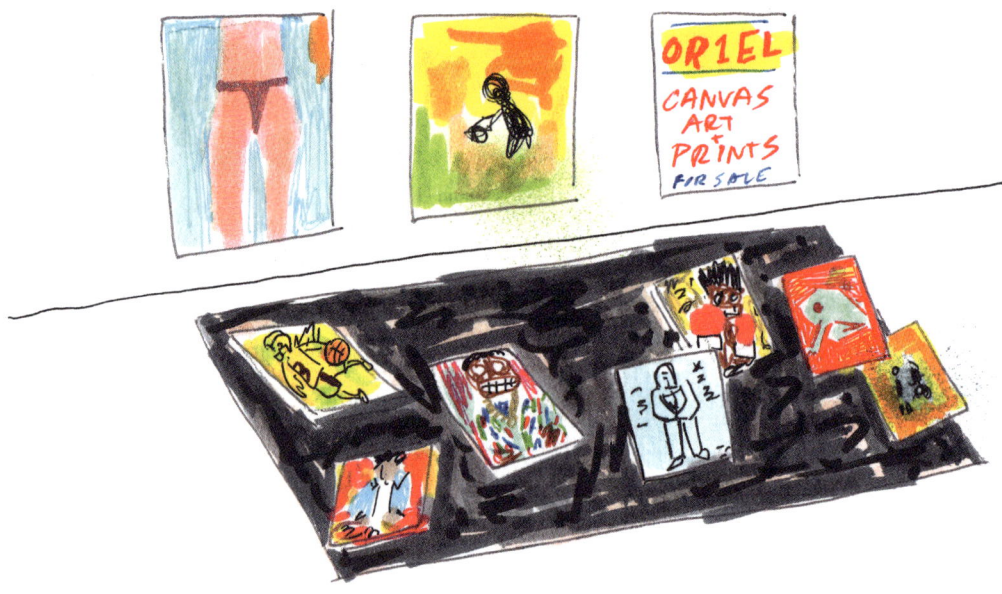

Times Square Performers

During the 2010s these performers became as much of a fixture in Times Square as the massive billboards and flashing lights: people dressed like slightly off-brand versions of Elmo, Spider-Man, and Minnie Mouse who pose with tourists and their kids before requesting a tip. Bare-chested women known as "desnudas"—and wearing little more than a Vegas-style headdress and patriotic body paint—were a common sight, too, posing with tourists in exchange for a few dollars.

For old-school New Yorkers used to a much seedier Times Square throughout the 1970s and '80s, this was all child's play. But for a new generation of visitors accustomed to a post-Giuliani version of the area (with an M&M'S Store rather than BDSM peep shows), these performers caused quite a stir. Eventually Times Square teemed with so many of the characters that the city passed legislation in 2014 to regulate them. The rules designate specific areas where costumed characters can solicit tips from tourists, sparking spirited debate in the city about the balance between artistic freedom and public safety.

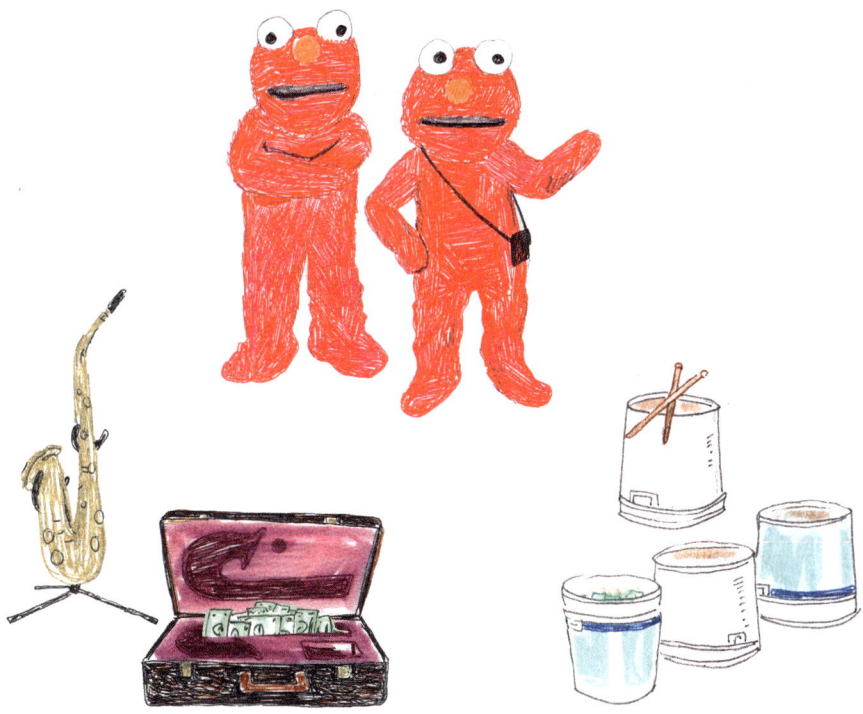

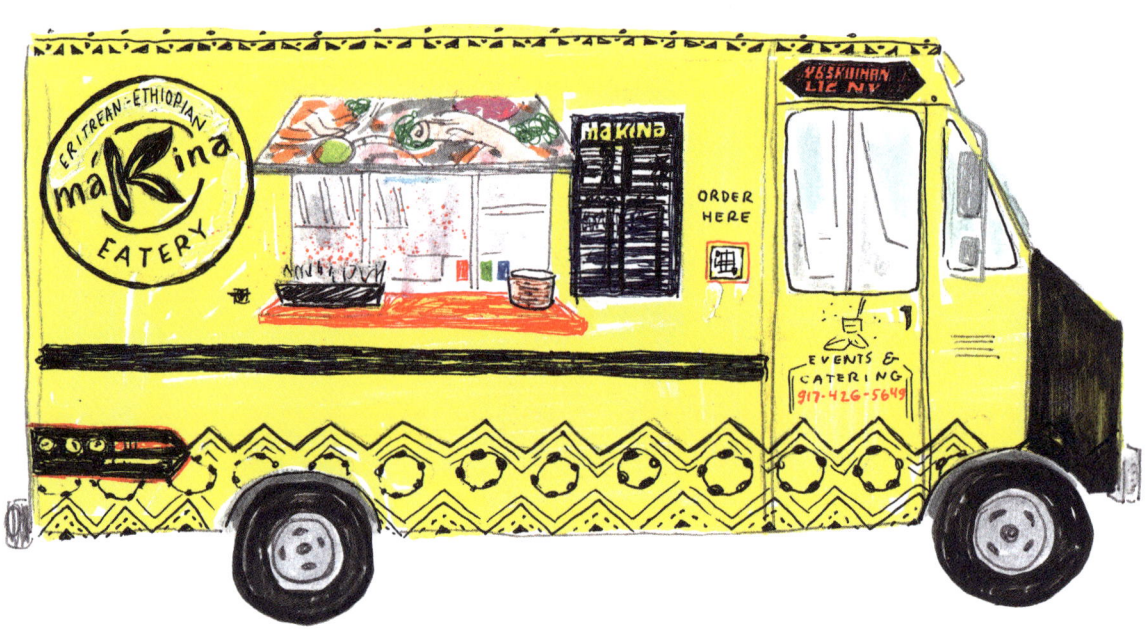

Makina

During the Eritrean–Ethiopian War, which took place from 1998 to 2000, the Ethiopian government forced anyone of Eritrean descent to leave the country. This included Eden Gebre Egziabher and her parents, who sought asylum in the United States. Here, Eden attempted to find harmony between the two opposing parts of her background through her main passion: food.

Makina was born in 2017, and Eden has been selling her take on Ethiopian and Eritrean cuisine from a bright yellow food truck ever since, which she says is the first and only one of its kind in the city.

She describes the food she cooks as Habesha, a term she uses to eliminate the distinction between different tribes of Eritrea and Ethiopia and to "celebrate the unity of people of the same region," she says on her website. The name of her business is also an ode to the area: From both the Amharic and Tigrinya languages, *makina* translates as "truck." Eden even continued to use the name when she opened her (immobile) Makina Cafe in Astoria, Queens, in 2022.

Depending on the day of the week, you can catch her truck on the corner of Old Slip and Water Streets in Lower Manhattan, uptown on 116th and Broadway near Columbia University, or on 30th Street in Long Island City, Queens. During warmer months you can even find Makina on Governor's Island. Eden's menu features staple dishes common throughout the region, including injera (a sour pancake-like flatbread), gomen wat (collard greens made with a spiced oil), and sambusas (a flaky dough filled with lentils and spices). Her "house" sauce is based on a recipe from her grandmother, and *The New York Times* called it "a jalapeño inferno that bestows divinity on all it touches." She also offers a nonthreatening option, made with lemon and oil, that may be more appropriate for some American palettes.

In 2022 Makina Cafe was featured on an episode of *And Just Like That . . .* , the reboot of the *Sex and the City* series. In the scene Sarah Jessica Parker, Cynthia Nixon, and Karen Pittman enthusiastically chow down on plates full of her food. The way the cast "was killin that makina food was not an act," Eden wrote in an Instagram post.

Shoe Shiners

Shoe shiners—once ubiquitous street vendors in New York who stationed themselves outside busy transit hubs or Midtown office buildings— reached their peak in the early to mid-twentieth century.

Changing fashion trends, however, as well the advent of at-home shoe-care products, have led these stands to all but vanish.

Don Ward, a shoe shiner who worked for years at the corner of Forty-Seventh Street and Sixth Avenue in Manhattan, was a notable and beloved proprietor of this type of business. Known to some as the "Midtown Heckler," Don made a name for himself by jokingly insulting pedestrians whose footwear he deemed in need of a little love—a strategy which could earn him up to nine hundred dollars a shift on a good day, he told the *New York Post* in a 2017 video interview. "You can do better than that," he might say to a man wearing a distressed pair of loafers, or, "You can't look neat if your shoes look beat!" The philosophy behind this is simple, he explained. "How do you catch good fish? You've gotta use good bait."

Leather Spa, with six locations across the city, including two at Grand Central Station and one at Saks Fifth Avenue, is a notable exception in the downward trend in shoe shining. While online reviewers say these spots are pricier than some you can find inside the stores of more traditional cobblers, at least one woman was impressed with their work. "They're expensive, but they do fix everything pretty much perfectly. They even got blood off a pair of old ballet flats for me!"

Shoe shiners have long captured the imaginations of New York–based artists. In the 1860s Horatio Alger Jr.'s serial novel *Ragged Dick* helped popularize the rags-to-riches narrative common in American storytelling, with a New York City shoe shiner as its protagonist. In 1947 a teenage Stanley Kubrick captured the life of Mickey, a twelve-year-old Brooklyn shoe shiner, as part of a photo essay for *Look* magazine—offering a portrait of a young boy forced to work to support his family, which included nine brothers and sisters.

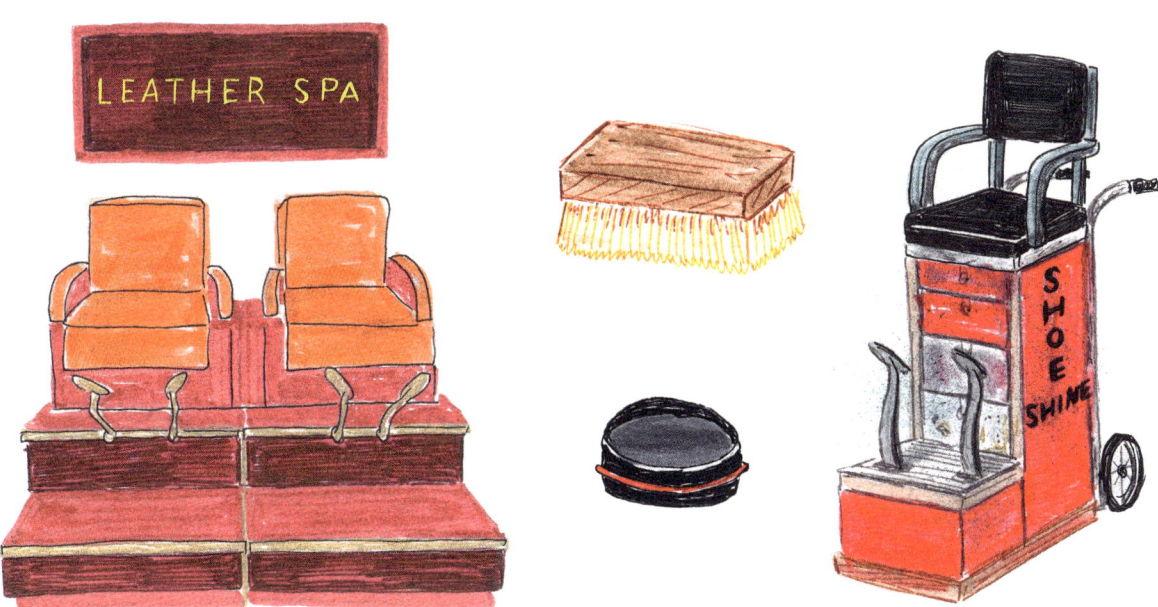

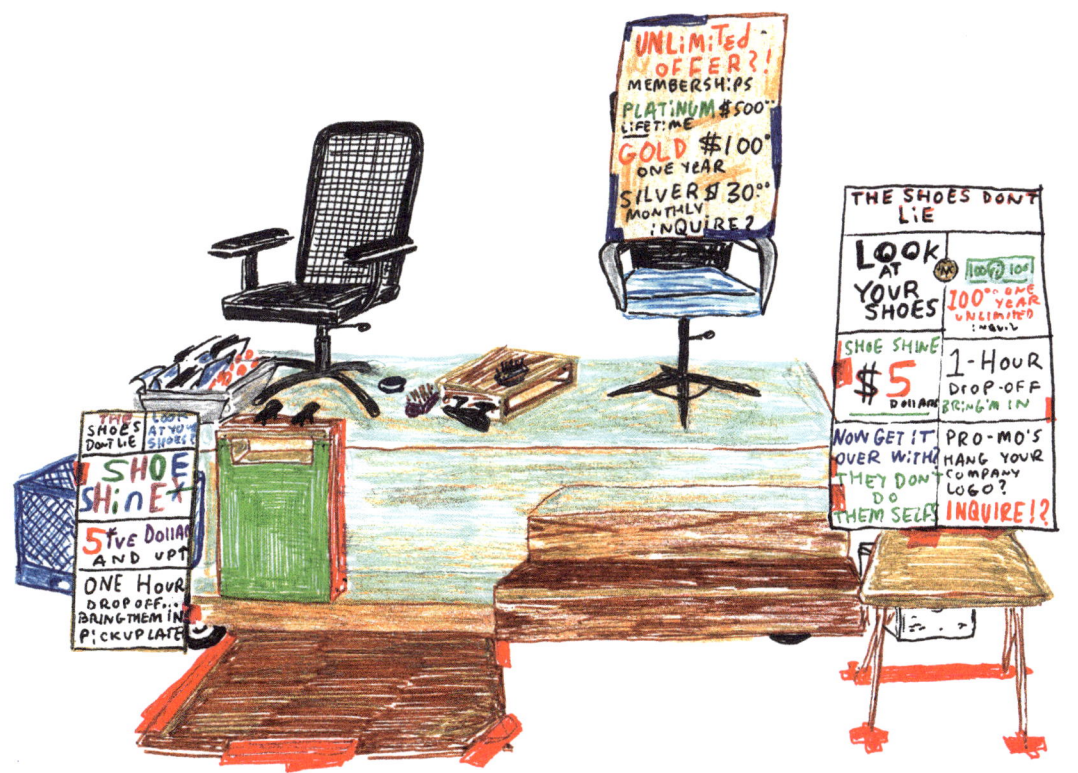

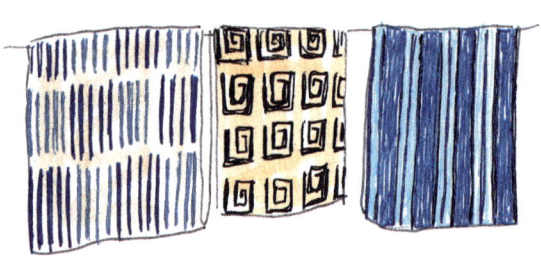

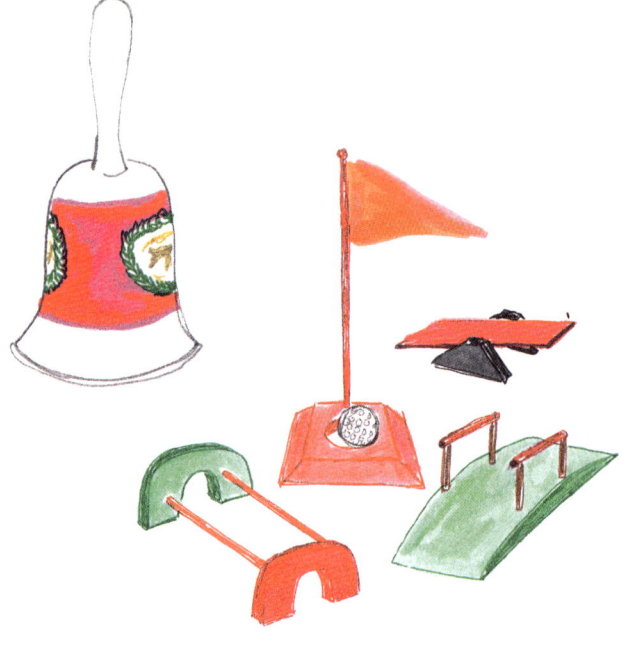

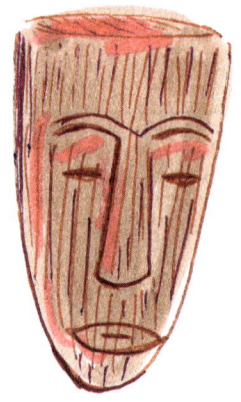

Chelsea Flea

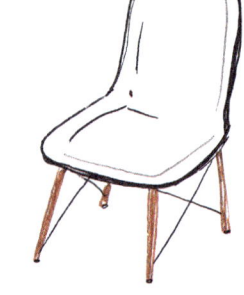

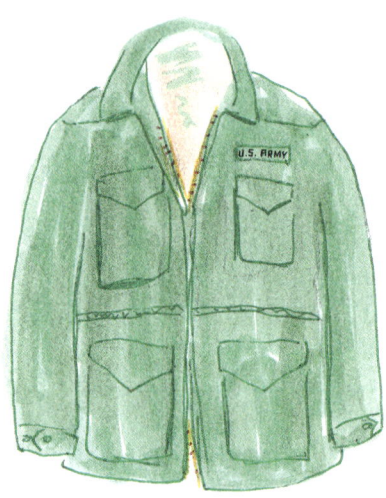

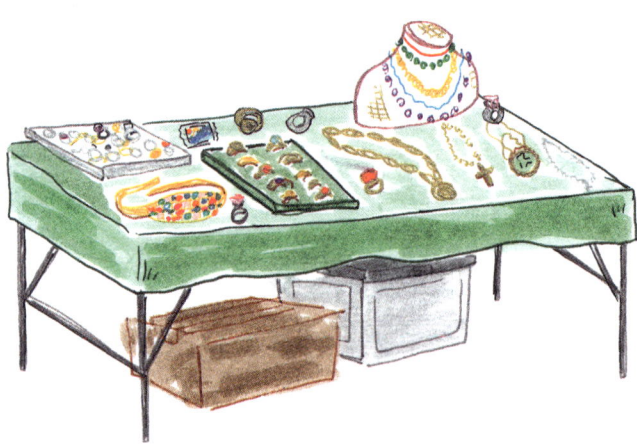

This market has operated on West Twenty-Fifth Street, between Sixth Avenue and Broadway, since 1976. Its founder, Alan Boss, started the venture with just eleven vendors. At its peak hundreds of sellers covered every nook and cranny of its footprint and much of the surrounding sidewalks, offering up a wide array of high-quality antiques, furniture, art, and other collectibles. In recent years the Chelsea Flea has shrunk to less than one hundred vendors, but it stays open year-round on Saturday and Sunday, rain or shine.

Many credit the market, which draws in the city's creative community, for helping turn Chelsea into one of New York's most popular arts districts.

Andy Warhol was a common celebrity sighting at the Chelsea Flea during the 1980s—he often visited in search of vintage cookie jars to add to his collection. "A friend told him you need to go to the flea market to get new and great ideas," Alan told *The New York Times* in 2019—and for Warhol, apparently, that idea was cookie jars: By the time he died, he had 175, which sold at auction for a total of $247,830.

Under its original owner, the Chelsea Flea managed to hold on for decades, even amid the neighborhood's gentrification. In 2019, however, Alan finally lost his lease. Fortunately, just a year later Jonathan Butler and Eric Demby—the duo that started the popular Brooklyn Flea in 2008 (p. 26)—came to their fellow market's rescue and continue to operate it under their umbrella today.

Lulu's Vintage Lovelies, where owner Yardena Lulu offers an eclectic mix of vintage items, has been a part of the market for years and is among the more popular current vendors. At her stall you might find collectibles like a lion necklace from the 1960s, complete with emerald eyes and long gold-plated foxtail fringe for the mane, or a six-inch 1990s butterfly brooch by Bettina von Walhof decked out in Swarovski crystals.

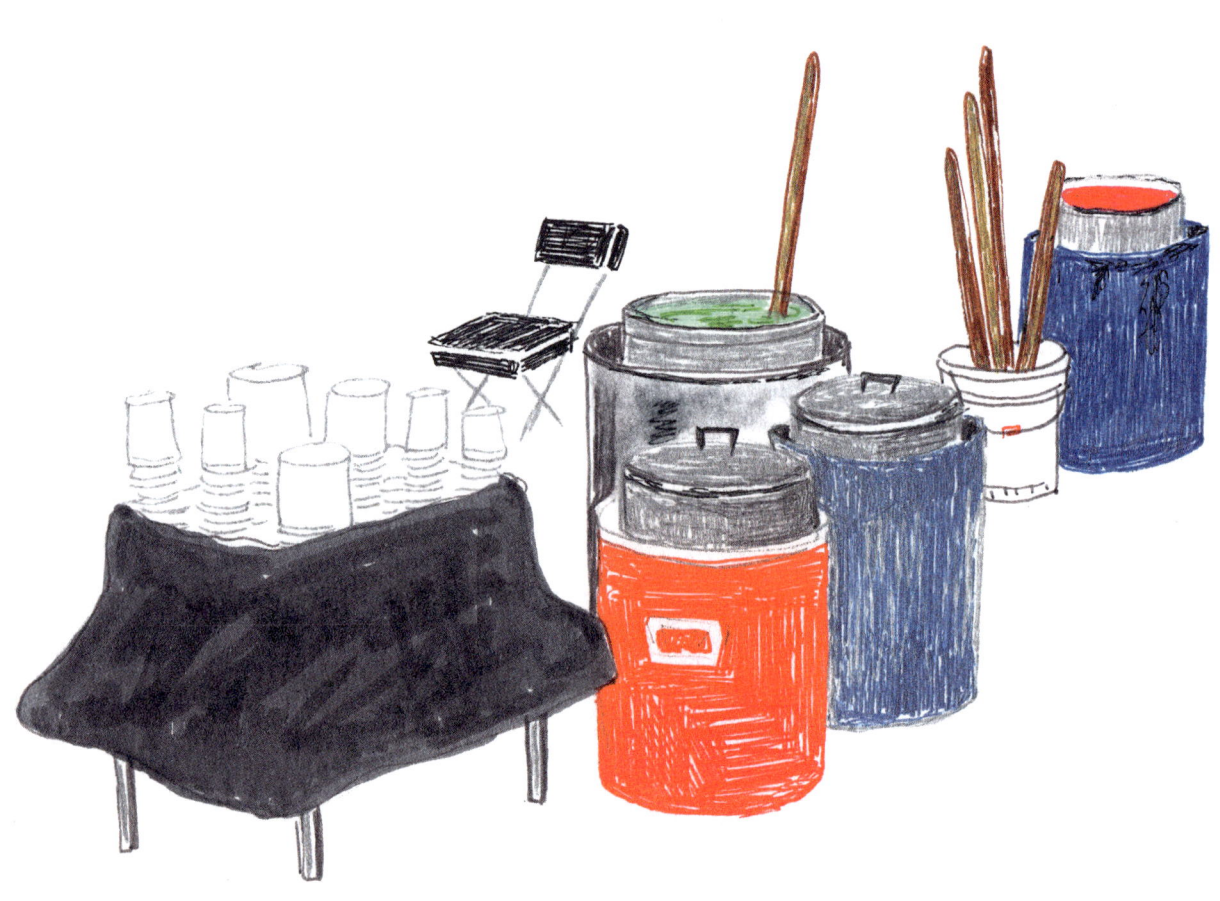

Nieves Cortés

Since 2020 Fidel Cortés Jr., originally from Pueblo, Mexico, has been giving sweet relief to New Yorkers during the sweltering summer months. When his hours were cut back at his previous job at a supermarket, he began selling ice-cold nieve (also called *nieve de garrafa*—Spanish for "jug of snow"), a traditional Mexican dessert that tastes like sorbet, to make some extra cash. His sweets quickly took off, however, and what started as a side hustle soon became his main focus. During the hottest time of the year, you will find Fidel at the intersection of Knickerbocker Avenue and Suydam Street in Bushwick, Brooklyn, near Maria Hernandez Park, often with a crowd of kids (and, let's be real, adults) gathered around him.

To make the nieve, Fidel and his family spend up to three hours blending fresh, ripe fruit every morning. The juice then sits in big wooden barrels, packed with ice and salt, for another two hours until it's ready to serve. Popular flavors include cantaloupe, watermelon, mango, pineapple, cactus fruit, and tamarind.

The secret to achieving nieve's smooth, creamy texture is constant stirring—it's a workout for the arms, but at least there's an icy treat as a reward at the end.

Making the sweets from scratch using real fruit has garnered Fidel a loyal following both in person and online, thanks to the Instagram-friendly, eye-catching colors of his iced treats. The business is a family affair, with Fidel's father and mother popping up on his social media accounts, helping stir the sweets and interact with customers.

Though he loves making and selling nieve, Fidel's work is, for the time being, more of a passion project. The problem, he explained in a TikTok video posted in January 2025, is that it's very seasonal. "When it gets cold, I have to find other work so that I can survive here, pay the rent, pay bills," he said in the clip. One day he hopes to open a permanent, year-round location where he can sell nieve, in addition to some Mexican staples his mother makes, including masa, tortillas, and tlacoyos.

Soft Pretzel Vendors

The pretzel's journey to New York started in the nineteenth century during a wave of European immigration—particularly from Germany, where the twisted, baked bread has been a staple snack for centuries. According to one theory, the pretzel was invented in Italy in the seventh century, created by monks who incorporated three holes into it to represent the Holy Trinity. Another theory holds that monks devised the snack as a doughy representation of hands crossed against a chest in prayer. The exact origins are a mystery, but at least we seem to know monks were involved.

At first pretzel vendors in New York sold their goods from open-air wooden wagons they wheeled around pedestrian-packed parts of the city. Today you can typically find them selling from metal carts equipped with heating elements that help keep the bread warm; many also offer up other snacks, like hot dogs and sodas.

There are still dozens of these mom-and-pop vendors operating in the city, some of which have been in business for decades.

One of these vendors, named Chris, originally from Greece, has sold pretzels from the same corner on Forty-Third Street in Manhattan for more than a decade. He sells around fifty pretzels a day, he told the blog *Time Travel Turtle* in 2023, for $2.50 each. "You get to see all these people who come here from around the world," he said of the job. "They stare at the buildings. It's fun."

These days, even Auntie Anne's, a pretzel company started in 1988 and sold today in hundreds of stores internationally, has gotten in on the street vending business, launching a food truck version of its empire in New York (mostly for catered or private events). The truck is painted a vibrant blue and adorned with massive pretzel shapes—but just in case you happen to miss those, you'll likely spot the four-foot-long blow-up pretzel that's on top of the truck while it's doing business.

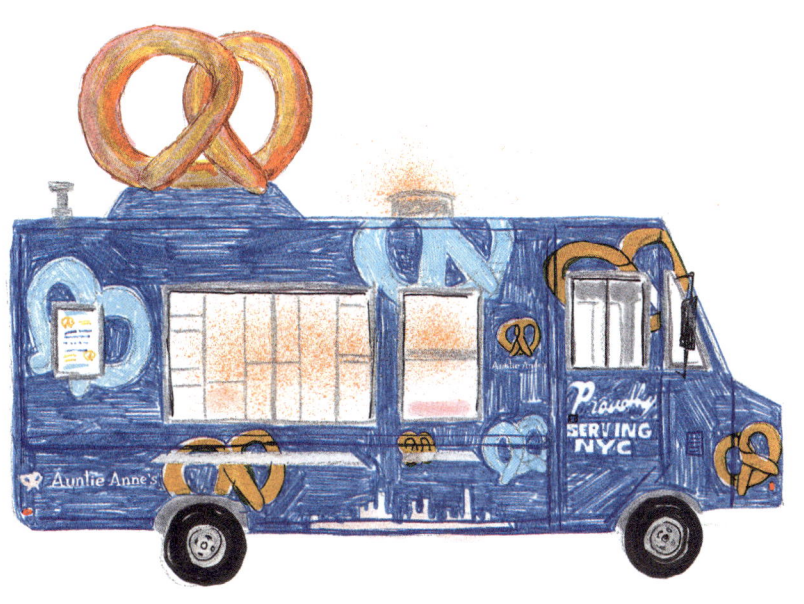
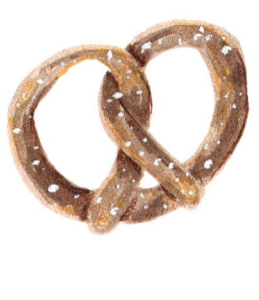
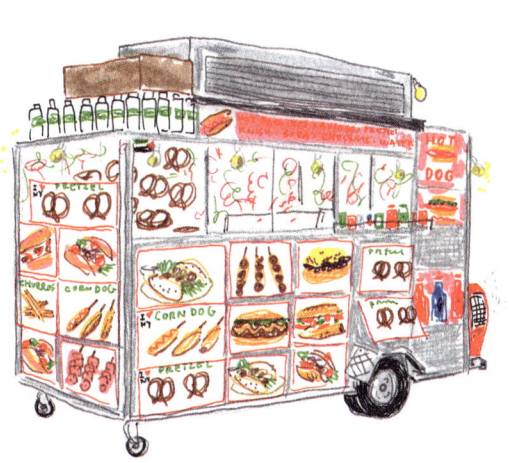
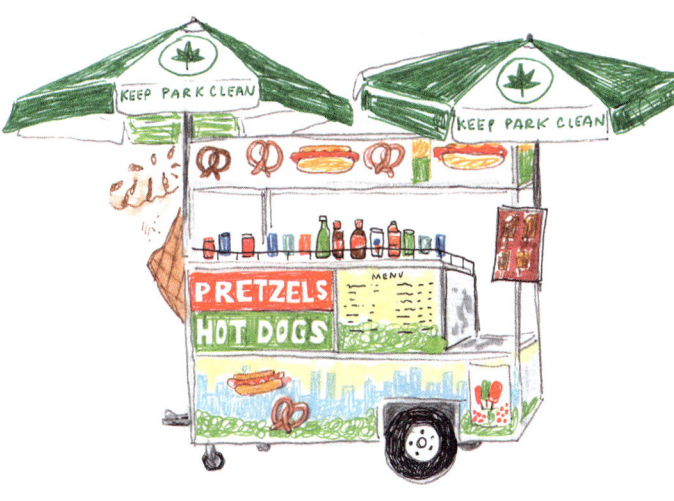

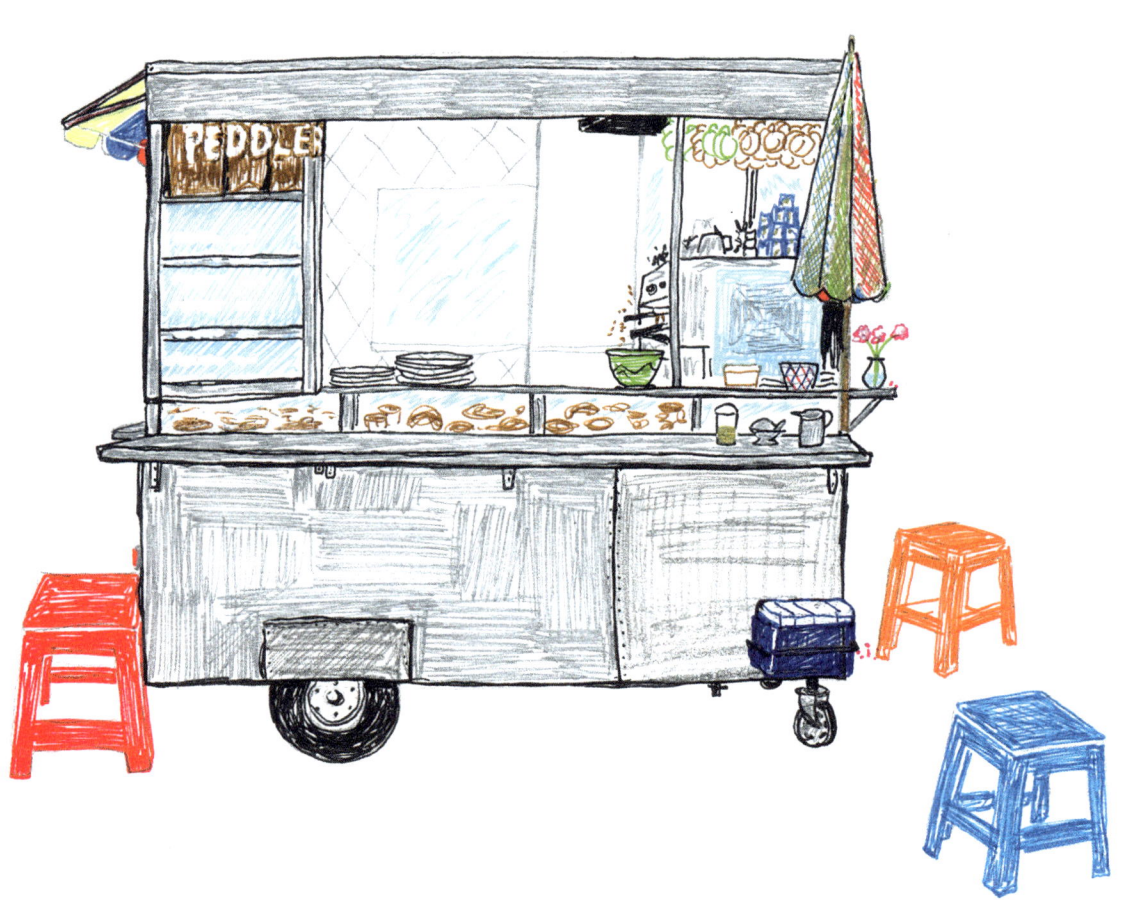

Peddler 2000

For years, if you passed by the northeast corner of Lafayette and East Houston Streets in downtown Manhattan, you couldn't miss Peddler 2000, a quirky local coffee cart from the brains of its proprietor, Australian-born Byron Kaplan. A collection of random teacups dangled from the cart's ceiling, and bright plastic stools dotted the nearby grounds. Don't be fooled by Byron's ragtag operation, though. As one regular told *The New York Times* in 2015, Peddler 2000's coffee, sourced from the Brooklyn-based roaster Sey, was "very bright and fruity, and . . . super consistent."

Byron started the business in 2012, using a cart he created himself from discarded glass siding and scrap metal he found around the city.

It was his second version; the first was made using the base of an old nut-roasting rig. "Most shops I took it to didn't want to touch it, or if they did they were asking for too much money," he told the website *Daily Coffee News* in 2018. Eventually Byron found "a guy" willing to transform it at an affordable price—and he continues to work with him to this day on what has become an expansive fleet of coffee ventures around the city, under the umbrella name Peddler. Over time Byron's street-side coffee business grew to include locations in SoHo and the Flatiron and Financial Districts. As word of his quirky enterprise got out, however, he began focusing more on catering, working events for Google, MTV, HBO, Netflix, and even New York Fashion Week.

As part of Peddler's purpose, Byron also enjoys working with local artists to help bring their talents to New York's streets. He teamed up with designer Makayla Wray, for instance, to open Pedal (p. 94), a mobile tailoring stand in SoHo converted from the nut-roasting cart that Byron used himself in his early days in business. With his colleague Tatiana DeOliveira, he launched Cici (p. 95), a gold-themed coffee cart in Manhattan's Financial District. He has collaborated outside of New York too: In 2016, working with artist Tom Sachs, Byron created a space-themed coffee experience, called Logjam Cafe, inside a tricked-out Winnebago at the Yerba Buena Center for the Arts in San Francisco.

Pedal

When seamstress Makayla Wray began to lose work during the COVID-19 pandemic, she did what many New Yorkers do when trying to get the word out: took her business to the streets. Using a converted nut-roasting cart that belonged to her old boss, Byron Kaplan, the proprietor of Peddler (p. 93), she set up a mobile tailoring shop on the corner of East Houston and Mulberry Streets in Manhattan. To make the cart work for her needs, she welded in an ironing board and attached vintage Abraham & Strauss and Singer sewing machines.

Fortunately, the economy has rebounded since the early days of the pandemic. Makayla now works for an upscale fashion designer based in Chinatown during the day—but each Wednesday she still returns to her corner of SoHo, from roughly 5:30 p.m. until dark, mending garments and fixing hemlines. As she told the *New York Post*, "In the morning I make runway clothes, then I come in at night to hem the little guys."

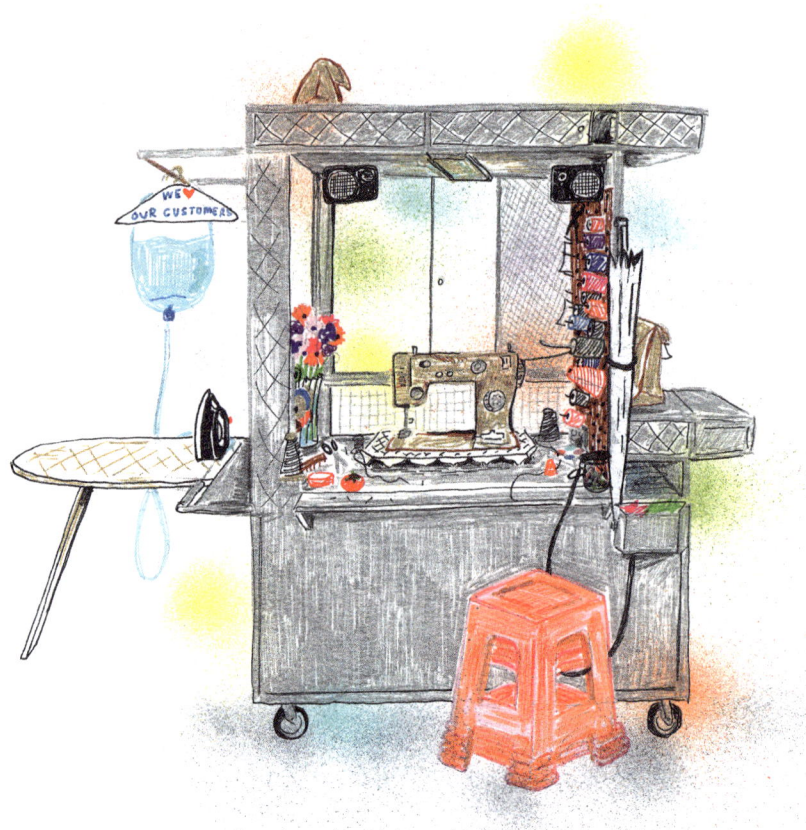

Cici

Tatiana DeOliveira started this coffee cart in 2021 with Byron Kaplan of Peddler (p. 93) and Pedal fame. This one, called Cici, is located at 20 Pine Street in front of Fosun Plaza in Manhattan's Financial District.

Originally Tatiana was pursuing a career as a chef but enjoyed working at the cart so much she decided to do it full time. The cart's design, which is dripping in gold, takes inspiration from the surrounding neighborhood. While Tatiana does serve many of the area's white-collared and well-heeled, including financiers, lawyers, and architects, she says Cici's customer base is mostly locals who live in the area. Her offerings include coffee from Sey and fresh-baked croissants and buns from Otway Bakery, both sourced locally from Brooklyn. The cardamom bun is a favorite, though Tatiana says the jam croissant, with homemade strawberry-raspberry jam, is the true showstopper.

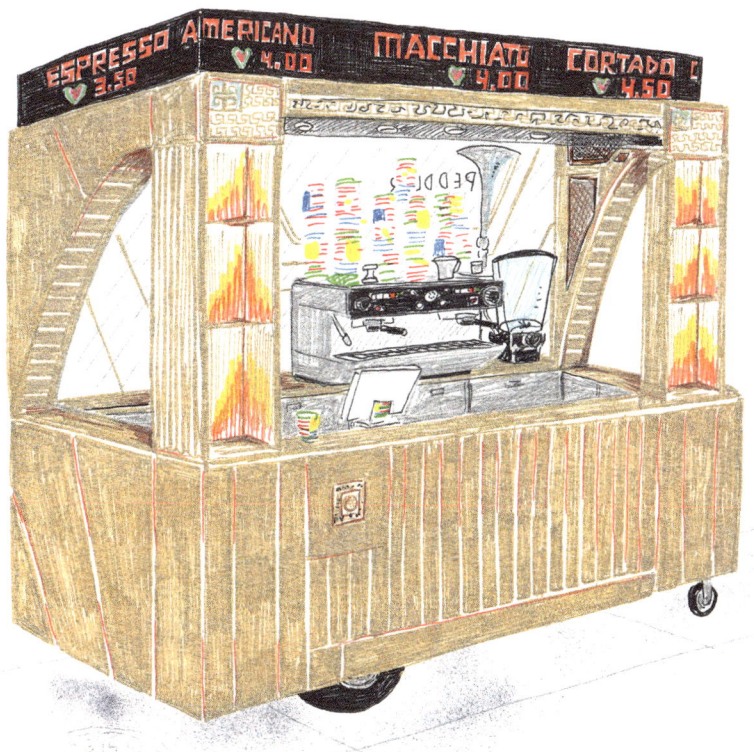

Calexico

Brothers Jesse, Brian, and David Vendley started this Cal-Mex culinary venture in 2006 with a simple cart on the corner of Wooster and Prince Streets in downtown Manhattan.

They named the business after their small hometown on the border of California and Mexico, where "everything is a hybrid," as they say on their website: "The people, the language, and especially the food." The brothers have long roots in and around Calexico (which, if you didn't catch on yet, is a portmanteau of "California" and "Mexico"), where their family has lived for generations.

After moving to New York City, they were "blown away," their site explains, by the diversity and quality of the food. "But no matter where we looked, we couldn't find anything that could satisfy our craving for our hometown cuisine." They decided to fix that glaring omission in the New York food scene themselves by setting up a tiny street cart in SoHo.

Word quickly spread about the brothers' new business. Lines stretched down the block, filled with lunchtime crowds eager to place their orders before favorites—like Baja fish tacos topped with a signature "crack sauce," and carne asada tacos served with avocado and pico de gallo—were completely gone. The same year the brothers opened Calexico, they won the Street Vendor Project's competitive Vendy Award. Several years later, they again won, this time for "Street Vendor of the Decade." *Newsday*, apparently, agreed, naming Calexico in a roundup of "The Most Influential Restaurants of the Decade," a list that also included the likes of beloved institutions Roberta's and Per Se.

The brothers have continued to cement themselves as a fixture in the city's competitive culinary scene with several brick-and-mortar locations, which include Brooklyn spots in Greenpoint, Park Slope, and Red Hook, as well as Manhattan's Upper East Side; they even have an outlet in Bahrain, the island country off the eastern coast of Saudi Arabia.

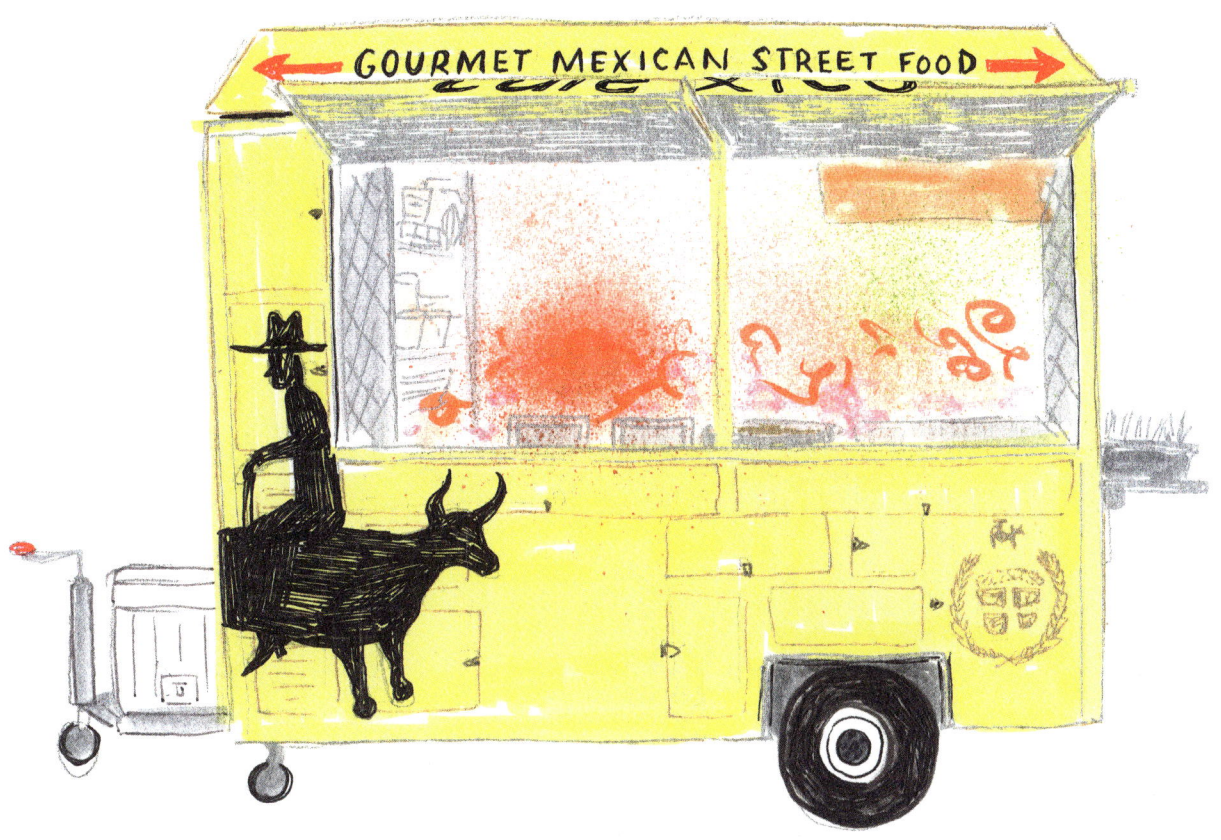

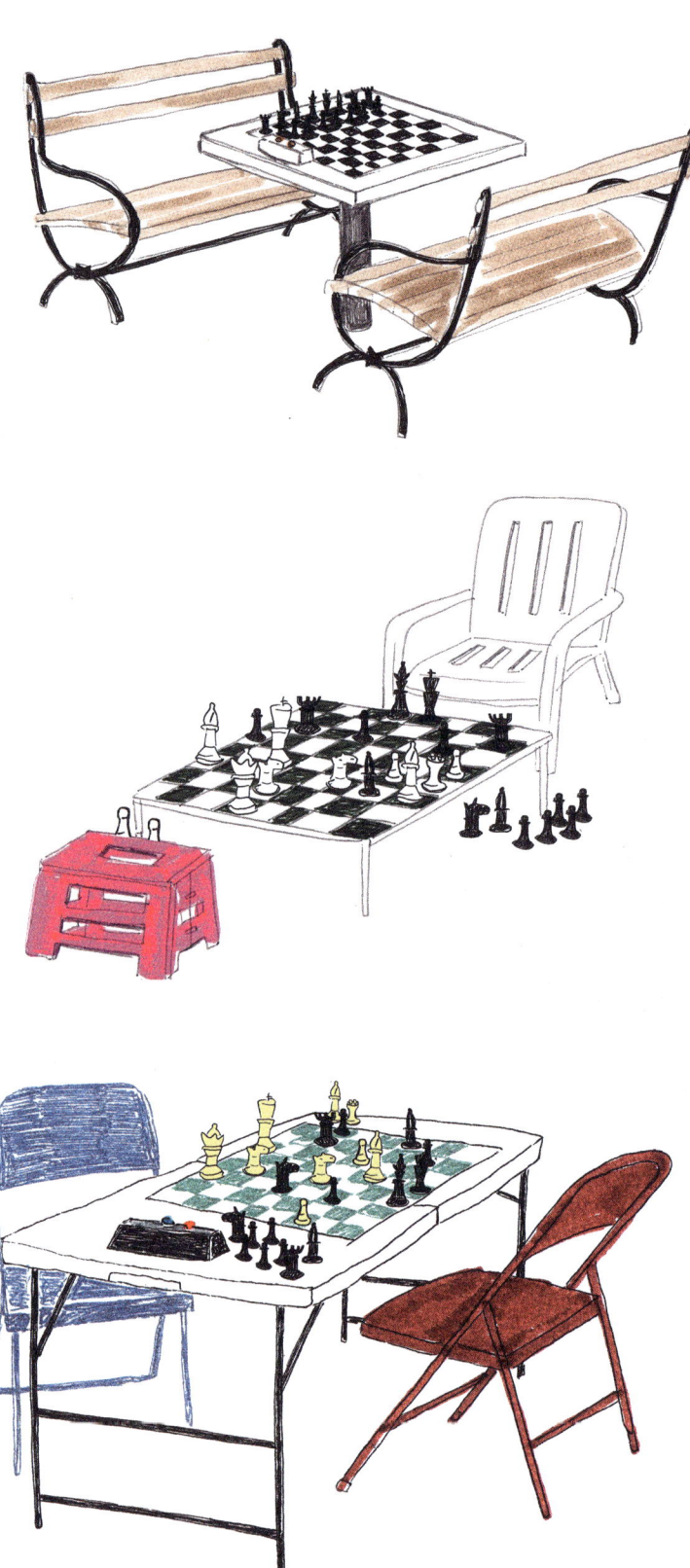

Chess Players

In Manhattan's Washington Square Park, New York University students come and go over the years, as do the different musicians, dancers, and guys whispering "smoke, smoke" as you walk by. A nearly constant presence amid all this happy chaos, however, are the chess players situated at the park's southwestern corner. They often play well into the night, beckoning tourists and other passersby to try and best them under the light of portable lamps. For practiced players, many of whom specifically seek out this corner for a game, it's a point of pride to get even a single win.

These chess players are not just confined to Washington Square Park; they are regular fixtures at several of the city's green spots, including Bryant Park, Central Park, and Union Square. While people must bring their own equipment to some of these locales, the tables at Washington Square are permanent—and the players here are known as much for their skills as their mouths.

In 2022, when a *New York Times* reporter asked one of the regulars at Washington Square how long he'd been playing, he replied, "Longer than you've been alive."

Several of the players there have adopted, or been given, nicknames. There's one who goes by Johnny the Loser, for instance (and if you fall for that one, you might as well forfeit your wallet to begin with). Another is known as Russian Paul, who told that same heckled *New York Times* reporter that, on a good day, he can walk away having made up to four hundred dollars.

Some call the players who station themselves here "hustlers," but chess enthusiasts admit they are quite up front about the arrangement: Come try your hand at beating them in a game of chess. If you win, you pay nothing, but if you lose, you fork over five dollars. Certain players may offer you friendly advice on how best to beat them—but that'll cost you, too, of course. In the end, if you find yourself twenty dollars or more poorer, who's left to blame but yourself?

Mo's Famous Burgers

Many establishments in New York City are guilty of falsely bestowing the adjective "famous" onto their names. Mo's Famous Burgers, a canary-yellow food truck typically parked on Malcolm X Boulevard between West 117th and 118th Streets in Manhattan, is an exception that manages to live up to the hype. Founded by veteran Maurice "Mo" Robinson, it has been serving the Harlem community since the 1990s. With business booming, Mo even bought a nearby barber shop at one point (which he has since sold) just so he would have a place to "keep my refrigerators and freezers," he told *New York Amsterdam News* in 2024.

Mo is known for his affordable, frills-free menu which includes classic items such as burgers and hot dogs for less than five dollars. However, he attributes part of his staying power in the community to his gift of gab. "I just like to talk with people, push people's buttons," he said to the *Amsterdam News*. "I can never have a bad day at Mo's Burgers. It just works. People come out and support me."

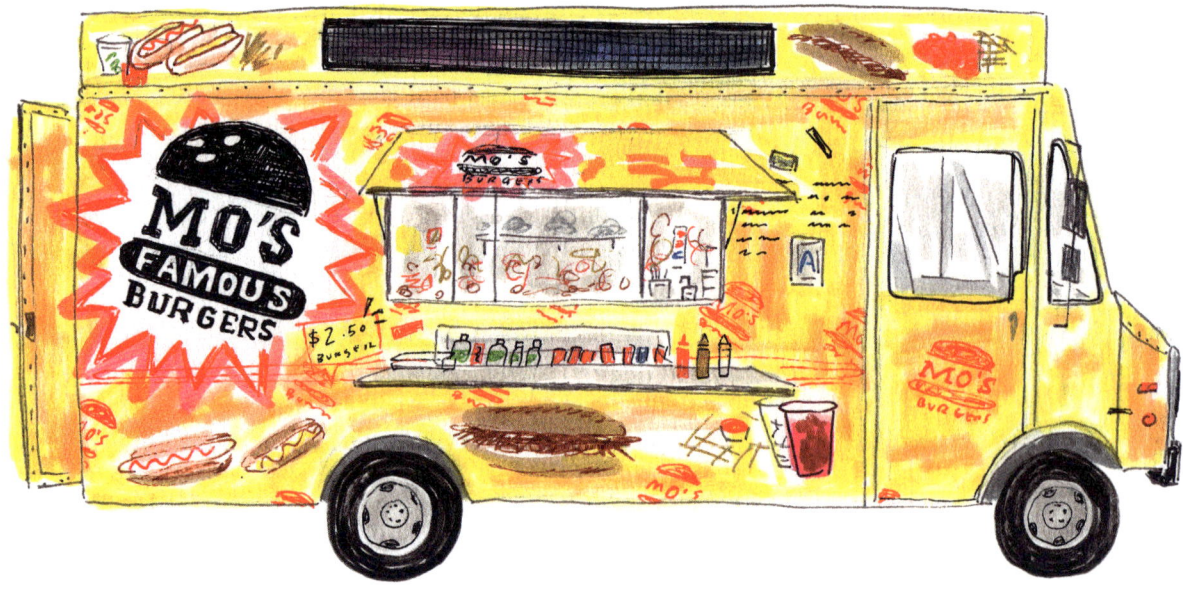

Banh Mi Cart

Since the early 2010s this Vietnamese food cart has been serving up banh mi, sandwiches featuring a variety of salty meats, vegetables, and tangy sauces on a crispy baguette, as well as other classic dishes, including pho. Typically parked at the corner of Hanover Square and Water Street, the unassuming business has become the go-to lunchtime spot for many a harried office worker in Lower Manhattan. "This place is magical," one online reviewer wrote. "It's still a mystery to me how a delicious, authentic hot bowl of pho can come from a tiny truck!"

Today locals and tourists alike make the trek to the tip of the island for a chance to sample what some say is the best banh mi you'll taste outside of Vietnam. A review on the website *New York Street Food* called the sandwiches here the "perfect combination of crunchy, mushy, crispy, gooey, sweet, salty, and spicy."

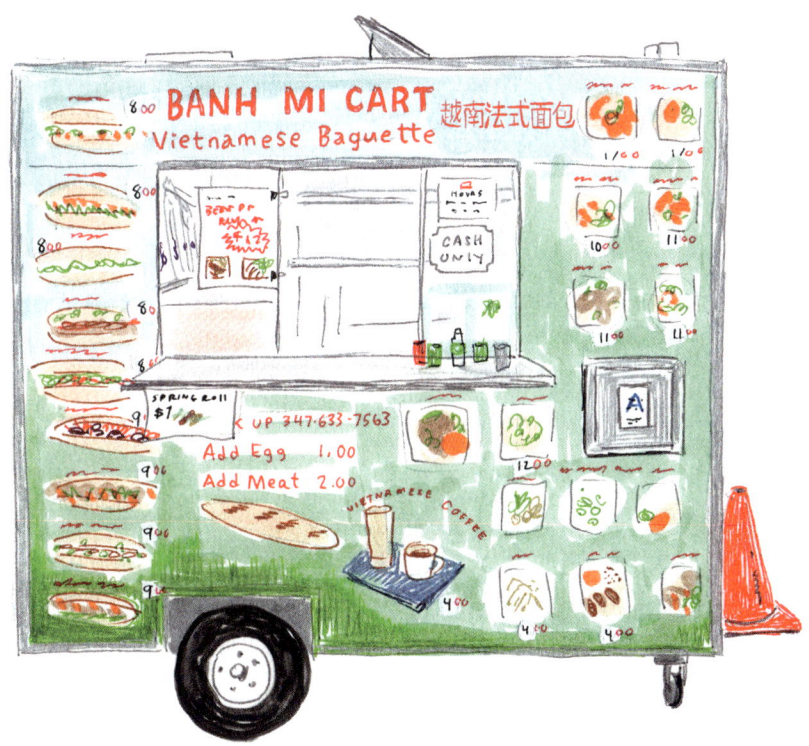

Mobile Tire Shop

"When you need tires, we come to you," this company writes on its website. The mobile shop installs new tires, fixes flats, and rotates tires, working out of trucks that are equipped with all the necessary tools. Their technicians meet customers at home, the office, or wherever else you can park a car (legally, anyway) in New York City.

You can book an appointment online, specifying your car's year, make, and model, and within hours a Mobile Tire Shop technician will be on the way to upgrade your ride, wherever it may be. "It's like I'm in the future," one online reviewer said of not needing to make their way to a brick-and-mortar tire store. "And the future is not lifting a finger or even moving!!!" From the many five-star reviews this business has received, it appears numerous drivers throughout the city agree.

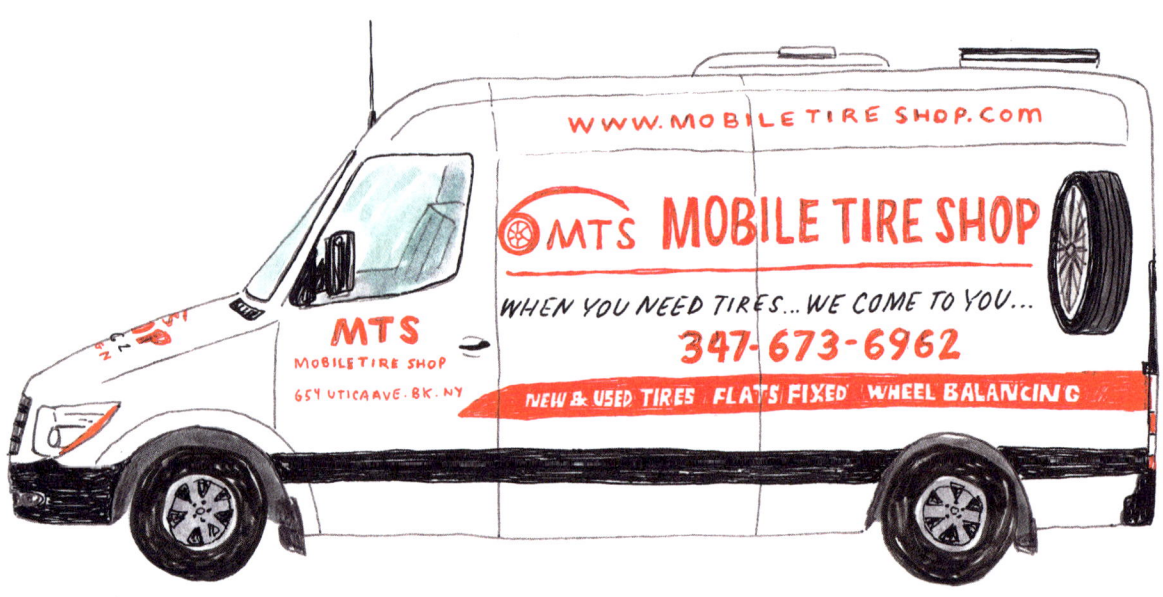

La Cocina Tropical

This food truck, located most days on Bay Street in Staten Island, offers a variety of specialties from various Latin American cuisines. Menu items include Mexican-style tacos, Dominican burgers called chimis, Salvadoran pupusas, and classic Tex-Mex burritos. However, the birria here is a fan favorite. It can come in its traditional taco incarnation or (even better, according to some regulars) heaped on top of cheesy nachos. During rush hour it can take forty minutes or more to place your order—which prompted the business to gently remind some of its more impatient fans on social media that "we are not a fast food truck."

La Cocina Tropical maintains a playful online presence, with one post attempting to goad their followers into a spirited argument over which is the best flavor of agua fresca, a drink made from real fruit blended with water, lime juice, and sugar. According to the responses, it's a toss-up between two contenders: piña and tamarindo.

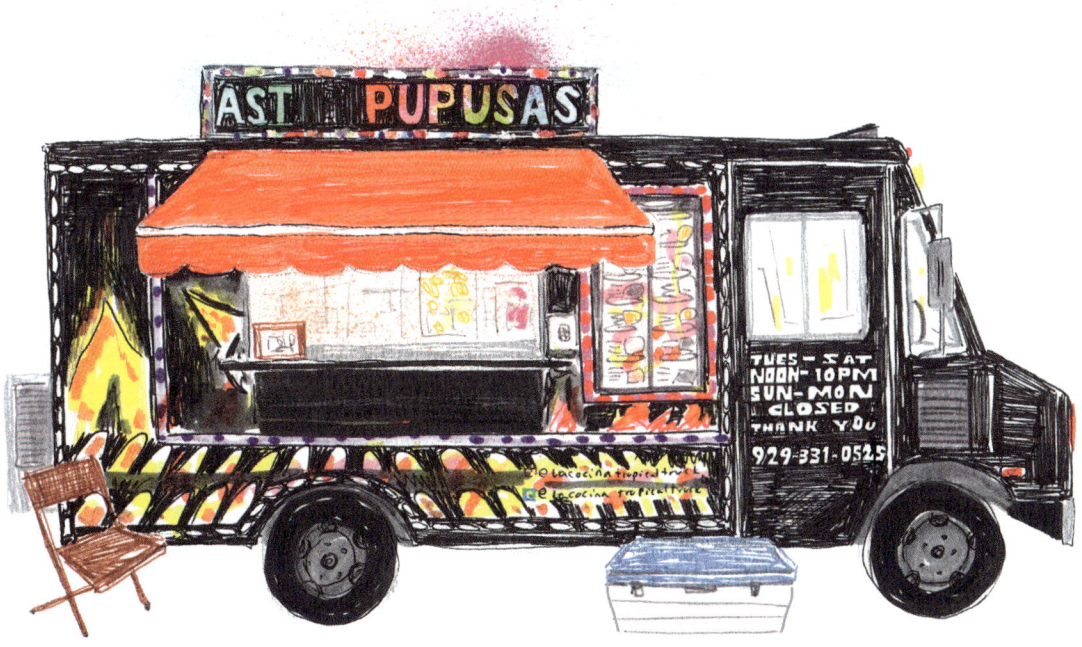

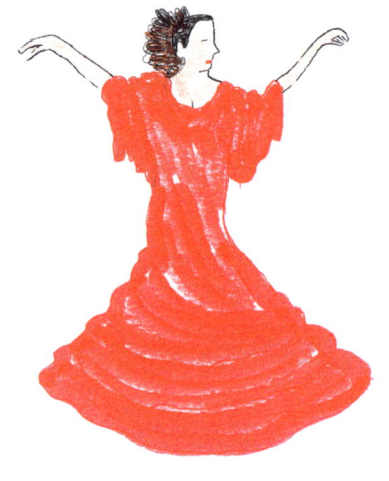

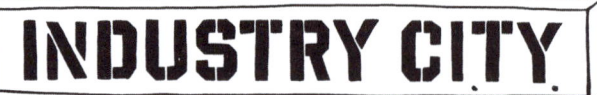

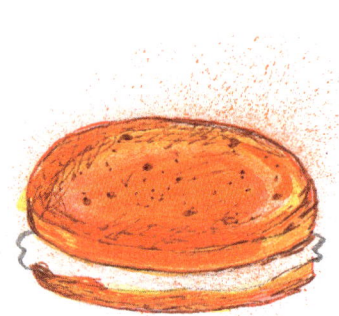

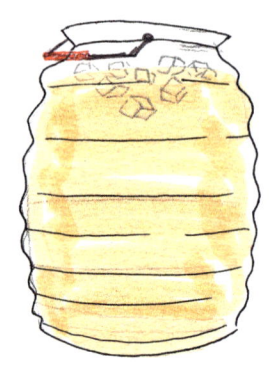

Latin Food Fest

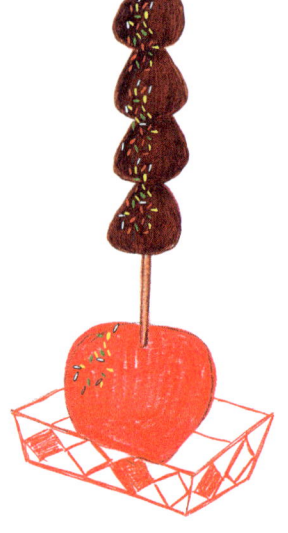

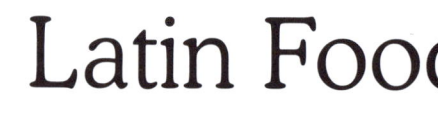

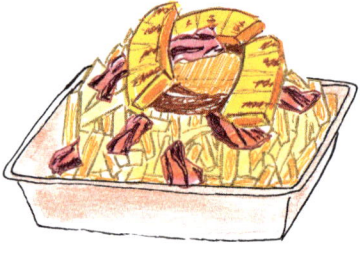

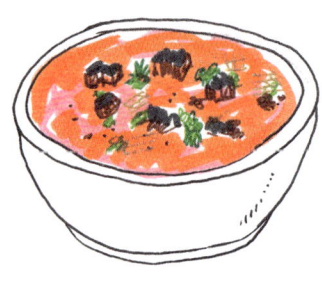

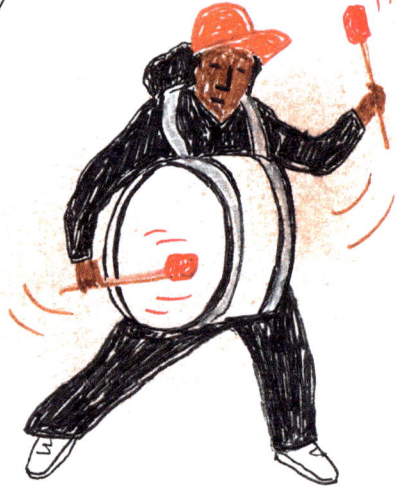

This festival started out as the Latin Night Market, a venture organized by Marco Shalma (p. 55). It debuted in the summer of 2023 with dozens of vendors and attracted nearly twenty-thousand visitors to Quisqueya Plaza, on Dyckman Street, in Manhattan's Inwood neighborhood. According to the website *Secret NYC*, the festival is the US's first-ever large-scale food and culture celebration exclusively dedicated to representing Latin America. In 2025 it moved locations to Industry City in Sunset Park, Brooklyn.

"The Latin Food Fest isn't just an event," the organizers write on their website. "It's a cultural phenomenon."

Previous vendors have included Tacos El Guero, known for its mozzarella arepas and skewered meats, and Criollo Burgers, which offers a Latin take on North American food (the "loaded fries" here come covered in cheese and topped with roasted pineapple). Wash it all down with horchata—a creamy, plant-based drink popular throughout Latin America that is made from rice, water, cinnamon, and sugar—and make sure to leave room for dessert, too, provided by vendors like Chocolicious NYC, which specializes in strawberry arrangements and pancakes.

The event, which now takes place over one weekend in September, also features live musicians performing genres that span Latin America, including salsa, reggae, rumba, hip-hop, and more. Past entertainers have included dancers from the Xianix Barrera Flamenco Company, and drummers and dancers from the Marching Cobras, a youth-focused music program that also has performed at the Super Bowl and accompanied superstars like Rihanna.

"It's always a great time with great food, friends, and atmosphere. The DJ was playing all of the latest tunes," one online reviewer wrote. A post on the event's Facebook page, however, makes the case for it even more simply: "Vamoooossss."

Charles Mysak Bookseller

Charles Mysak, an Upper West Side bookseller, has been stationed at various corners of the Manhattan neighborhood since the late 1990s.

In recent years you can find him most often on Columbus Avenue between Sixty-Seventh and Sixty-Eighth Streets. He's become such a fixture of the area that *The New York Times* has featured his outdoor used bookstore not once, but twice, first in 2005 and again in 2010.

When Charles first started selling used books on the street in the neighborhood, he was far from alone. The Strand, New York's largest surviving independent bookstore, maintained a stall nearby. Back then the city held an annual street fair called New York Is Book Country, Charles told the website *I Love the Upper West Side* in a 2020 interview. The event involved periodically closing parts of Fifth Avenue to car traffic to let book publishers and sellers set up stalls. "It was quite an affair," he said. "Of course, they haven't done that in decades, unfortunately."

The fascination with Charles's longevity comes not just from being an outdoor operation (after all, how do you sell books in the rain?). It's also because he's managed to escape—thus far, at least—the fate of hundreds of independent and corporate bookstores across the country, many of which have long shuttered their doors with the rise of online shopping. It's additionally impressive given the over "20 years of hostility" that he's experienced from the police for vending outside without a license, frequently landing him in court, he said in the interview.

Charles is still around, in part, because he knows his right to sell books is one protected under the First Amendment. And he is a vocal defender of everyone's right to make a living selling goods, food, and services on the streets. "What makes [New York] run are people like me, and the 10,000 other vendors," he explained.

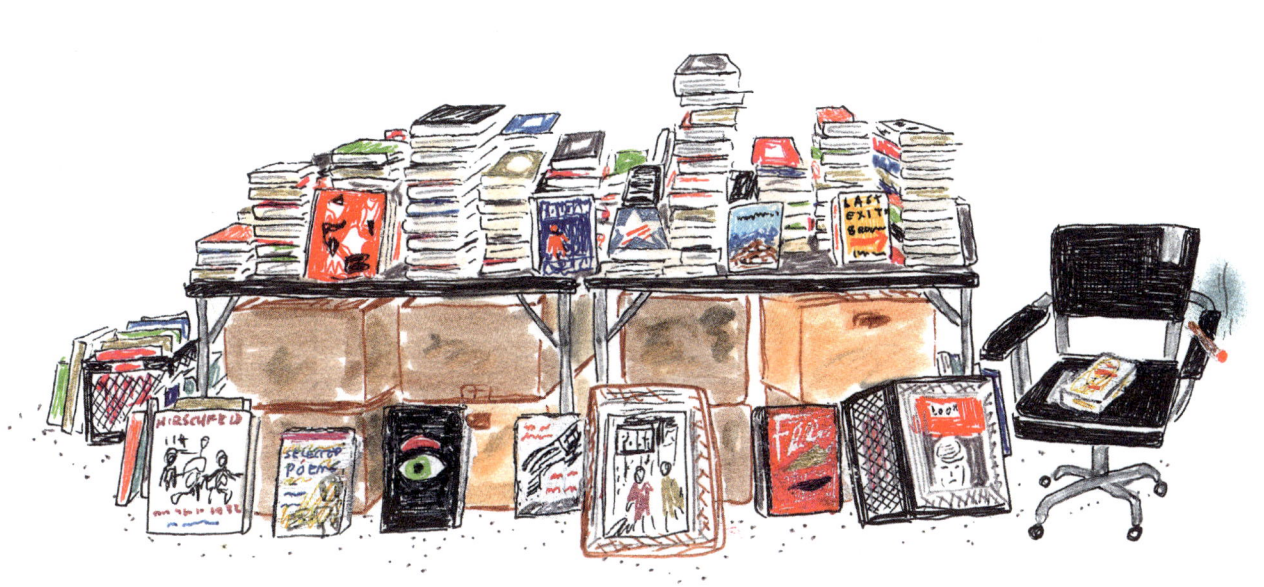

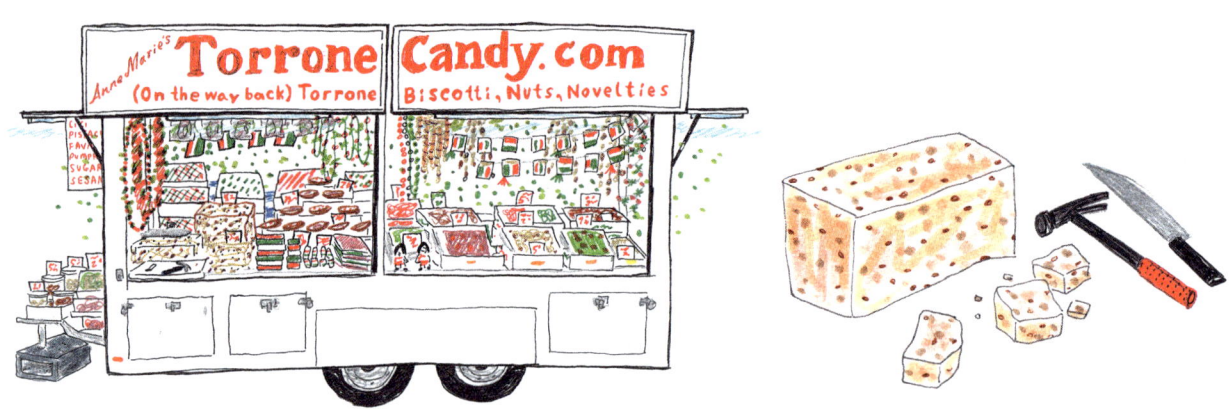

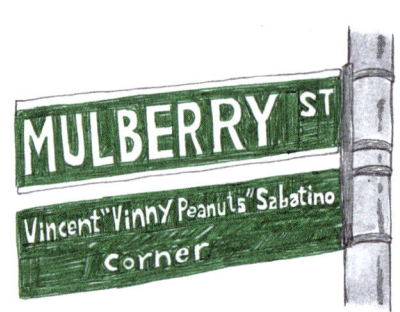

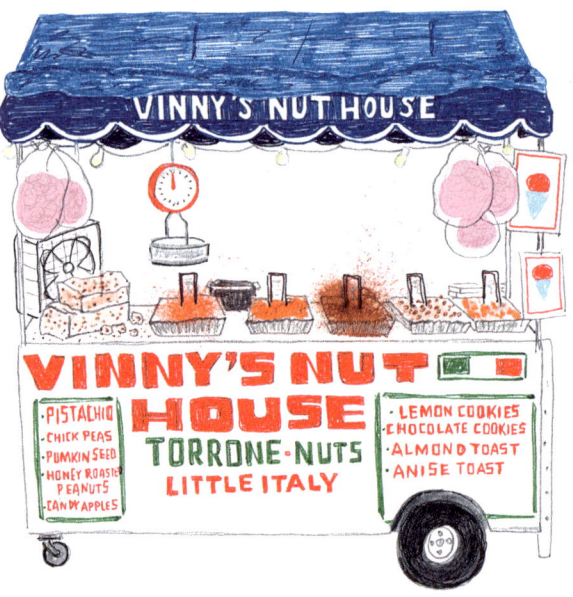

Torrone Vendors

A visit to the annual Feast of San Gennaro in Manhattan's Little Italy, during which dozens of street vendors sell goodies from the land of la dolce vita, isn't complete without buying a bit of torrone. This traditional Italian nougat candy is made from honey, sugar, egg whites, and nuts (typically almonds, pistachios, or hazelnuts).

The sweet is thought to have gained its name thanks to its likeness to the Torrazzo, a Gothic bell tower in Cremona, Italy, and was created to celebrate the marriage of a duke and duchess in 1441.

Since San Gennaro's inception in the city in 1926, Danny Fratta's family has sold torrone there each September. Today their stand is called Danny on the Corner (in more recent times, they've become known for selling other Italian treats, too, like zeppole—deep fried dough balls). The Frattas have been in business so long, the festival reserves the same spot for their cart every year, on the corner of Mulberry and Grand Streets.

Danny also now runs Vinny's Nut House, another long-standing torrone vendor with roots dating back to the 1920s (as you might have guessed, it sells nuts too). It was named after Danny's uncle Vincent Cirelli Sabatino, better known as "Vinny Peanuts," who manned it for decades until his death in 2020. A few years later, the local community board changed the street sign at the Frattas's corner, naming it after Vinny Peanuts.

Torrone Candy is a newer entrant into the world of torrone street vending—but only by comparison. Tony Andriola started this business in 1970, originally calling it Anne Marie's Concessions, after his daughter. The stand mostly sold seafood and sausages at Italian festivals in New Jersey. In 1988 he decided to add torrone to his list of offerings, and "Tony Sausage," as he was previously known, became "Tony Torrone." Anne Marie, who used to work with her father at the stand as a child, now operates the business. Its current name dates to 2006, when the Andriolas first started selling torrone—in addition to other Italian goodies, like biscotti, chocolates, and panettone—through their online market.

Blue Dove Coffee

Casee "Amadeo" Falce, a US Army veteran and founder of Blue Dove Coffee, wakes up every morning at 2:30 a.m. at his home in Brighton Beach, Brooklyn—leaving him enough time to set up his cart in Manhattan's Union Square and sneak in a workout at a nearby Equinox before the morning rush hour. Despite having no previous experience in the coffee industry, or street vending, Amadeo has quickly made Blue Dove a fixture in one of New York's most iconic squares since it opened in 2024.

Amadeo has also become a presence on social media, with over forty thousand Instagram followers, thanks to his inventive content—like recurring "crazy customer" posts featuring a purposefully annoying regular and coffee neophyte whose supposed ignorance helps provide insights into the coffee trade. In one video the regular orders a "16-ounce macchiato," something that, according to traditional Italian standards, doesn't exist, Amadeo explains. Made properly, a macchiato contains just a shot or two of espresso with a small dollop of steamed milk. "Starbucks, take notes!" the caption reads.

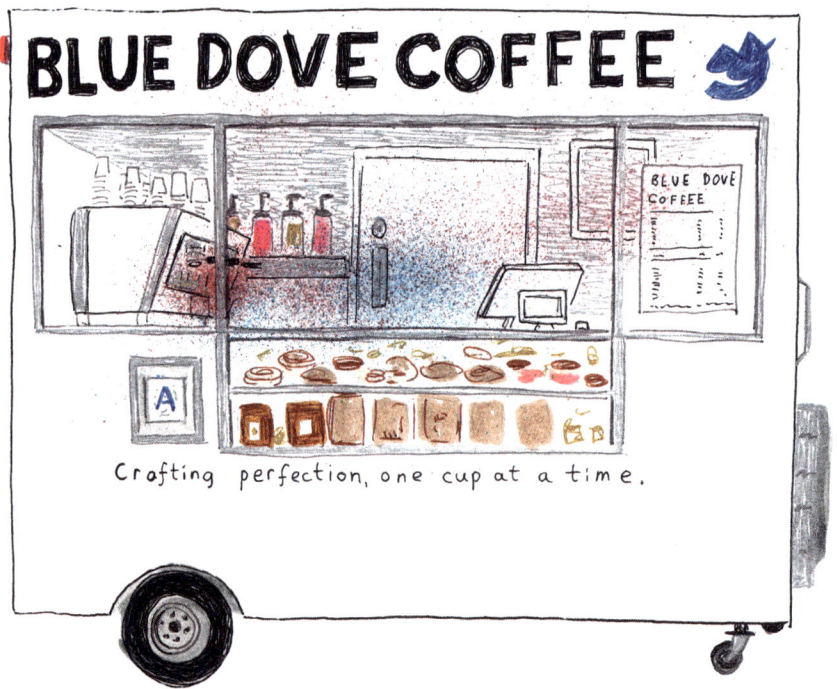

The Casbah

This Moroccan food cart, typically parked at the intersection of West Sixty-Sixth Street and Columbus Avenue, has become a mainstay for locals on Manhattan's Upper West Side—and a must-try destination for halal fans across the city and beyond. One patron even offered a controversial "pro tip" online, saying he's fond of smuggling a "few plates" of this tasty, fragrant food into the nearby Lincoln Square AMC theater. "Your movie neighbors might be jealous," he wrote, "but your stomach will be very, very happy!"

Known for its blend of spices and massive portions, the Casbah's menu has typical offerings like the lamb gyro sandwich. According to regulars, though, the Royal Combination Plate—which heaps generous amounts of chicken, lamb, and falafel over rice—is particularly rockin'. And remember, if you're not quite bold enough to sneak your plate into a theater, Central Park is close by and has plenty of seating too.

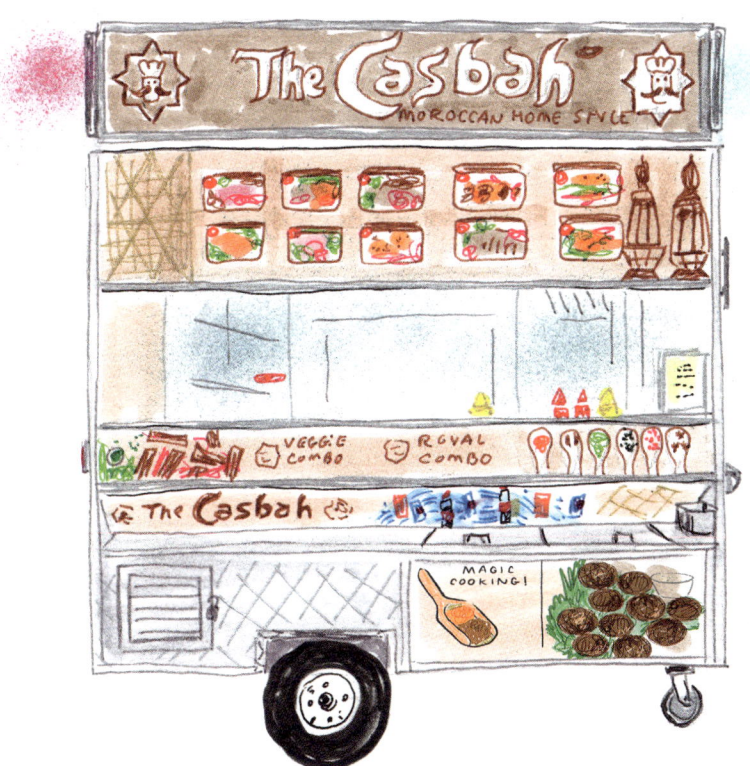

Harlem's First Mobile Barber

In 2019 Linwood Dillard, a longtime Manhattan barber based in Harlem, found himself priced out of the storefronts available in the rapidly gentrifying neighborhood. Though his space at Lenox Avenue and 128th Street was successful, his landlord raised his rent from $3,500 to $8,500 a month, he told ABC News, making the business untenable.

Rather than retire his shears, he instead got creative and put his barber shop on wheels. After Linwood purchased an old, beat-up Ford E-350 bus for $2,500 and retrofitted it to meet his haircutting and styling needs, Harlem's First Mobile Barber was born—perhaps even the first of its kind in the city. Though he hasn't been seen around the neighborhood recently, when he's active, his preferred spot is not far from his former storefront, along Lenox Avenue.

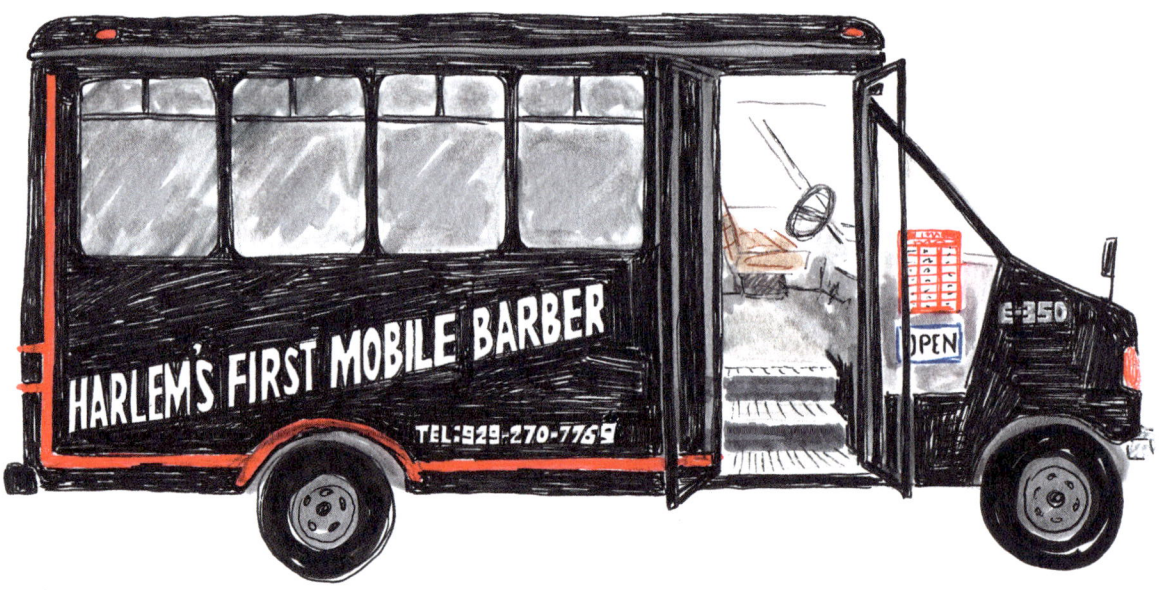

Musubin'

Founded in 2023, this street vendor specializes in omusubi (also known as onigiri), traditional Japanese rice balls shaped into "delightful triangles," according to its website. The business name is derived from the Japanese word for "to tie" or "to roll." Offerings include varieties made with soy-infused bonito flakes mixed with smoked radish pickles; tuna and creamy mayo; and the classic, which is adorned with nothing more than "a touch of salt" and some black sesame seeds. The vendor's nontriangle shaped food, according to regulars, is just as delightful—like the wagyu skewer, made with "award-winning full-blood" beef from Japan's Iwate Prefecture, and takoyaki, savory octopus balls that are crispy on the outside and "soft and gooey" on the inside, as per the menu.

Whatever shape its food takes, Musubin' is on a mission to redefine what it calls New York's "grab-and-go street food scene" with options that aren't just quick and easy but also health-conscious. Catch the cart at any number of local markets as well as pop-up locations throughout the city.

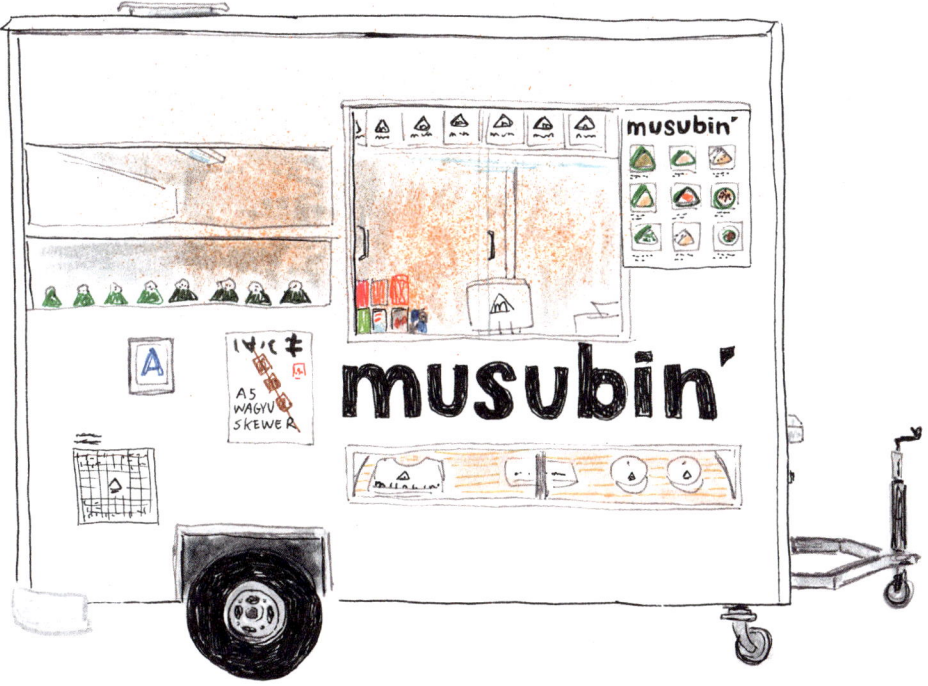

Kwik Meal

After years of working in fine dining, including at the Russian Tea Room in Midtown Manhattan, Mohammed Rahman, originally from Bangladesh, decided in 2000 to bring his talents straight to the streets of New York. His food cart, which he positioned on Forty-Fifth Street, quickly gained attention in Midtown thanks in part to his commitment to fresh foods—you'll find no processed meat products here. Mohammed may be in a cart now instead of a full-sized restaurant kitchen, but you will still see him cooking and serving his food outfitted in a chef's jacket and hat.

As one online reviewer put it, "The yogurt sauce is actual yogurt, and the lamb is actual cubes of marinated lamb." The standout here is indeed the lamb, which is seasoned with cumin and coriander and served over rice or in a pita. For fans of a little heat, don't forget to ask for an extra squeeze of Mohammed's trademark jalapeño hot sauce.

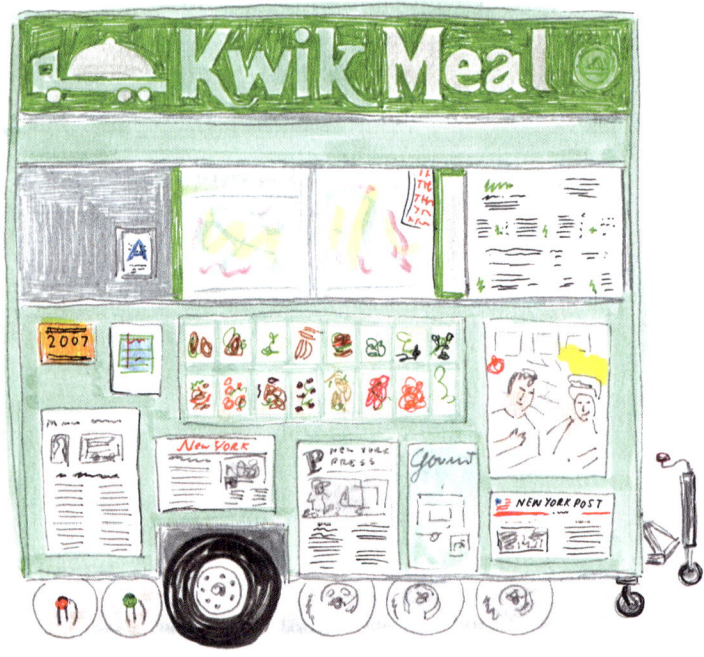

Old Traditional Polish Cuisine

———

True to its name, this street food vendor offers an array of authentic Polish gastronomic treats, like grilled kielbasa and pierogi filled with potato and cheese, seasoned meat, or sauerkraut and mushroom. The misleadingly named Lite Combo is a popular choice for hungry customers and comes with a grilled kielbasa, four potato-and-cheese pierogis, and pickle salad.

New York has no shortage of spots for Polish food, even boasting a Little Poland neighborhood in Greenpoint, Brooklyn. Nevertheless, friends Grzegorz "Greg" Gryzlak and Przemyslaw "Mek" Motyka, both originally from Poland, started this street food venture in March 2011 with the goal of bringing classic cuisine from their homeland straight to the city's streets. Greg and Mek park their truck at various locations but are most often in the Bryant Park area of Midtown Manhattan. Regulars say not to sleep on some of the traditional drinks on offer here, like the Tymbark cherry-apple beverage.

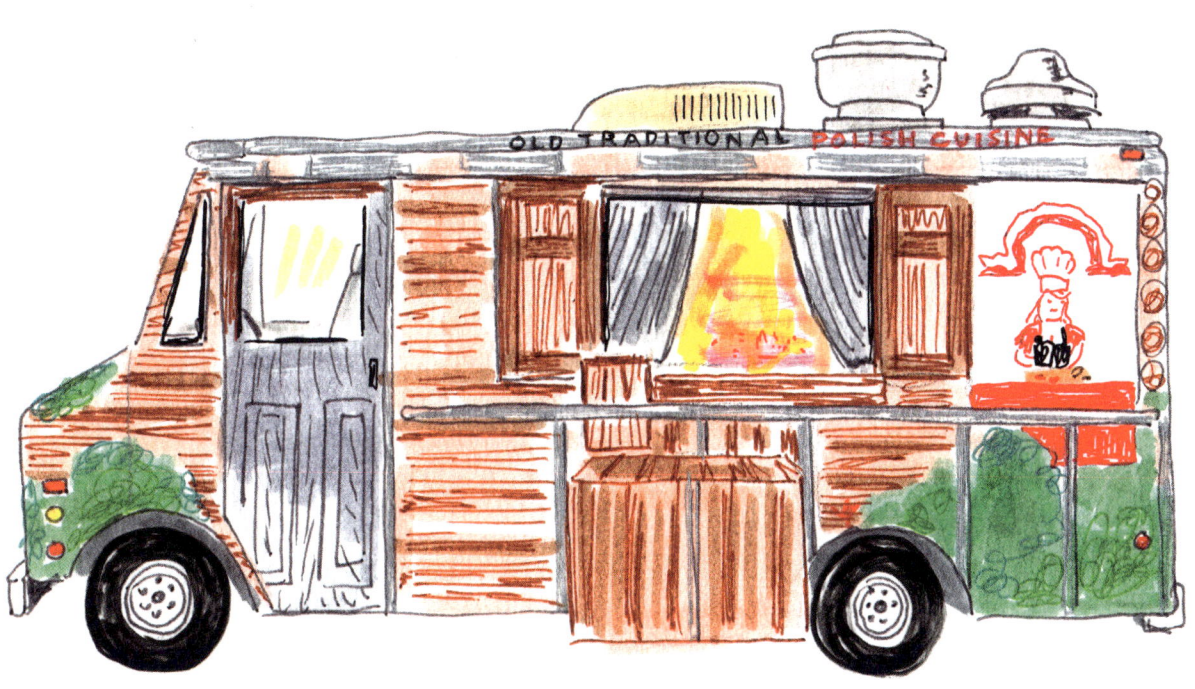

Pamphleteers and
Street Canvassers

You can't get too far inside one of New York's major transit hubs without being stopped by an overly friendly stranger, often outfitted in a bright vest, asking if you might "have a moment for gay rights." Or for women's rights. Or for children. Some of the country's largest nonprofit advocacy organizations—like Save the Children, the Human Rights Campaign, Greenpeace, the American Civil Liberties Union, and Planned Parenthood—employ these street canvassers to do their best to solicit donations from commuters. Public spaces like Washington Square Park in Manhattan or Grand Army Plaza in Brooklyn also have long been popular spots for promoting various issues, raising money for causes, and disseminating information.

Many harried New Yorkers are annoyed by the practice, often faking a phone call or averting their eyes to avoid interacting with canvassers, but the practice is protected by the First Amendment's free-speech clause. Requiring permits for this type of work has been deemed unconstitutional by the Supreme Court.

Aggravating or not, the tradition works; street canvassing has played an important role in helping raise money and spread the word about many social causes.

Politicians, who often must collect thousands of signatures to run for office, frequently rely on these low-wage workers when trying to meet deadlines. Entry-level canvasser positions often earn no more than minimum wage in New York City. At least one description on Indeed lists ideal qualities in candidates as "energetic, motivated, professional individuals" willing to collect signatures for a petition "that will affect New York residents significantly."

Over the decades, social and digital media activism has led to some decline in street-based canvassing—though particularly, come election time, you can still expect to see a smiling stranger with a clipboard on your morning commute to work. Even if you don't have time to talk to these bright-eyed optimists, the least you can do is give a quick, "No thanks, but good luck"—and not just to be polite. Anyone who has the guts to stop disgruntled New Yorkers during rush hour is very likely on their way to bigger and better places.

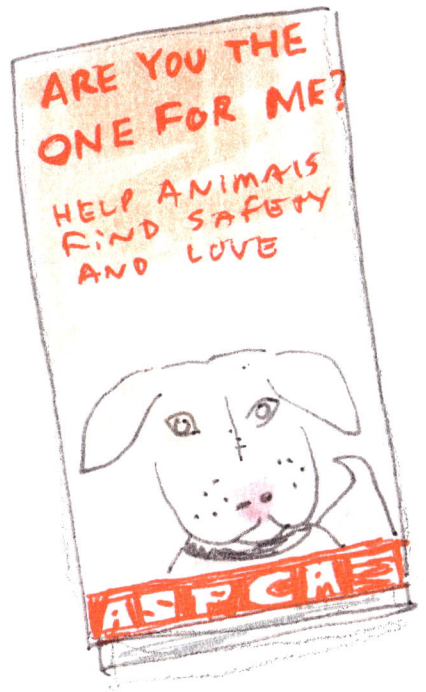

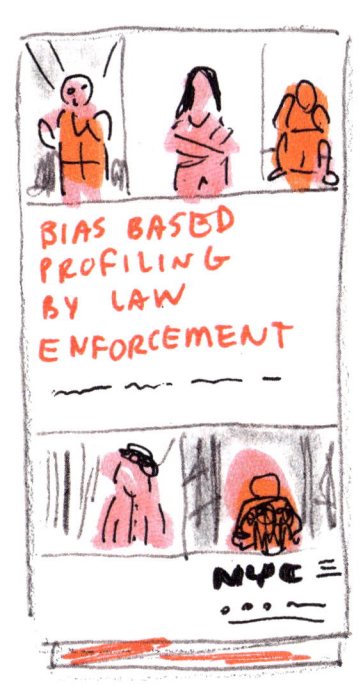

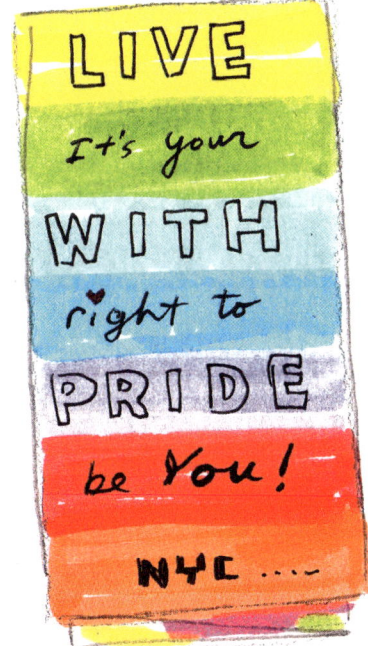

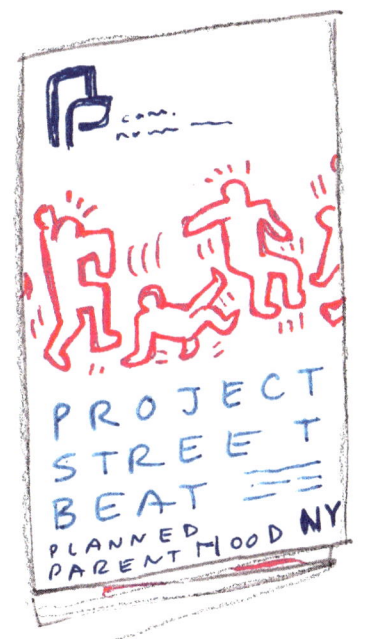

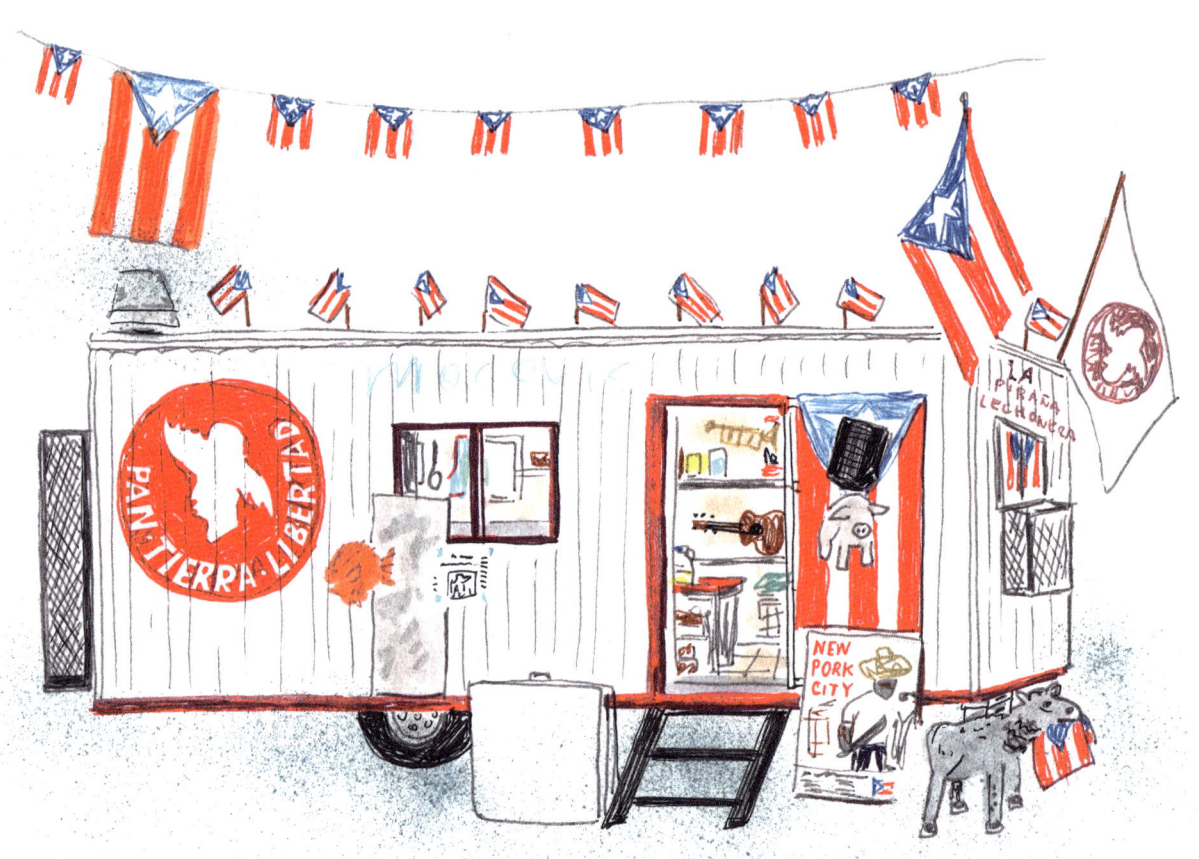

La Piraña Lechonera

Succeeding his father, who started the business in the 1980s, Angel "Piraña" Jimenez has been helming this Puerto Rican pig-roasting operation since 2000.

Every Saturday and Sunday, you can find his food truck (which, technically speaking, is actually a trailer) on the corner of Wales Avenue and East 152nd Street in the South Bronx.

In 2022 *New York Times* food critic Pete Wells gave La Piraña three out of four stars—making it the only three-star eatery in the "inexpensive" category among the paper's notoriously fickle recommendations. The food truck, he wrote, "packs more joy into two days than most restaurants do into a week."

Angel earned such distinction in large part thanks to the strength of his famous lechón asado, or slow-roasted pork. He cooks it in a custom-built pit for eight hours, until the skin is crispy and the meat tender and flavorful. (According to regulars, his adherence to this traditional preparation method makes his lechón asado the best in the city.) Patrons can pair their pork with a variety of other Puerto Rican classics on the menu, like the pulpo, a cold octopus salad with bell peppers, and mofongo, typically made with deep-fried plantains mashed and mixed with meat or seafood. Angel's comes covered in a garlic sauce so popular that some customers refer to it as "God juice."

The buzz around La Piraña arises not only from Angel's food but also from the ambiance he creates. Salsa music blares from speakers set up outside the trailer, keeping the vibe upbeat during what is often a substantial wait. (Pro tip: Bring a lawn chair—many regulars do.) When it finally comes time to order, customers climb inside the trailer to find a good-spirited Angel, often covered in meat juice, hacking away on hunks of pork with his machete. Most stick around even after they've devoured their food to enjoy the atmosphere. "People dancing, eating, having fun, like Puerto Rican style," Angel told *VICE* in a 2019 article. "I've been making it like that since I started. They sit down, eat, feel like family."

The Hip Hop Food Truck

Alfredo Estrada, a chef with over two decades of experience, opened this hip-hop-themed food truck in October 2020. After being furloughed from his job during the COVID-19 pandemic, he began the venture, most days stationed on White Plains Road in the Bronx, to help make ends meet—while also finding time to donate meals to essential workers. Menu items are inspired by the legends of New York's hip-hop scene, whose music Alfredo blasts from his truck while serving customers. The Gordo Burger, for instance, pays homage to the late Fred the Godson.

On Fridays Alfredo often parks his truck outside of IN-Tech Academy, a Bronx high school on Tibbett Avenue. Here he's managed to not just become a favorite lunch option for the students but also a valued member of the community, offering student discounts and specials to make his food affordable.

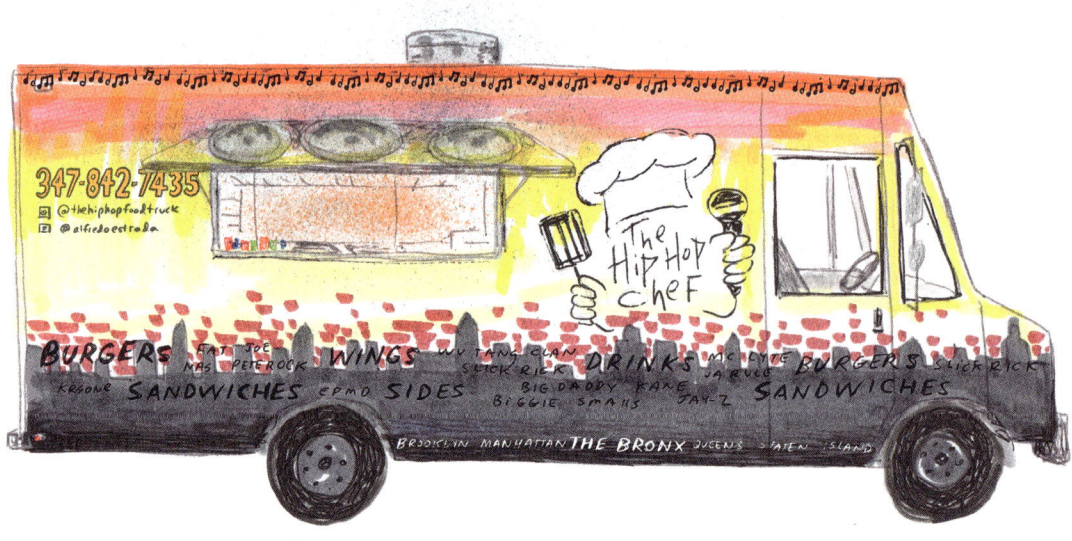

Stan's Taco Bike

In 2018, when Stan Tankursley closed his Manhattan restaurant, Tortilla Flats—a notorious West Village Tex-Mex spot known for its raucous trivia nights and tequila shots—longtime regulars, including Sarah Jessica Parker, were distraught. "The corner of West 12th and Washington Street will never be the same," she wrote in an Instagram post.

Fortunately for Carrie Bradshaw and Stan's many other fans, this restaurateur—who has opened and closed around twenty different eateries in his career—always has ideas brewing. His latest culinary adventure, launched in May 2024, is on wheels: Stan's Taco Bike. At seventy-two years old, he began serving Austin-style breakfast tacos with fillings including scrambled eggs, crispy tortilla chips, chorizo, and spicy beef directly from his bike basket, bringing a taste of Texas to the streets of Lower Manhattan. More recently he has teamed up with Casa Next Door—the coffee shop associated with the iconic Casa Magazines, on the corner of Eighth Avenue and West Twelfth Street—to offer his tacos there.

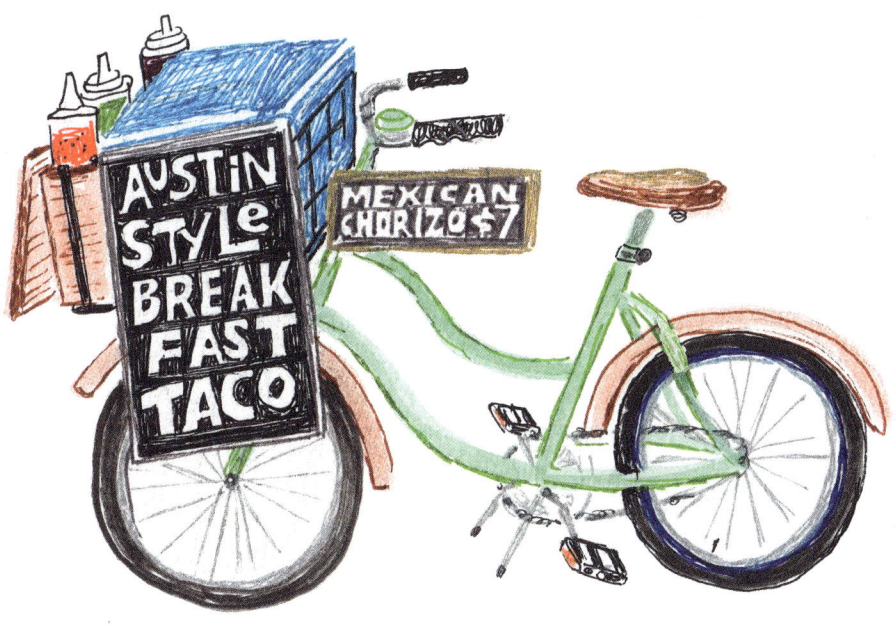

Mikey Likes It

While many New York restaurants got their start in the city with a simple pushcart or food truck before expanding into a brick-and-mortar spot, Mikey Likes It—a local ice cream favorite—took the opposite route. Michael "Mikey" Cole first started his business in an East Village storefront in 2014, eventually expanding to Harlem and Hell's Kitchen. He differentiated himself from his fellow cone-based competitors with imaginative flavor profiles inspired by pop-culture icons. Favorites include Foxy Brown (mocha with crushed chocolate wafer cookies and caramel sea salt) and the Brady Bunch (banana pudding with vanilla wafers).

In 2022, due in part to challenges brought on by the COVID-19 pandemic, Mikey decided to shutter all of his storefronts to focus on a pushcart and food truck, which New Yorkers can rent for their private events, festivals, and parties. "Book us!" the business proclaims on its website. "We'll come to you."

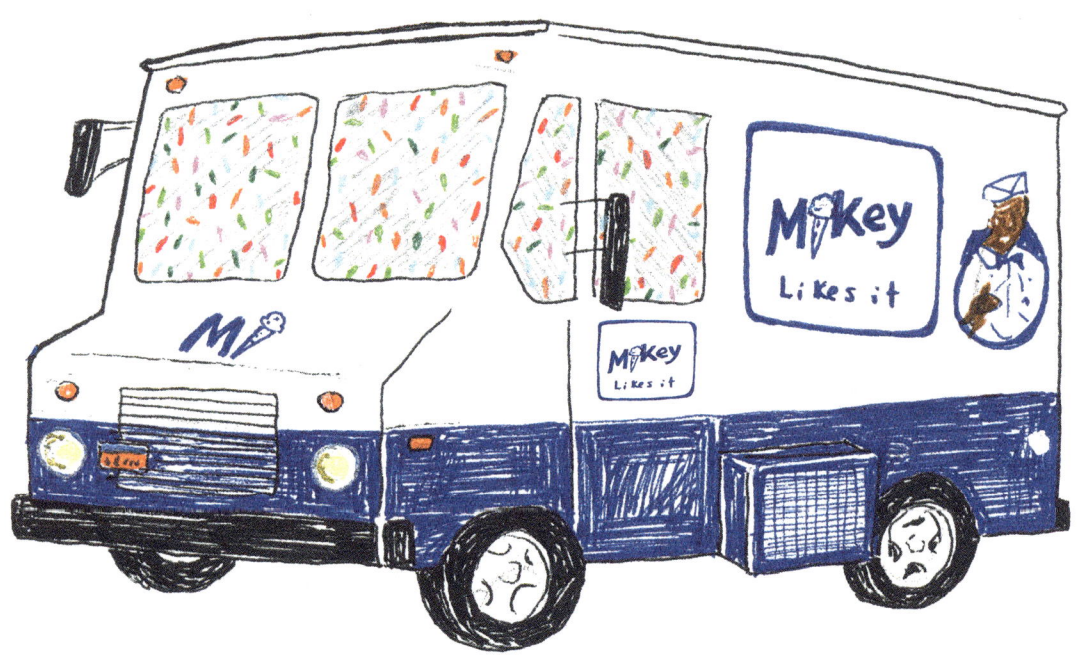

Steak Freak

On any given weekday, busy New Yorkers eager for a quick, quality bite descend from Midtown skyscrapers and swarm one of the half-dozen food trucks parked along a stretch of Fiftieth Street between Sixth and Seventh Avenues. The most hurried office workers, however, may have to skip this local favorite—known for its steak and chicken dishes served over rice or noodles—where lines are consistently the longest.

Steak frites is the specialty here (as it well should be, with a name like Steak Freak). Other standout items from the eclectic menu include kimchi sesame steak, chimichurri steak, and honey-glazed chicken. Regulars know to get there on the early side of the rush, before they run out of the most popular items. According to one online reviewer who frequents Steak Freak at least two days a week, "in good times and bad," it's the glazes and sauces that sets this food truck apart from the competition.

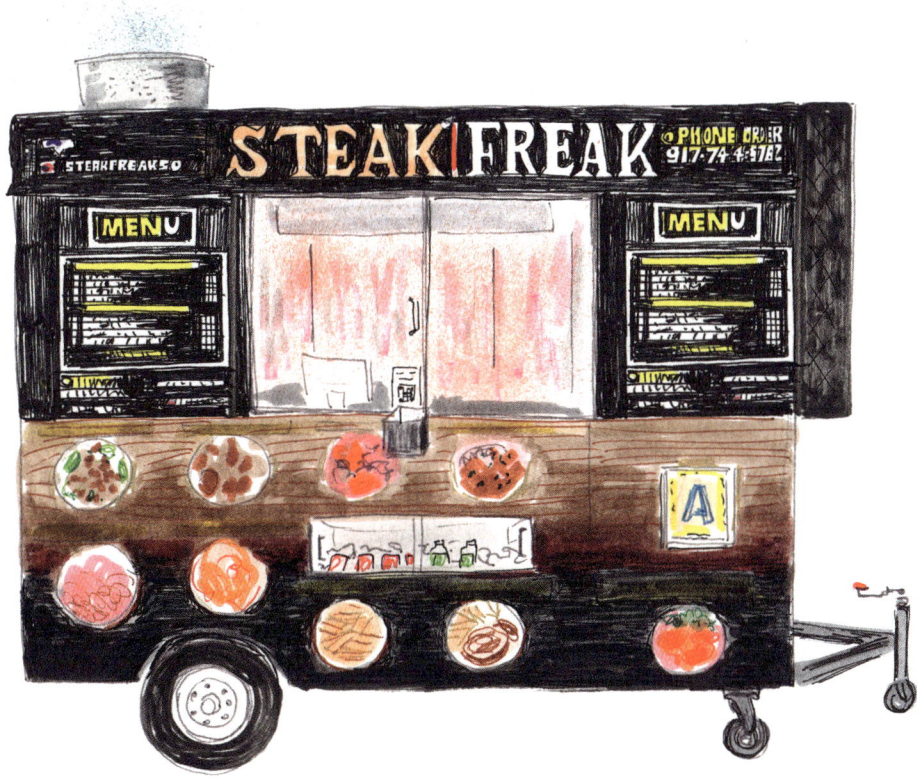

Mobile Sharpening Services

In New York the tradition of mobile sharpening services took hold in the early nineteenth century, following a wave of immigration from parts of Italy where homemakers, butchers, and tailors have long relied on *arrotinos*, people who sharpen tools on grinding wheels attached to their carts or bikes.

For decades New Yorkers needing to fix their dull knives or scissors could simply run into the streets (though hopefully, with sharp objects, they walked) in search of one of these mobile grinding services.

Mike & Sons, a family business with roots extending back to the early twentieth century, is the longest-running mobile sharpening service in the city. Today it's operated by Mike Pallotta, a third-generation owner who took over from his father in 1971. His grandfathers from both sides of his family immigrated to New York from Italy during the 1920s and made their livings as knife grinders. By the 1950s more than twenty of Mike's relatives were operating sharpening trucks in the city. "Whenever I seen a scissor-grinding truck," he told *The New York Times* in a 2006 interview, "I knew that was a *paisan* of mine."

Dominick Del Re, originally from southern Italy, started his mobile sharpening business in 1987, after a Wall Street crash forced him to abandon the daily grind of commodities trading. True to tradition, Del Re's Grinding doesn't take reservations. "I'm like the fisherman. He doesn't make an appointment with the fish," he told *The New York Times* in 1997. Instead, customers listen for the old-school bell he clangs from his red paint-chipped truck (or they check his Instagram).

Meanwhile, the newcomer Green Point Knives is helping breathe life into a century-old tradition that has otherwise been in decline in recent decades. In 2023 Ryan White and Patrick Bradley left their careers in film and television in order to turn their passion for knives into a full-time gig, sharpening blades from a retrofitted truck and bus in Greenpoint, Brooklyn. The duo doesn't just vend from these wheeled vehicles, though—they also operate an online shop, where they sell luxury knives from brands like Kikuichi.

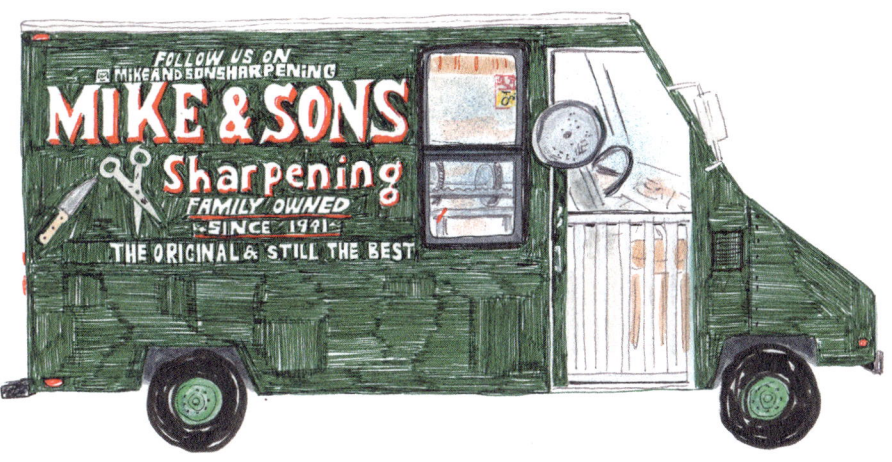

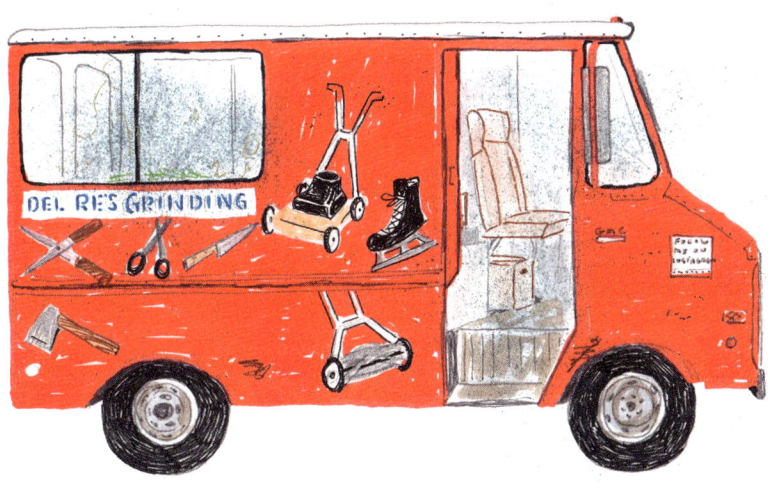

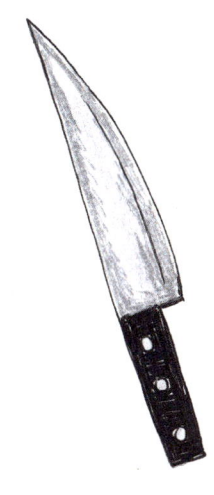

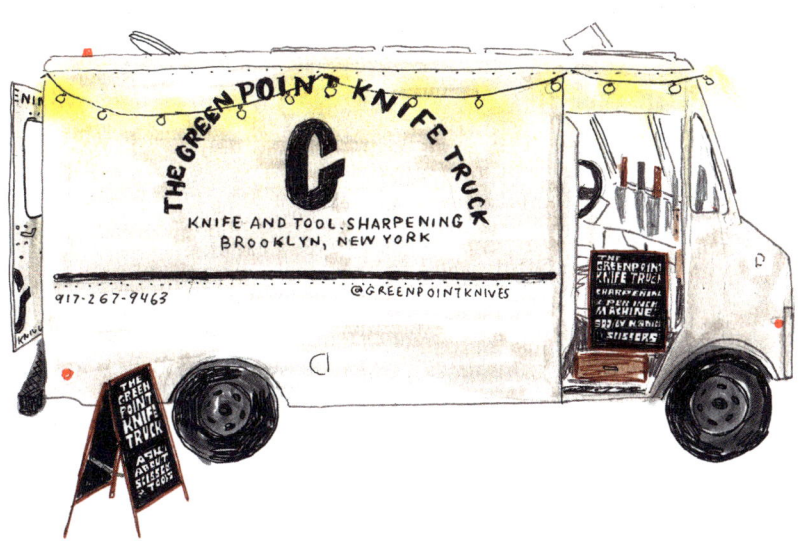

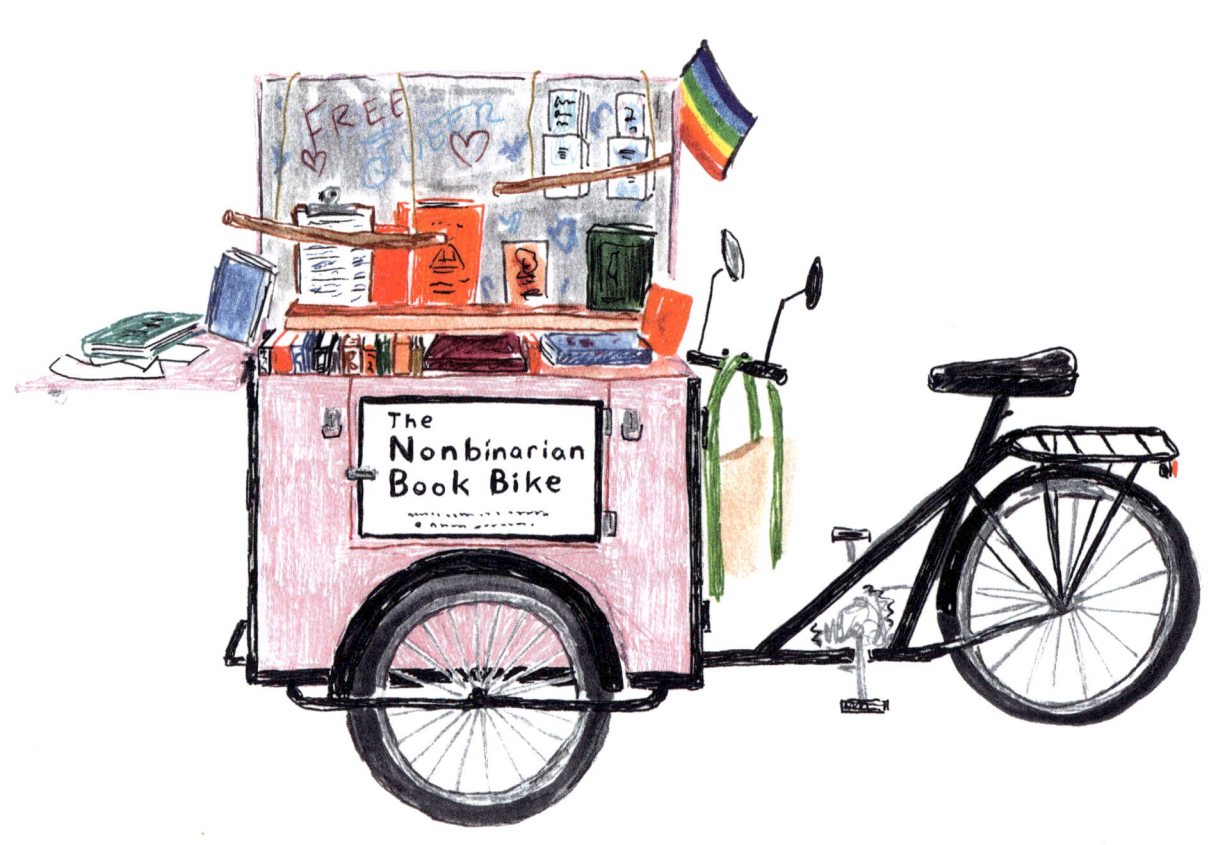

The Nonbinarian Book Bike

K. Kerimian—a veteran of the popular, independently owned Greenlight Bookstore in Fort Greene—started their own Brooklyn-based venture in 2022 with the aim to provide LGBTQ+ literature to communities throughout the borough. To accomplish this goal, they enlisted the help of a bike outfitted with a bright pink cargo box.

The mutual-aid initiative started out with K. delivering free books to spots they deemed to be "book deserts," particularly for queer and transgender-inclusive literature.

The idea proved so popular that K. opened a brick-and-mortar bookstore on President Street in Crown Heights in November 2024. In addition to stocking an impressive collection of queer and trans fiction, nonfiction, and poetry, the storefront also hosts events like a queer writer's group, a Sapphic speed-dating event, and the Bi Wives Club Weekly Knit-Along, a community-building event exclusively for "bisexual comrades that often don't feel 'queer enough.'"

The business also offers many of its titles as audiobooks through the platform Libro.fm, which includes themed playlists curated by Nonbinarian's staff. Collections include audiobooks celebrating Trans Day of Visibility, Black History Month, and banned queer books.

In 2023, before the launch of the store, K. had already given away over fifteen hundred free books on their bike. At the shop, though, not all the offerings are free—but K. is adamant that cost should never be a limiting factor preventing LGBTQ+ people from accessing books that feature topics, authors, and themes inclusive of their community. As a result, they offer a "gay-what-you-can" sponsored wall of books. Even then, if customers have nothing they can pay, "we're still going to be doing free," they told the website *Brownstoner*.

The store has not led K. to give up their first love, the bright pink book bike. During seasonally appropriate weather, you will still find this pink library on wheels delivering free books through Brooklyn, and K. hopes to expand its operations in the future.

Latino Bites

John Bedoya started this food truck, known for its distinctive blend of Colombian and Mexican flavors, in 2014. He began with what he refers to on his website as a single "mini truck"—which has grown into a fleet of three, with perfectly normal-sized trucks now regularly stationed in Queens, the Bronx, and Manhattan. The success of the business also led him to open his own brick-and-mortar spot in Jackson Heights, Queens, on Northern Boulevard.

Offerings differ slightly by location. The Bronx truck caters to the morning crowd and serves mostly breakfast food. The Queens truck is open late, and makes comfort food like perros, a decidedly Latino take on the hot dog that comes covered in a variety of sauces, including rosada (a mix of ketchup and mayonnaise), garlic, and pineapple—and sprinkled with mozzarella. The Colombian burger comes with the same ingredients but adds some ham, as does the open-faced arepa burger. For the Mexican-inspired part of the menu, they offer quesalupas, among other items, that meld the cheesiness of a quesadilla with a crispy chalupa shell.

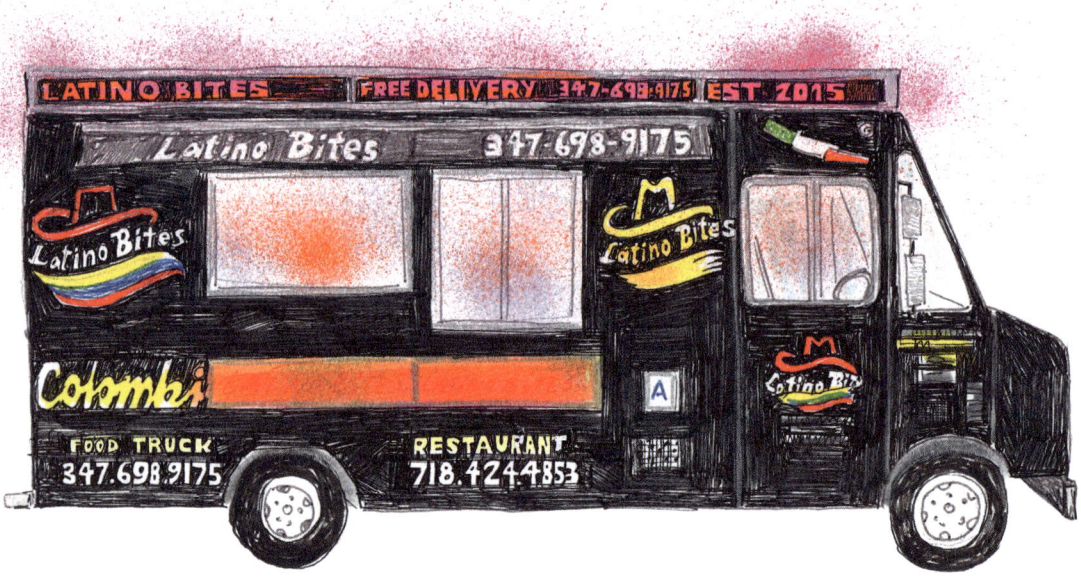

Steve's Authentic Key Lime Pie

Steve Tarpin's walk-up pie spot has been bringing a taste of the Florida Keys straight to Brooklyn's remote Red Hook neighborhood since 1995. At first Steve, a Floridia native, just made pies for friends and family. When he moved to New York, however, he started baking them in his small apartment and delivering them to customers. (Today he uses a vintage, key-lime-colored Ford truck to make his deliveries.) As demand grew, he moved operations to a brick-and-mortar location, establishing a permanent presence in the community.

Steve sells his pies, each made using fresh-squeezed key lime juice and hand-formed crust, in a few sizes: the traditional ten-inch, a "wallet and waistline-friendly" eight-inch, and a bite-sized four-inch. He also uses the latter size for the Swingle, a frozen pie dipped in rich chocolate and served on a stick. If you don't regularly find yourself trekking to Red Hook, no worries: Today dozens of markets across the city stock his wares as well.

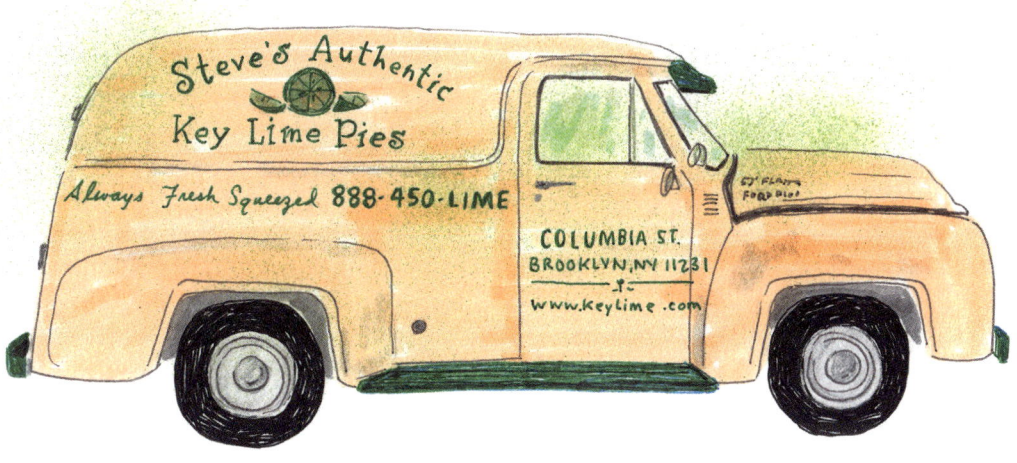

Mama Hattie's Kitchen

This mobile business offers up hot soul food, often from its preferred location on Fortieth Avenue in Long Island City, Queens. Run by the Williams family and named after their grandmother, Hattie McMillian, the truck got its start in 2023. Inspired by her home cooking, the team fries up chicken wings and catfish each day, served with sides like mac and cheese, collard greens, and candied yams. As one online reviewer said after a healthy sampling of Hattie's, "This soul food puts the soul back into food."

According to the food truck booking service Roaming Hunger, Mama Hattie's menu "sports loads of stick-to-your-ribs cuisine." A "MUST TRY," the site proclaims—which you know they really mean, since it's in all caps—is the chicken and waffles. "Crisp-on-the-outside, chewy-on-the-inside waffles topped off with succulent chunks of chicken all smothered in maple syrup. Yum." The truck is available for catered events as well.

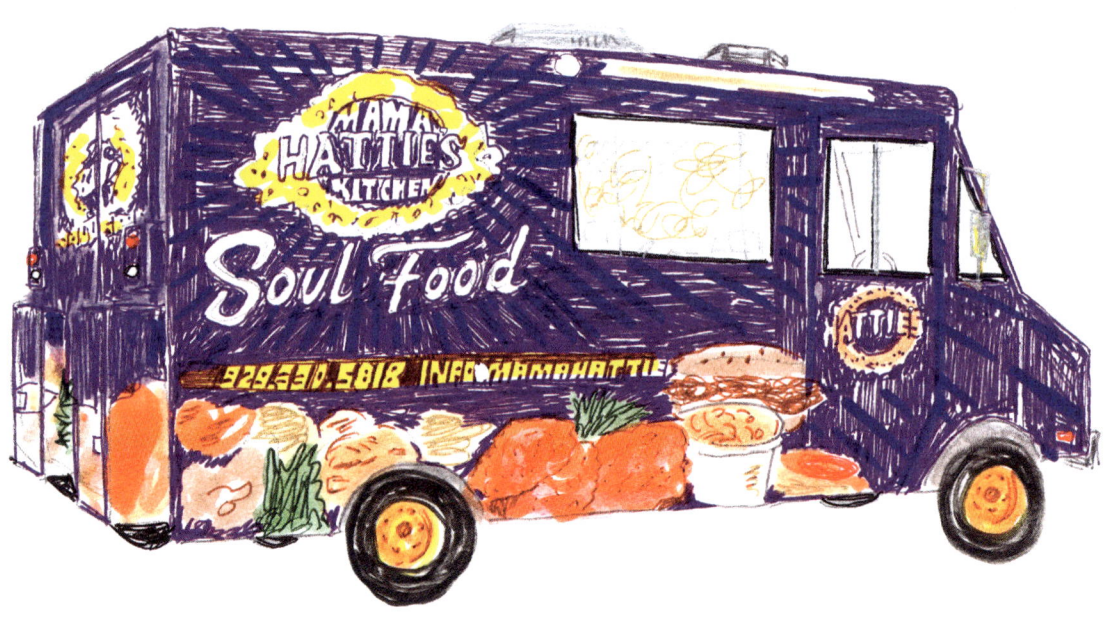

The Halal Guys

Today this halal stand is one of the best known in the city. It started in 1990 after three Egyptian immigrants—Mohamed Abouelenein, Ahmed Elsaka, and Abdelbaset Elsayed—opened a humble hot dog cart in Manhattan. Recognizing a demand among taxi drivers eager for quick, affordable, and authentic halal meals, they soon began changing their offerings, laying the foundation for the Halal Guys' takeover of New York's streets. Their menu, though concise, has garnered a devoted following. Protein choices include chicken or beef gyro (or both! Why pick?), which can be served on a platter over rice, or wrapped in a pita. They serve falafel too. Their signature sauces include a white sauce—a creamy, tangy blend that complements the savory meats—and a spicy red sauce, for those seeking an extra kick.

The success of the Halal Guys has been instrumental in popularizing halal street food, now ubiquitous across New York City. In the years since first starting the business, its founders have opened several brick-and-mortar stores and franchises across the US, and even international locations as far away as Jakarta and Seoul.

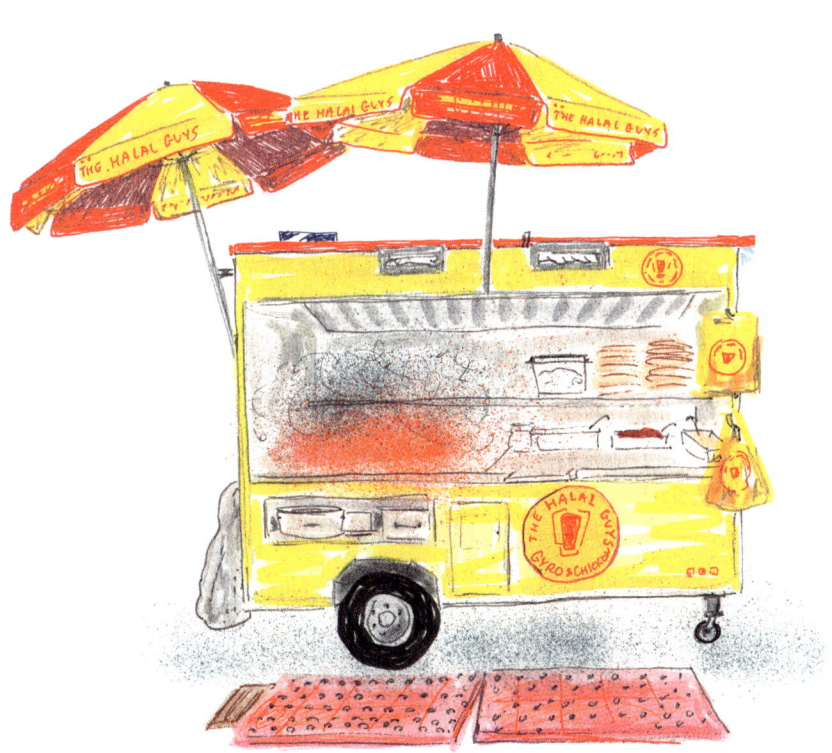

Mango Vendors

If you've spent any time in New York, you've likely come across one of the city's famous mango sellers, who are mostly women and therefore better known to locals as "mango ladies." Primarily hailing from Latin American countries, these vendors offer peeled and sliced mangos—sometimes artfully carved into floral shapes and served on sticks or in cups, and topped with a squirt of lime and a dash of Tajín seasoning.

The mango vending business, while seemingly straightforward, involves meticulous planning and long hours.

Vendors typically start their day early, purchasing boxes of the fruit from a wholesale market, such as the Hunts Point Produce Market in the Bronx. Each box, containing multiple mangos, costs between $7 to $9 wholesale. After peeling, slicing, and packaging the fruit, vendors sell each mango for a few bucks, yielding a substantial profit margin. However, their earnings are tempered by expenses such as transportation, supplies, and far too often, fines.

María, a vendor in downtown Brooklyn who's originally from Ecuador, shared her experience selling mangos in a 2019 article for *The Wall Street Journal*. A typical day for her begins at 7 a.m. with a visit to a Queens wholesale market, where she spends about $50 on fruit and ice. She then prepares the mangos at home before transporting them to wherever she decides to set up shop. On a good day, if she manages to sell all her prepared fruit, María can make a profit of approximately $150.

As with many street vendors, operating without the necessary permits (which are hard to come by in the first place) leads to frequent confrontations with the police. Each fine can range from $100 to over $1,000, posing a significant financial burden. In May 2022 María Falcon, another mango vendor from Ecuador, went viral due to a video her daughter took of her being arrested. "We can't stop working, we're not hurting anyone," she told the food news site *Civil Eats* following the incident. "My family needs me here. For this reason, I keep working."

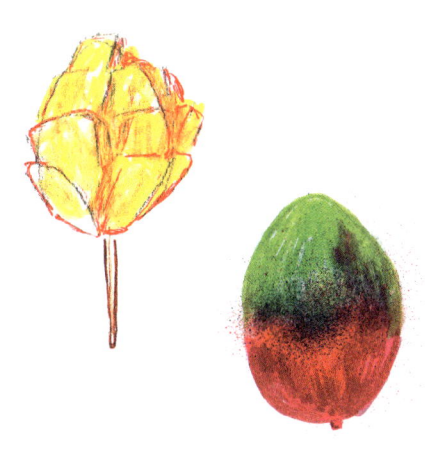

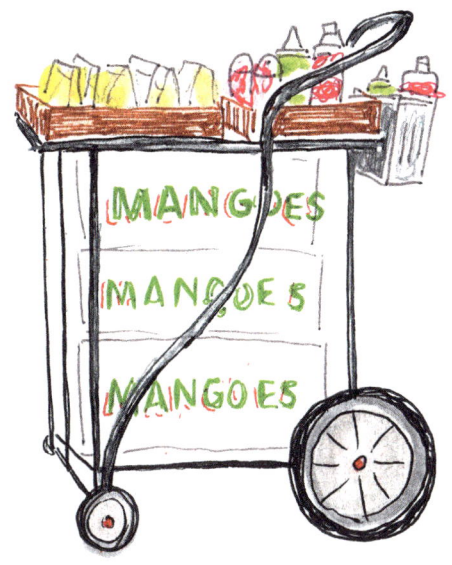

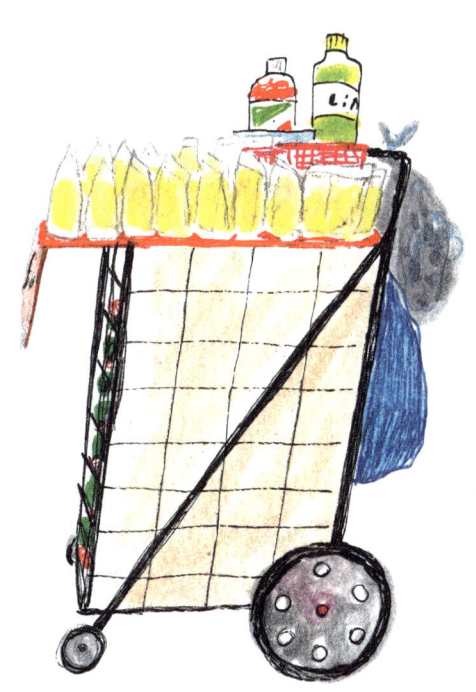

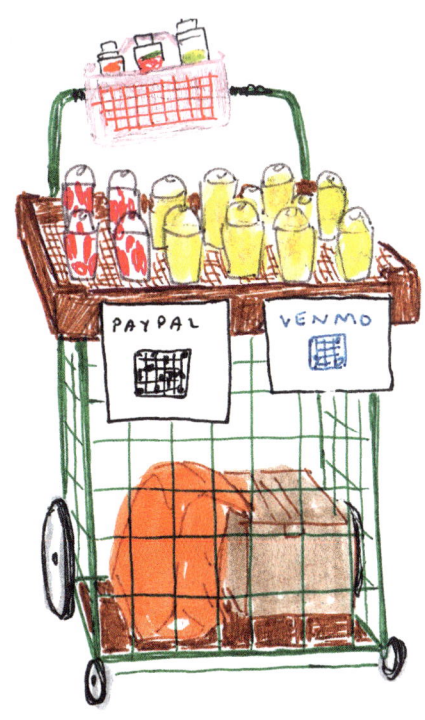

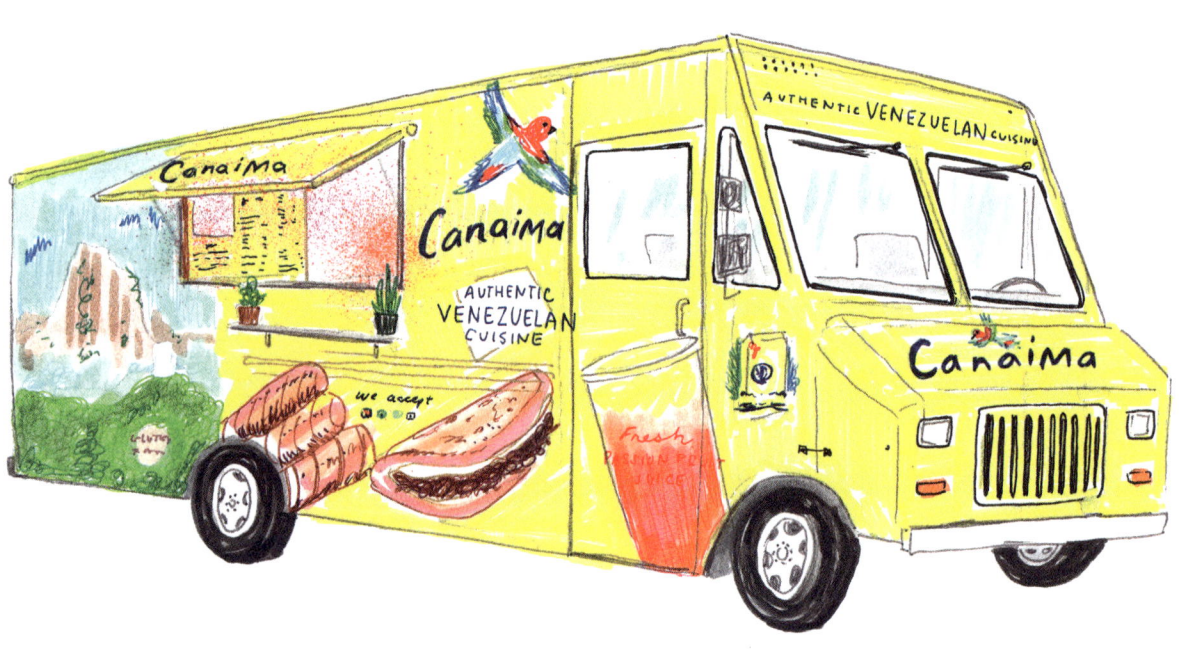

Canaima Food Truck

Andrés Baffigo has been selling Venezuelan street food like arepas, cachapas, and empanadas on the streets of Williamsburg, Brooklyn, since 2021. He operates his food truck seven days a week with the help of his wife and brother. The business is also part of the family's larger wholesale venture, Salto Angel Food Corp.

Well before Andrés became the proprietor of the successful truck, he was a young prodemocracy activist in Venezuela. As the country became increasingly unstable, he made the difficult decision to immigrate to New York in 2018, when he was twenty-four years old. Leaving Venezuela was not something he wanted to do, but ultimately he feared staying meant risking death or imprisonment because of his activist work, he told the website *VoyageLA* in a 2023 interview.

The transition to the US was challenging, but Andrés attributes his grassroots organizing skills with helping him make it in New York's "concrete jungle." "I went from leading political movements to navigating the complexities of running a food truck," he said, which shares a name with a national park in southeast Venezuela. "Each challenge has been a stepping stone, shaping who I am today and making every success, no matter how small, feel even more significant."

According to regulars, the cachapa—made from fresh corn batter, cooked on a griddle until golden brown, and then stuffed with cheese, meat, and other fillings—is a standout here.

Cachapa options include queso de mano (a soft, fresh Venezuelan cheese), shredded beef, ham, and chorizo. The fresh passion-fruit juice is also a palate pleaser. Many of Canaima's reviews online are from expatriated Venezuelans who attest to the authenticity of Andrés's cooking. "I've been coming to this place for a while now and I can confidently say that this is the best place I've been to that serves the best Venezuelan food," said one reviewer. "I'm from Venezuela and I always go here for a taste of home and it never misses."

Flushing Xinjiang BBQ Cart

Xinjiang BBQ carts are a common sight in Flushing, Queens. One such business, located on 39th Avenue and 138th Street, is a "staple" in the neighborhood, said an online reviewer. Another described the cart's lamb and chicken skin as "absolutely fire," adding that "the spicy is hella dank."

An integral part of New York's street food scene, Xinjiang BBQ carts typically offer grilled and skewered vegetables and meats, including lamb, beef, pork, and chicken, topped with a cumin and cayenne spice mix popular in western China. As skewers cost less than two dollars each, customers are often able to sample a variety of the affordable snacks. Meats and veggies will typically be made to order, over charcoal, rather than using the griddles installed in many mobile food trucks. As a result, it might take longer to get your food here than at some other street vendors—but it'll be well worth the wait; the slow-cooked meats come out perfectly smoked and juicy.

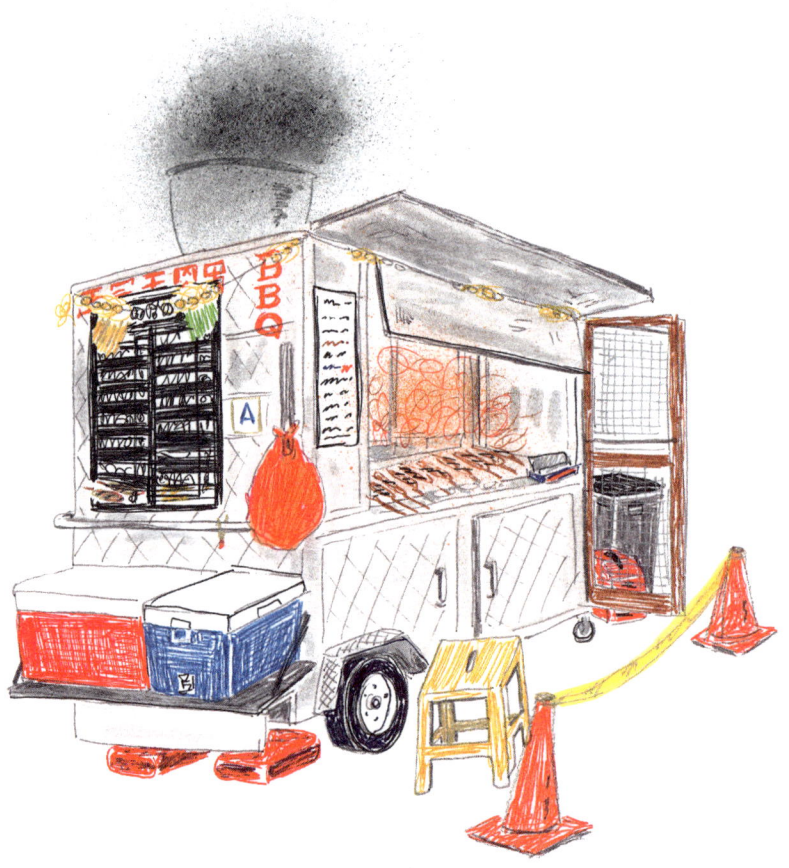

Red's Hot Dog Stand

Laura LoBuono and her son, Danny Tesoro, have run this beloved hot dog spot, located on Arthur Kill Road in Staten Island, since 2018. At that time Laura had been working on Wall Street for twenty-five years, but she quit to open her own business. Its name is inspired by her trademark fiery hair color (which also matches the paint job of the cart), and its logo features a cartoon image of Laura and her shock of red hair, waving from inside the buns of one of her hot dogs, or barkers, as she calls them.

In some ways, working the hot dog stand is an ode to her childhood. As a kid Laura frequented the very same business she now owns, which was located in the exact same place. When her brother learned the cart was for sale, he bought it and ran it for ten years before turning it over to her. "Now, I'm like, 'Heyyyy, here's your barkers!,'" she told the website *SI Live* in 2023.

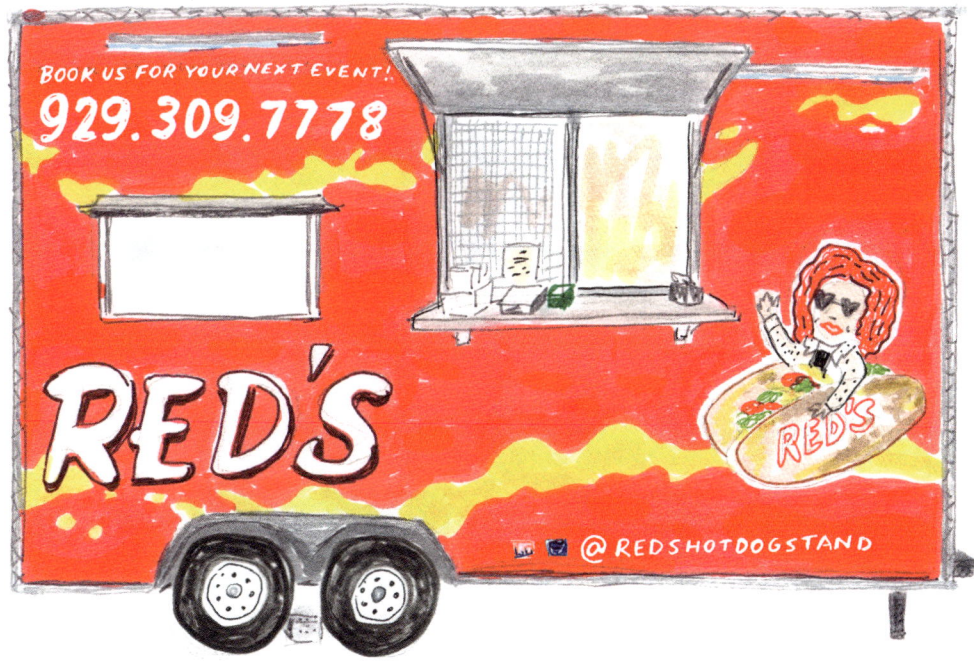

Kali Cooks

In 2024 chef Kaliope Tjutjulis opened this food cart, which offers American fare like smash burgers, hot dogs, and chicken sandwiches, on Cedar Grove Avenue in Staten Island—strategically located right across from the beach. If you can't spot the dark blue cart featuring an illustration of Kaliope with her arms confidently crossed up top, just look for the inflated "wacky wavy guy" beckoning customers in, she told the YouTube channel One Bun Burger Reviews shortly after opening.

A native Staten Islander, Kaliope got her start in the food business in Manhattan, working at spots like Upland. When she and her sister found an old hot dog cart for sale, however, she jumped on the opportunity to start a venture closer to home. During the colder months, she closes up shop but is still available to cater private events and parties.

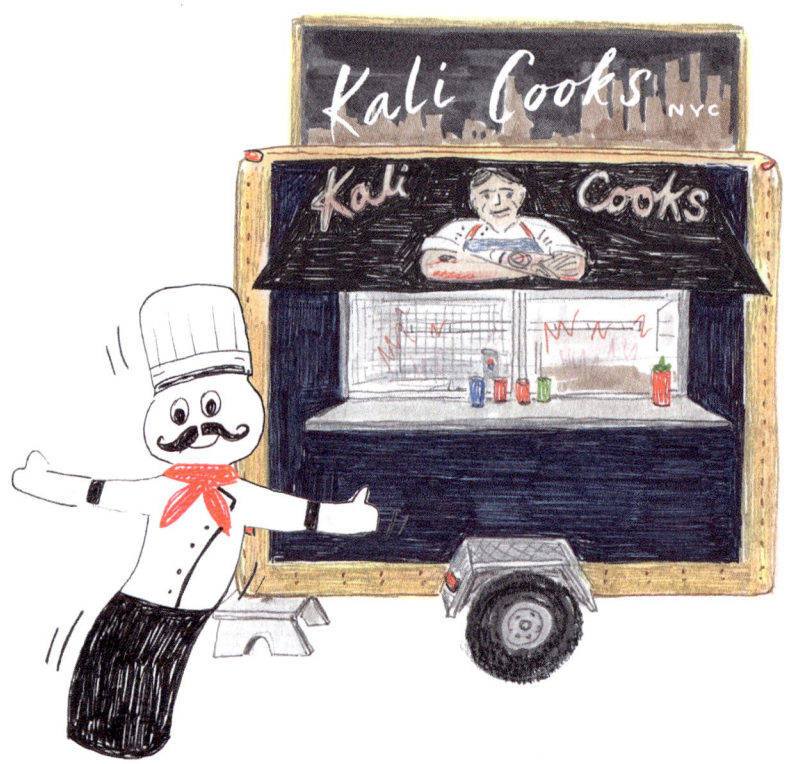

Father & Son's Kitchen & BBQ

Luis Rivera Jr., better known as "BBQ Lou," first got the idea to open a spot that blends traditional American barbeque with Puerto Rican flavors in 2009, while he was enjoying a pulled-pork sandwich at a Mets game. A trained chef who had spent decades working in the food industry, Luis at first set out to create the stadium's sauce as precisely as he could. In the process, however, he invented something he liked even better—which is now his signature sauce, the Sweet and Tangy.

His innovations didn't stop there. Other creations came to include barbecue sauces made with passion fruit and spicy guayaba, part of his Mi Gente, Mi Tierra line of sauces honoring his Puerto Rican heritage. Whichever dressing you choose, squeeze a generous portion over your chicken, ribs, or brisket, all of which are slow cooked over wood. You can often find Luis's truck at Broken Bow Brewery in the Bronx, but check his schedule online for other appearances throughout the city.

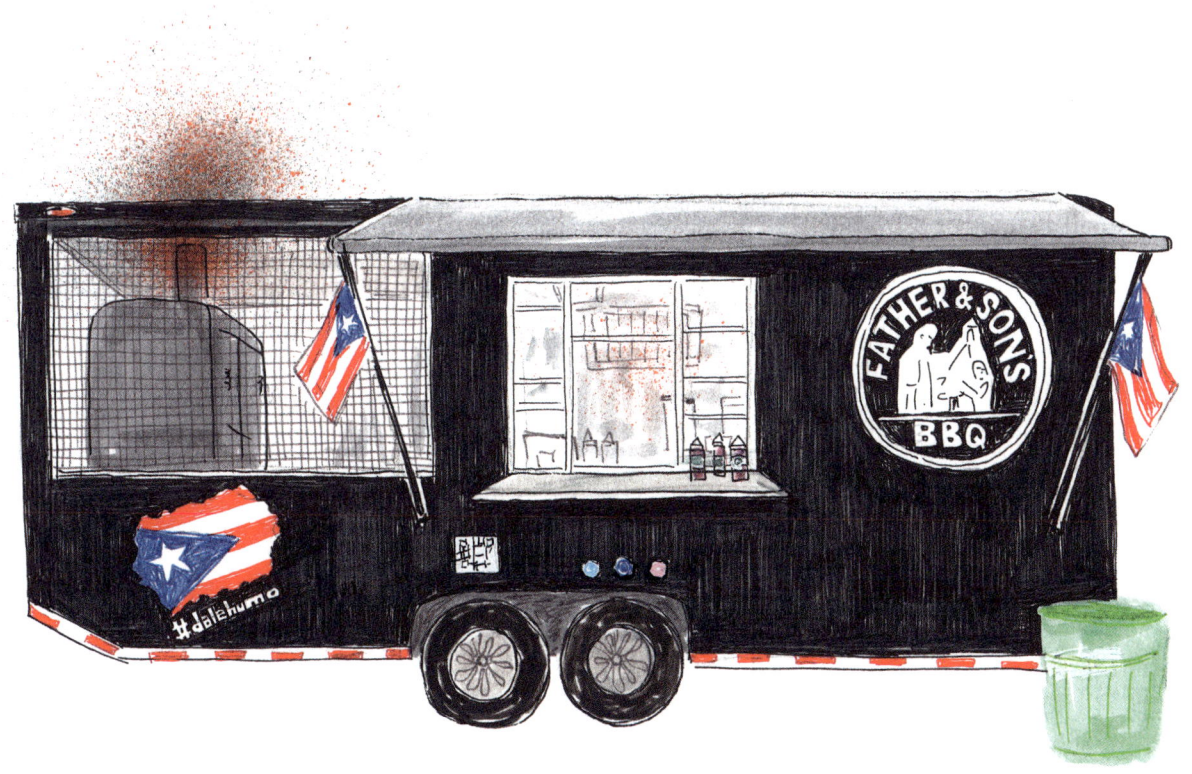

Harlem Seafood Soul

After surviving cancer and being laid off from her job, Harlem native Tami Treadwell started paying attention to what she realized was her true calling. As she writes on her website, "I love feeding people. I know that's the huge part of my purpose here on this Earth." In 2016 she began to do exactly that with her new business, a "state of the art eco-friendly mobile kitchen" that blends the best of seafood and Southern cuisine.

Tami's cart may be stationary—most often situated outside the state government building at the corner West 125th Street and Adam Clayton Powell Jr. Boulevard—but word of her cooking began to travel in the years following her opening. Lines frequently snaked down the block. In 2025 she temporarily took her cart off the market and announced plans to expand into a bigger food truck, which she launched later that same year. She also maintains a stall at the DeKalb Market Hall in Downtown Brooklyn.

Customer favorites include Tami's garlic-butter shrimp and creamy grits, fish tacos, and chicken and waffles.

The po' boy sandwich, served on freshly baked potato bread with a special garlic aioli, is another. It comes with your choice of three fillings: fried fish, jumbo shrimp, or oysters. "Chef Tami represents the true soul and deep love that comes from Harlem, and that energy shows in her cooking, which makes it so wonderful," according to one online reviewer. "The vibe here is unmatched."

Many media outlets and TV shows have been eager to showcase that vibe too. In 2022 Tami was included in the Netflix series *Street Food: USA*, and the *Today Show*'s Hoda Kotb and Jenna Bush Hager featured her in a segment. "I tell people all the time, at my corner on 125th Street, there's nothing but love," Tami explained to them.

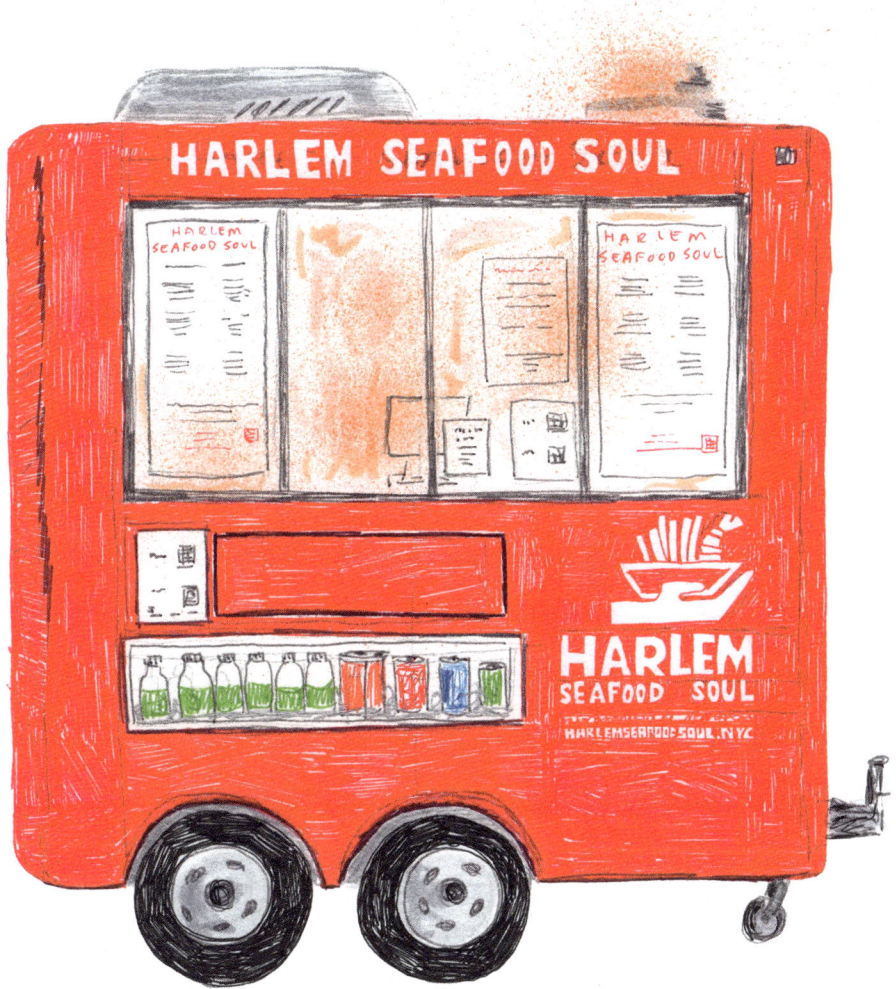

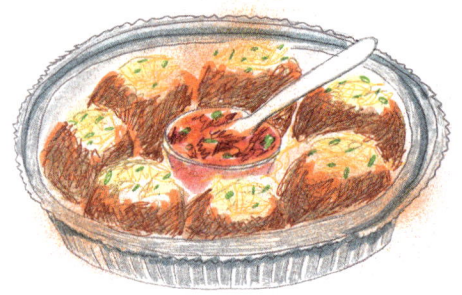

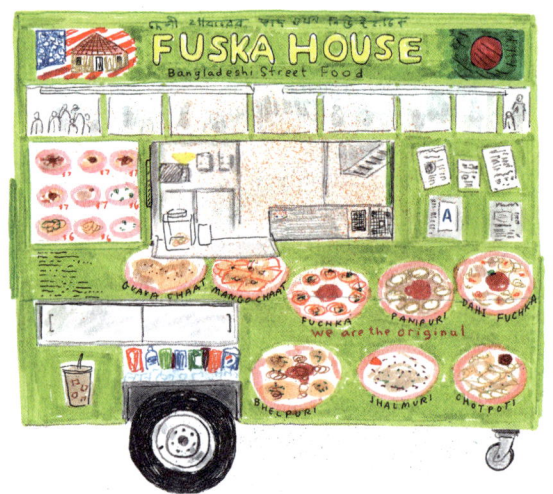

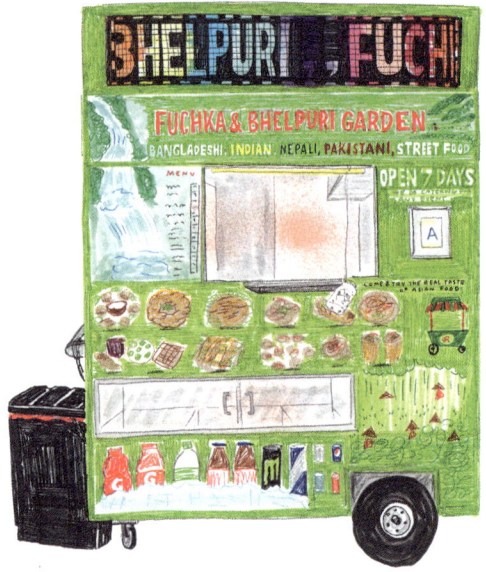

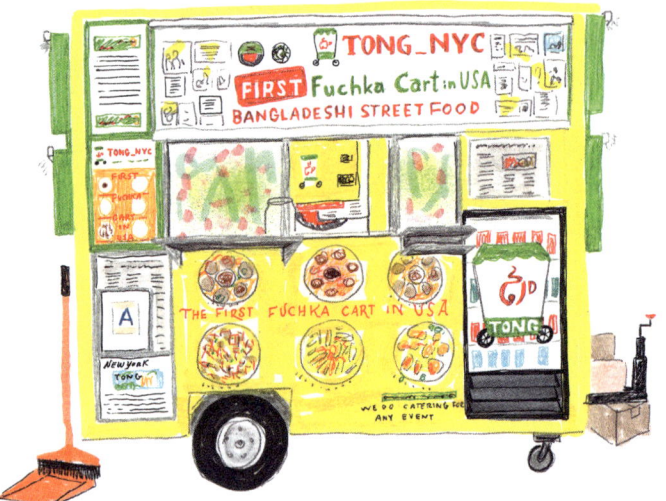

Bengali Snack Vendors

In 2017 Bangladesh native Md. Naeem Khandaker opened his food cart business, Tong, to sell the popular Bengali snack fuchka in Jackson Heights, Queens. (It's pronounced *FOOCH-ka*, in case your mind happens to be reading it more colorfully. And it's also known as fuska or phuchka.) The crispy treat is made with semolina shells filled with a savory mixture of potatoes, chickpeas, and a masala spice blend, all topped with bits of hard-boiled egg. Immediately before serving, the spherical balls are doused with tangy tamarind sauce, and they should be eaten right away. The result is a snack that "bursts into a slake of sour-sweet, cool and hot at once," as described by *The New York Times* in 2019.

When Masud Rahman, a fellow Bangladeshi native and Naeem's former roommate, saw long lines forming at Tong, he decided to get in on the action and in 2019 opened Fuskahouse on the same block. The two fuchkawala (as fuchka vendors are called) have nearly identical menus, except for their unique masala recipes, which both refuse to make public.

The men, it seems, have started a trend: Today there are several vendors along the same street selling the Bengali snack, sparking something of a friendly rivalry.

As competition increased over the years, Naeem hung a sign on his cart proclaiming Tong to be the first to sell fuchka on the block *and* in the entire country. Not to be outdone, Masud hung his own sign, claiming—despite being the second to the street—Fuskahouse is "the original." Fuchka Garden, a newer arrival, decided on a sign with a message that would be harder to disprove, stating simply, "We are real."

Naeem, for his part, welcomes the new entrants—all of whom, he told the *Times*, got their start at Tong before opening their own carts. Rather than become territorial, he's instead thankful for the increased attention they collectively bring to Bangladeshi cuisine, especially amid all the other options within the bustling Jackson Heights food scene. The competition also hasn't held him back in the slightest—he's since expanded his business to include additional carts and a brick-and-mortar location in Jamaica, Queens.

Los Amigos Chimichurry

This Colombian food truck, located between 108th and 111th Streets on Roosevelt Avenue in Corona, Queens, is a culinary landmark in the area. First-timers here are often at a loss as to what to order, since there is no menu. But frequent visitors know to simply strike up a conversation with the chef to see what's cooking, or to ask one of the many late-night revelers who line up here every evening.

According to regulars, who lovingly refer to this spot as the "Chimi Truck," standout items include dishes like the carne frita, empanadas filled with grilled meat, and tostones. Adorned with lighting around its perimeter, the business usually opens at 9:30 p.m. and often sells food until as early as 6 a.m. It's the "perfect place to end an adventurous night," according to one online review—or to "kick one off with a bang."

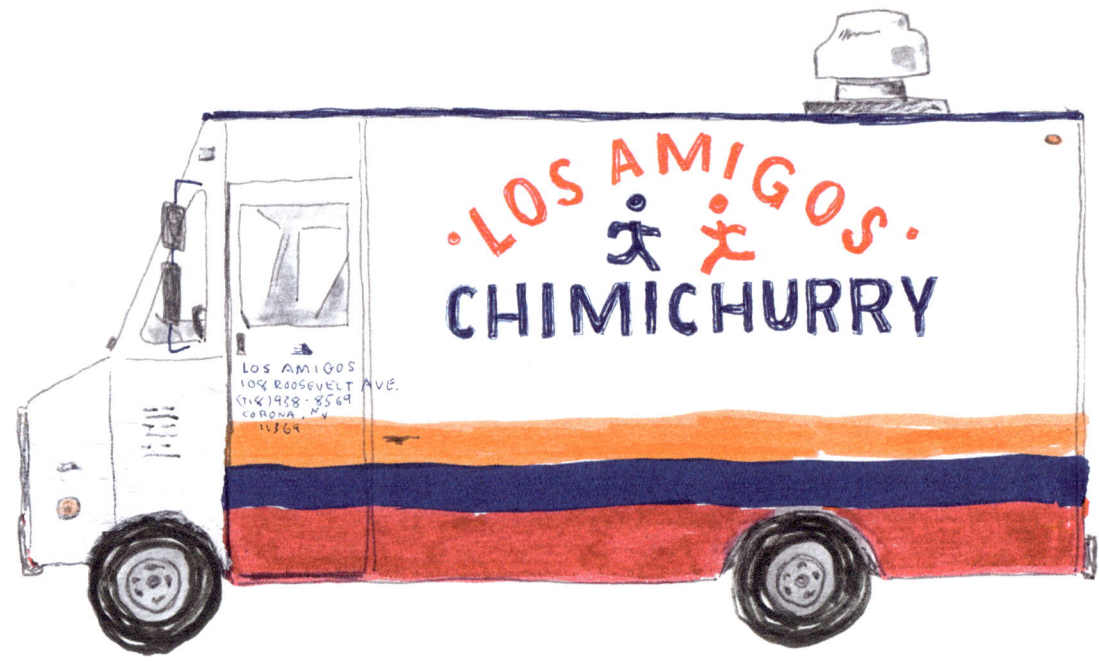

Jerk Pan

If you find yourself in Midtown Manhattan with a hankering for goat-head or cow-foot soup (and you would, if you've ever tried either), look no further than this Jamaican food vendor. A regular stop in the New York foodie scene since 2009, Jerk Pan parks most days on the corner of Forty-Eighth Street and Park Avenue. Can't spot the truck for some reason? Keep an eye out for the giant Jamaican flag, which is usually flying high off the back of it.

As you might expect from the name, the truck specializes in jerk chicken, but regulars also like the oxtail. Sides include cabbage, greens, and macaroni salad. Regardless of what you order, "If they ask you if you want gravy, you need to say yes," according to a review on *The Infatuation*. "It's for your own good."

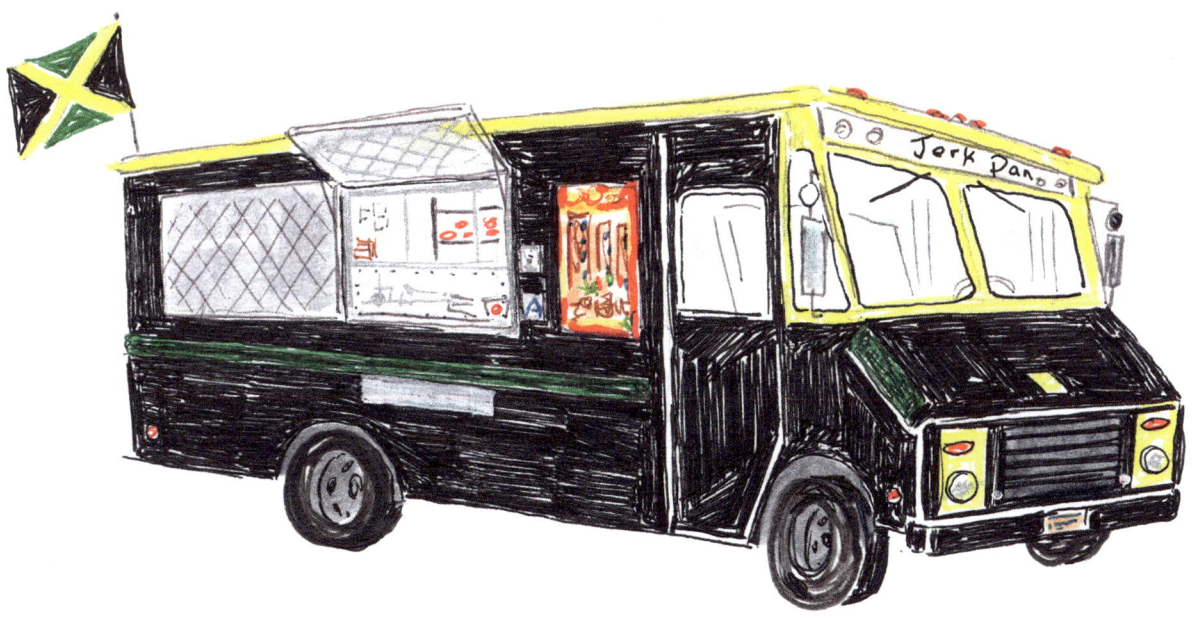

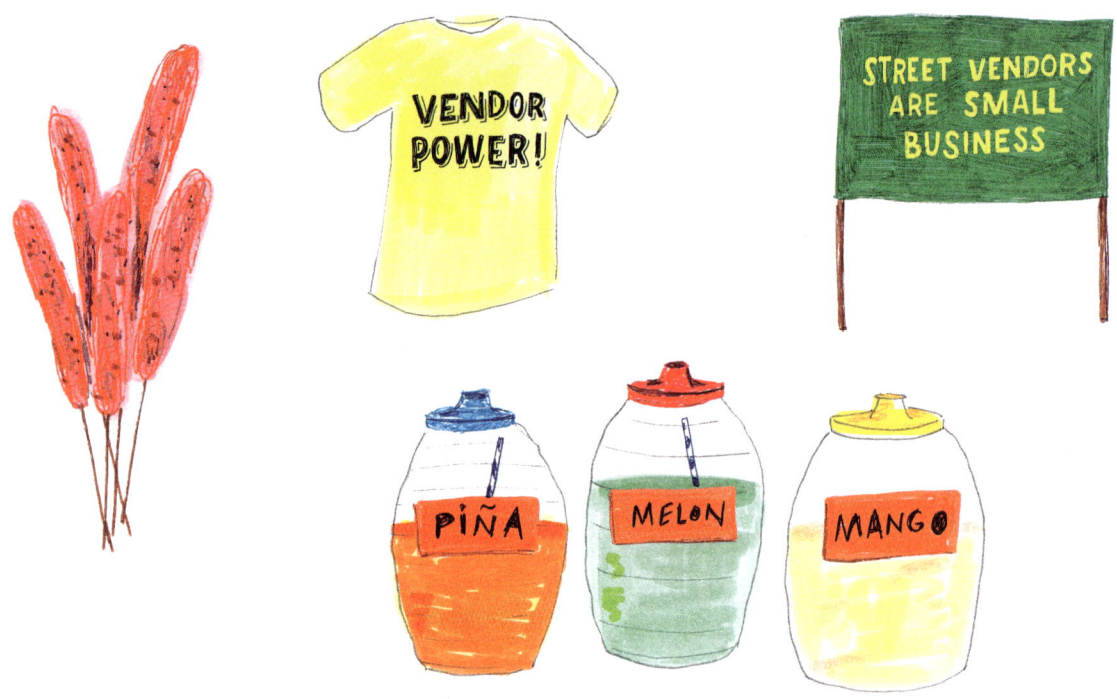

Corona Plaza Vendors

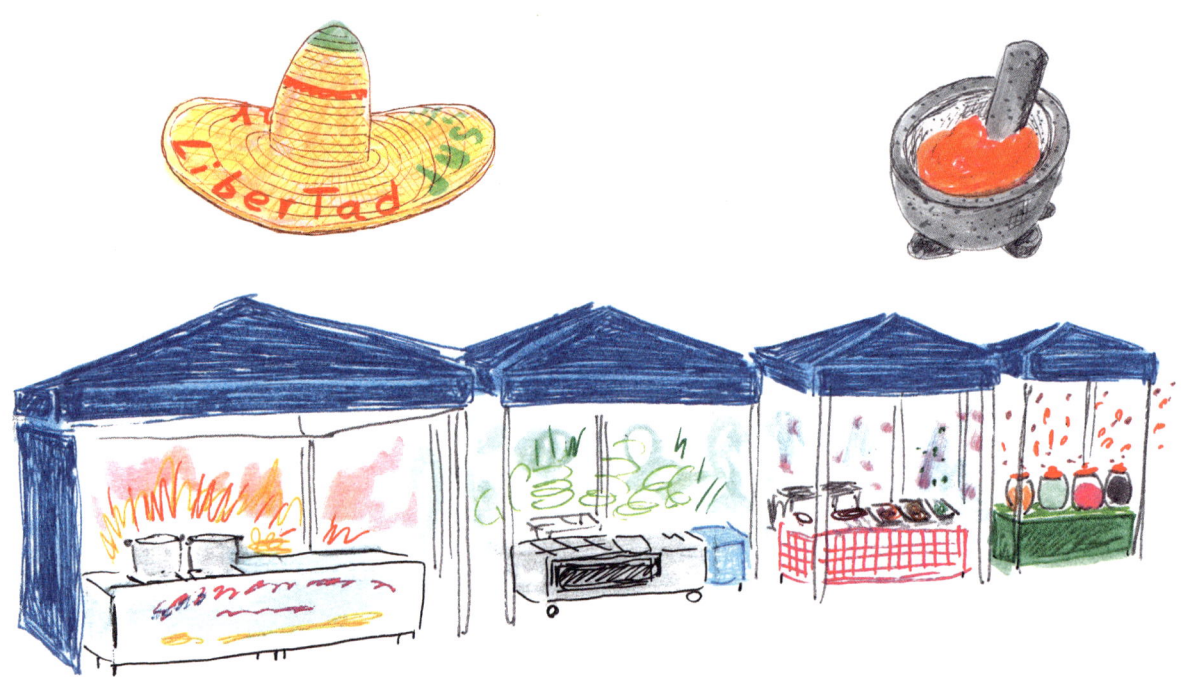

Corona Plaza in Queens is renowned for its extensive selection of street food, each stall offering a distinct taste of cuisines from Mexico and other Latin American countries. Looking for chilaquiles in the style made in Puebla, Mexico? Visit Norma's stand, Chilaquiles El Chingon, where you can try the "best chilaquiles outside of Mexico," according to at least one online review. In the mood for a tamale? Ana, originally from Guerrero, Mexico, makes and sells over two hundred of the masa-based meals on a good summer day.

This vibrant street food hub emerged during the early days of the COVID-19 pandemic, when vendors began to set up tents and carts here. The venture provided locals with a needed financial lifeline during tough economic times, and this once overlooked part of Queens transformed into a bustling city center.

By 2023 Pete Wells, food critic for *The New York Times*, included the vendors at Corona Plaza among the "100 Best Restaurants in New York City."

The plaza's success, however, led to increased scrutiny from the city. None of the vendors were able to secure one of the very few permits available that allow them to operate legally, for instance. Many of the food stall owners were subjected to ongoing policing as a result. In the summer of 2023, the city sent officers to stop nearly eighty people from selling on the plaza, sparking widespread outrage and concerns among the vendors, their customers, and the neighborhood as a whole.

However, the vendors decided to fight back. Through a new organization, the Asociación de Vendedores Ambulantes (Street Vendors Association), supported by the Street Vendor Project, they advocated for—and won—special permits to be able to sell at the plaza. A limited number of people are allowed to operate in Corona Plaza now at reduced hours if they pay quarterly sales taxes and meet additional health and safety requirements—moves that some say are overly stringent and have diminished the original spirit of the market. Still, it represents a rare victory in the movement to legitimize street vendors.

Street Preachers

Open-air preaching dates to ancient times (you may have heard of one such fellow who went by the name Jesus Christ), and the tradition has continued unabated over the centuries. Since the late 1800s preachers have been standing atop overturned soapbox crates every Sunday at Speakers' Corner in London's Hyde Park, opining on religion, politics, and everything in between. A similar tradition took hold in New York in the early 1900s, at 135th Street and Lenox Avenue in Harlem. Though the corner isn't used as often in the same way today, it was once where the likes of Marcus Garvey and Malcolm X gave rousing speeches for racial justice.

Though protected by the First Amendment, street preachers must often navigate complex legal landscapes to exercise their rights—particularly when they are espousing controversial or fringe ideas (looking at you, Westboro Baptist Church!). Still, organizations like the American Civil Liberties Union have historically defended the rights of street preachers, emphasizing the importance of safeguarding free expression even when the messages conveyed are unpopular.

Many creative and quirky people have taken up street preaching to communicate with the public in a way that combines political activism and performance art.

Reverend Billy, portrayed by performance artist William Talen, has preached in New York's streets since 1999, lecturing passersby about the evils of consumerism and corporate culture. He often stages theatrical protests with his Stop Shopping Choir, addressing issues like environmental degradation and economic inequality. His performance is equal parts satire and activism, leaving onlookers entertained—and often surprised to find themselves reflecting on societal values.

Another notable figure is politician Jimmy McMillan, founder of the Rent Is Too Damn High Party. Gaining national attention during the 2010 New York gubernatorial debate, McMillan centered his message on the unaffordability of housing in the city. His straightforward slogan and charismatic delivery resonated with many New Yorkers frustrated by escalating living costs. McMillan's advocacy highlighted the challenges of affordable housing and sparked discussions on economic disparities in urban areas.

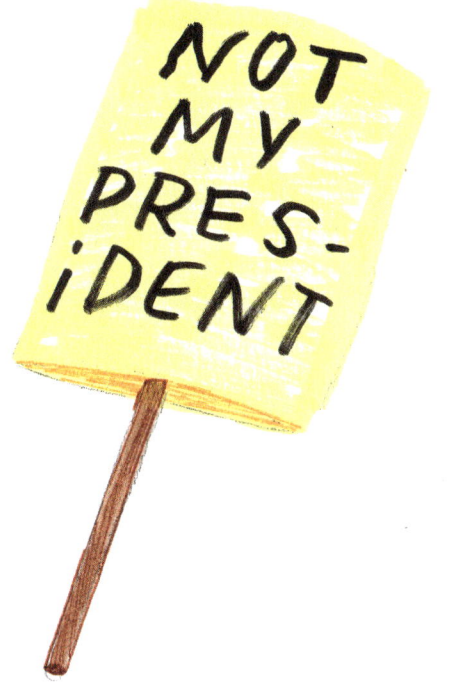

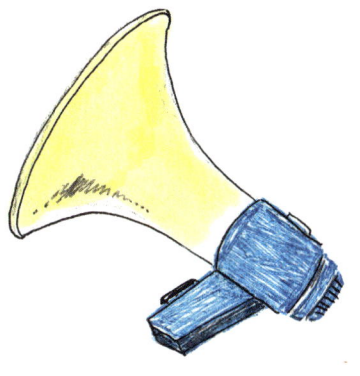

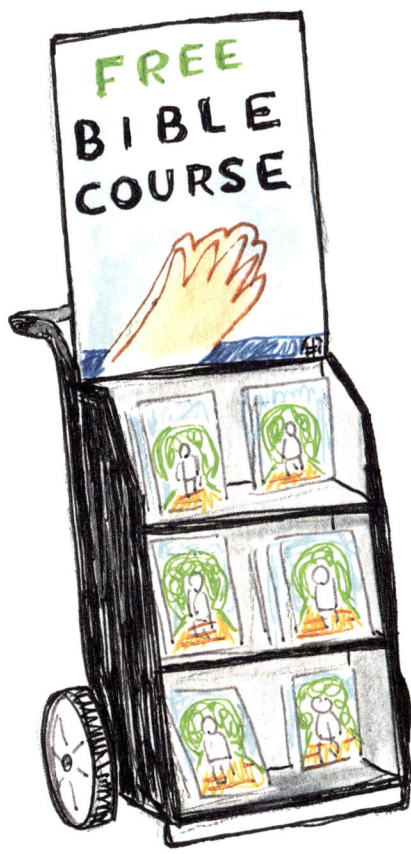

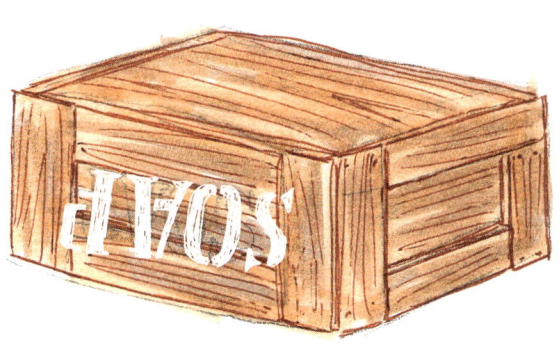

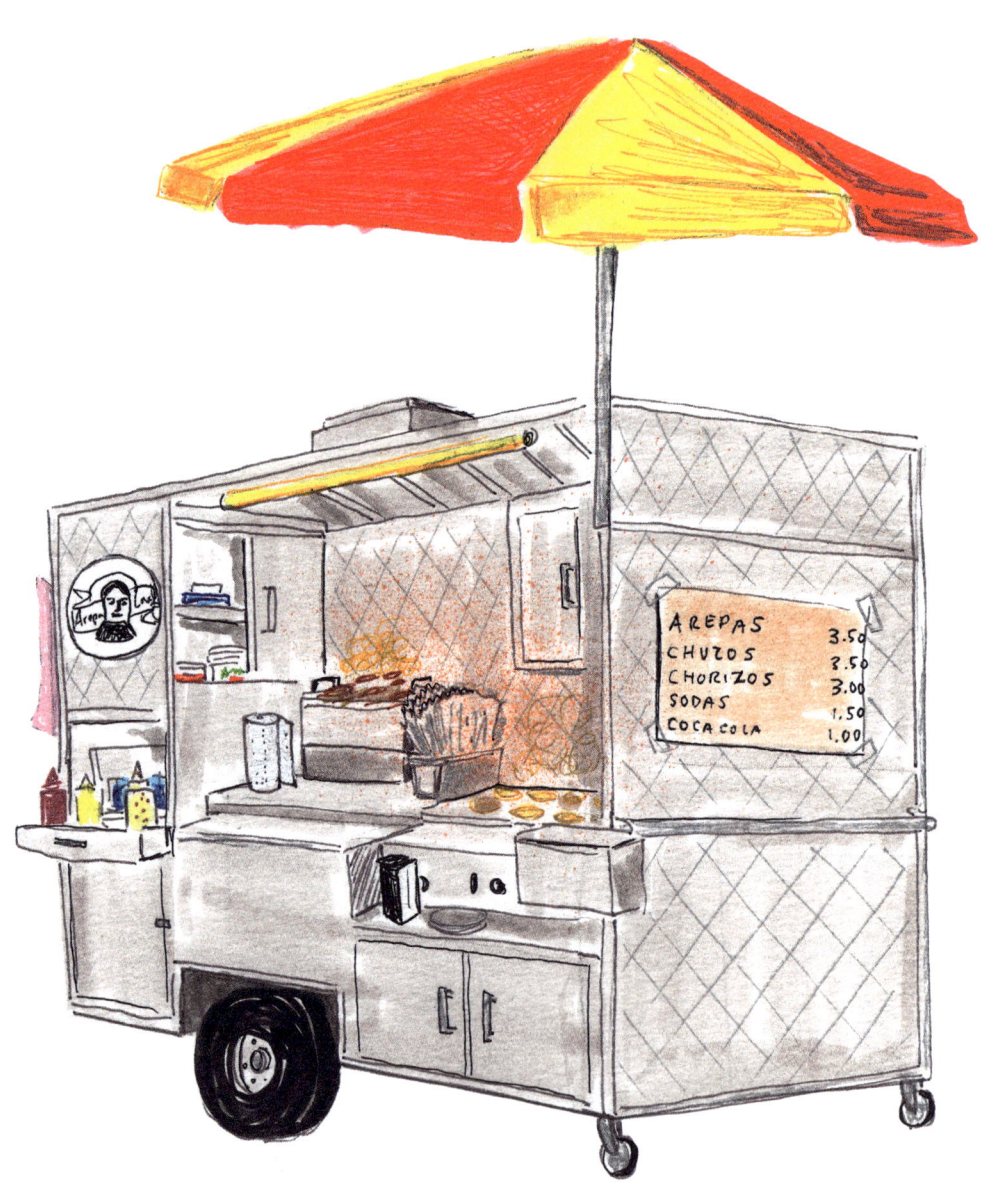

Arepa Lady

Maria Piedad Cano, better known as the "Arepa Lady," has been a storied figure on New York's culinary scene for decades. Originally from La Estrella, Colombia, where she worked as a lawyer, judge, and cofounder of the Universidad Autónoma de Medellín, Maria relocated to Queens in the 1980s to escape political unrest. To support her family, she began selling arepas—traditional Colombian cornmeal cakes—from a street cart in Jackson Heights around 1990. Initially stationed at the northwest corner of Roosevelt Avenue and Seventy-Ninth Street, Maria's arepa cart quickly garnered a loyal following.

In 1993 a *New York Press* article dubbed her the "Saintly Arepa Lady," a testament to not just her culinary skills but what regulars say is her warm, inviting presence.

That adoration has only grown in the decades since—a 2014 *New York Times* story on Maria, titled "The Comfort of Her Embrace," reads almost like a profile of a rock star: "I want to hug her," the article quotes one customer as saying.

However, Maria is much more than a nice lady who charms customers and food critics alike—her hype has as much to do with the "arepa" part of her moniker. Arepa Lady sells a variety of types of the Colombian staple, which can be served on their own or *relleno*, meaning "stuffed," with cheese, chorizo, chicharron, steak, or chicken. The menu also includes arepas de telo, a crispier flatbread version.

In starting her business, Maria didn't rely on long-standing cooking skills or a family recipe that had been handed down to her through the generations. "I had never made arepas before," she told CBS News in a 2021 interview. In a "desperation to pay rent, feed my kids, and satisfy the needs of an entire family," however, she saw an opportunity—and New York's streets are the tastier for it. Now she is mostly retired and leaves much of the day-to-day business to her two sons, who also helped her expand in recent years to brick-and-mortar locations in Jackson Heights and Astoria.

Piragua Carts

These shaved-ice treats, shaped into cones and doused with a variety of syrups, are a staple of the summer months in many New York City neighborhoods. Though versions exist throughout Latin America, *piraguas*—a portmanteau of the words for "pyramid" and "water" in Spanish—hold a special place in Puerto Rican culture. Syrup flavors include fruits commonly found throughout the island, like tamarind, passion fruit, and coconut.

Piragüeros, as the vendors are known, are especially popular throughout East Harlem, the Bronx, and parts of Brooklyn.

Piragüeros often become deeply integrated into the neighborhoods where they work. The "Piragua Lady," as she is affectionately known, has sold the sweet treats for decades, typically stationed on 116th Street and Lexington Avenue in East Harlem. During the summer, you can almost always find the "Slushie Man"—who combines traditional piragua flavors with modern slushie machines—outside the El Bohio Food Market in Corona, Queens.

Given piragüeros' importance in Manhattan's Washington Heights, local graffiti artist Snoeman—whose work decorates the facades of bodegas and storefronts throughout the neighborhood—hand-painted the menus on some carts in the area. The vendors themselves are also a regular subject in Puerto Rican art. In Lin-Manuel Miranda's musical *In the Heights*, for example, a piragüero calls out for customers while bemoaning competition from certain corporate ice cream companies. "So sweet and nice, piragua," the vendor sings (played by Lin-Manuel himself in the movie version). "It's hotter than the islands are today, and Mister Softee's trying to shut me down." Jean-Michel Basquiat, the neo-expressionist Afro-Puerto Rican artist, also created his own ode to piragüeros, drawing an untitled piece featuring a man pushing a cart.

In a 2023 article for the website *PS*, writer Kimmy Dole put into words the importance of piraguas for many Puerto Ricans in the city. The carts bring "a vibrant charm and sense of camaraderie to our neighborhoods," she noted, and are a "cherished part of New York City's summer traditions—one that I will continue to carry on for as long as I remain a New Yorker."

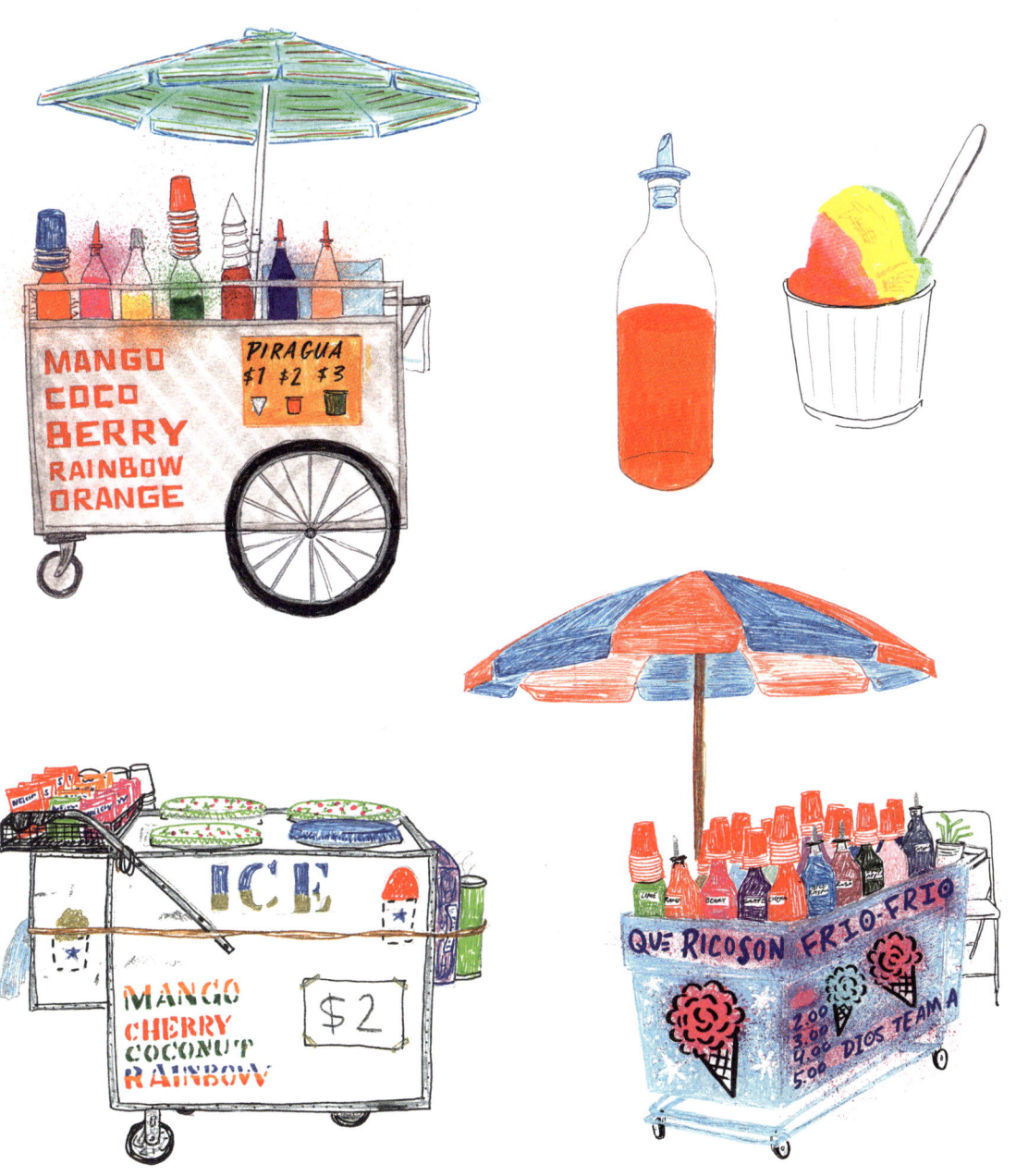

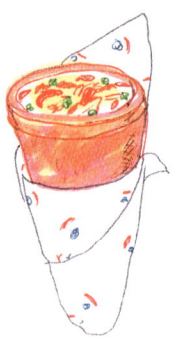
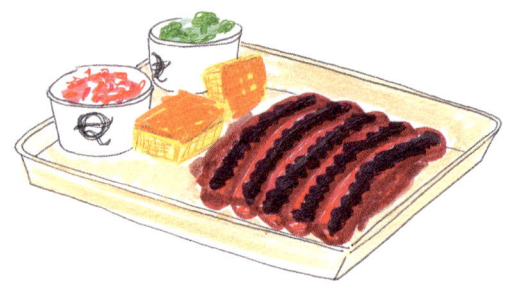
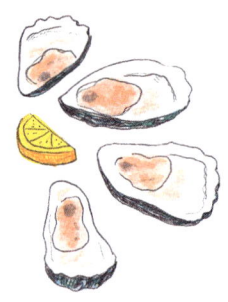
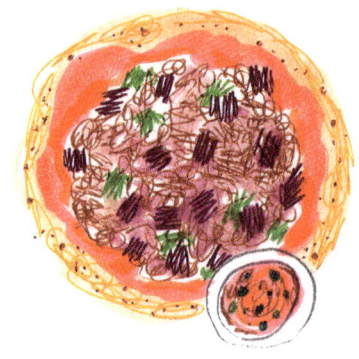
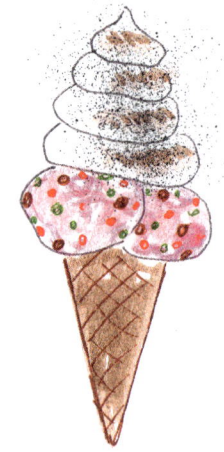

Smorgasburg

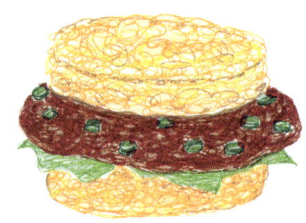

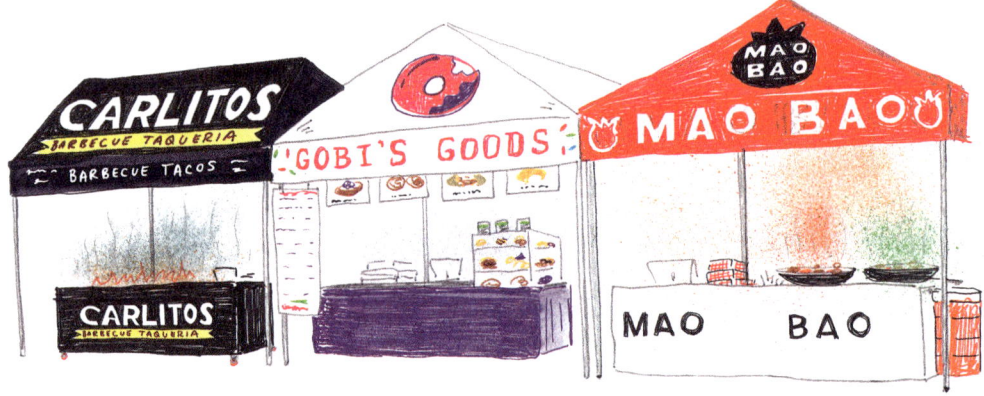

Jonathan Butler and Eric Demby launched this open-air market as an offshoot of the popular Brooklyn Flea (p. 26) in May 2011; the expansion was driven by the increasing demand of food vendors eager to set up stalls. Following a kickoff event that featured over sixty vendors along the Williamsburg waterfront in Brooklyn, a *New York Times* headline deemed Smorgasburg the "Woodstock of Eating." The market, which runs from April to October each year, continues to live up to that title today. It has since expanded to Prospect Park in Brooklyn, downtown Manhattan, spots in Los Angeles and Miami, and a bar in New Jersey. Together, the various locations welcome more than two million visitors annually.

Over the years competition among vendors to be a part of Smorgasburg has become increasingly fierce.

According to an *Eater* interview with cofounder Eric, only about 10 to 20 percent of applicants are invited in for a tasting—and even fewer of them will make it into the market. Today the tastings are conducted in secret to avoid unwanted attention from the public and press, to help out already anxious prospective vendors.

The nerves are well-founded—for some would-be food entrepreneurs, making it into the market can be a springboard into a full-time culinary career. At the Williamsburg Smorgasburg in 2013, for instance, chef Keizo Shimamoto's Ramen Burger kickstarted a craze by using boiled and pressed ramen noodles as buns. A few years later CNN dubbed him the "King of Ramen." Chrissy Teigen later said she was "over" any food that looked like it was just made for Instagram, except for the ramen burger. Another success story, Mighty Quinn's Barbecue now has five storefronts in New York, as well as locations in Connecticut, Florida, Maryland, and New Jersey, but had its humble beginnings as a Smorgasburg stall.

Of all their accomplishments, Jonathan and Eric say the market's ability to help up-and-coming chefs make their dreams come true, particularly in some of the most expensive parts of the country, is the thing they are most proud of. "Giving an entrepreneur . . . a less expensive/risky way to launch a business—and within a community of like-minded people to boot—is our most lasting legacy," they said in an online interview with clothing retailer ONS in 2018.

Bona Bona Ice Cream

———

Nick Di Bona debuted this artisanal ice cream company at the Williamsburg Smorgasburg in 2019—though he was no newcomer to the culinary world. In 2013 he competed on the Food Network's competition show *Chopped* and won by dazzling the judges with a maple gelato. Later that year he received a glowing *New York Times* review for his first restaurant, Madison Kitchen, located in Larchmont, a suburb of New York City. The review's closing line urged Nick to consider selling his homemade ice cream in pints to go.

Nick's inventive flavors and signature topping, a torched Italian meringue, have made his cups and cones a favorite at Smorgasburg. Today you can also find Bona Bona Ice Cream at a storefront in Baldwin Place, New York, and a flagship "dessert restaurant" in Port Chester, New York, complete with a "sprinkle shower"—which is exactly what it sounds like, except with clothes (and goggles).

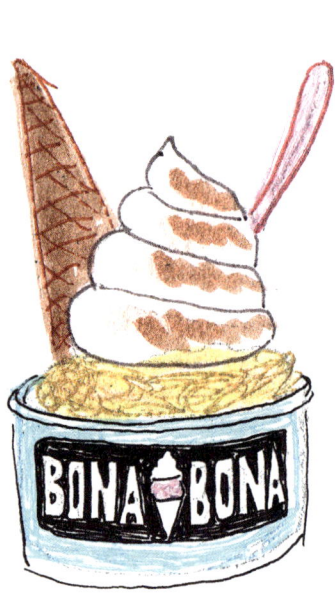
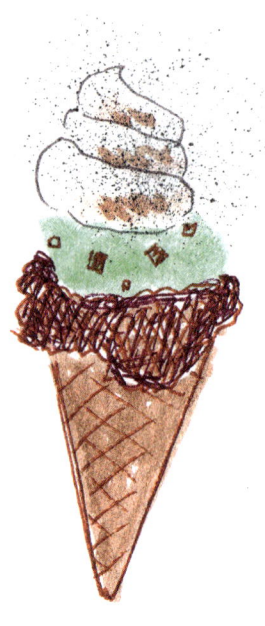

Mao's Bao

———

Eddie Mao started this mobile food venture in 2016, specializing in traditional Chinese buns known as shengjian bao, which are pan fried and filled with pork, beef, chicken, or lamb. (The business also offers "impossibao," a plant-based option using the Impossible-brand meat alternative.) The crispy exteriors are almost Easter egg–colored, with vibrant shades of blue, purple, and green.

Bao has been a part of Eddie's life since he was a child. In a 2023 Instagram post, he explained his mother used the buns as bribes to goad him into shopping with her. Today Mao's Bao is a regular at Smorgasburg's markets in New York. Eddie has also made appearances at the Smorgusburg spots in Los Angeles and Miami, making him one of the few vendors to pop up at each of the market's locations. You can also find Mao's Bao at Pearl River Mart Foods in Manhattan's Chelsea Market.

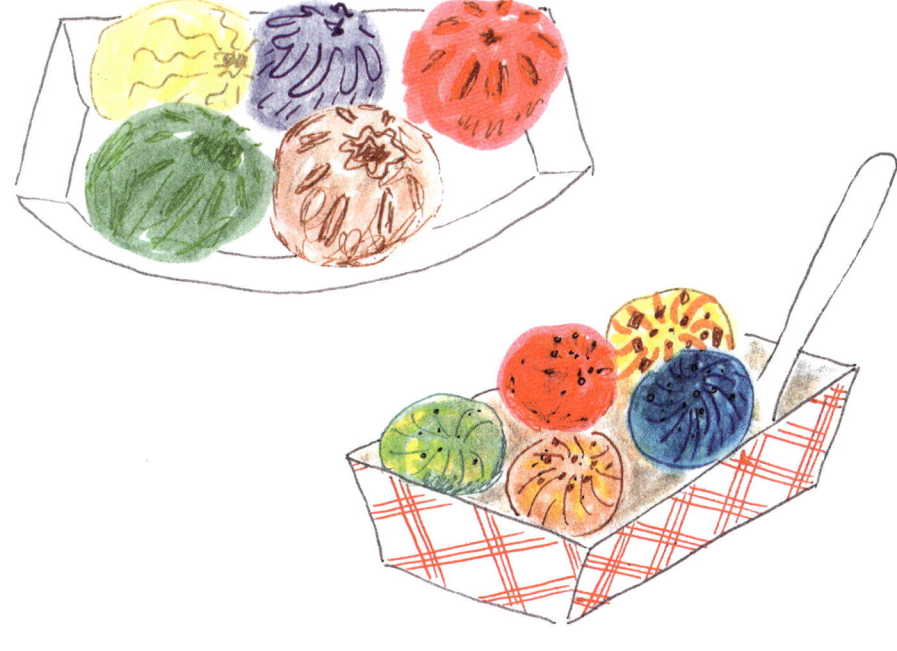

Carlitos Barbecue Taqueria

A trio of friends—Carlos, Fernando, and Martin—are the brains behind this Mexican-inspired mobile kitchen. Starting with a simple food trailer in Jersey City in 2017, they have dramatically increased their footprint with stalls at Smorgaburg's Williamsburg and World Trade Center locations, as well as several outposts in New Jersey, including at Newark Airport.

The menu is small but packs a punch; Carlitos is best known for its slow-smoked barbecue tacos, with pulled pork or brisket wrapped inside hand-pressed nixtamal tortillas. Regulars also rave about the nachos, doled out in generous portions, and elote (Mexican street corn). While the items on offer are consistent across locations, at least one online reviewer recommends the Carlitos spot at the Smorgasburg bar in Jersey City for a practical reason: "You get the best of both worlds," she wrote, "tacos from Carlitos and tequila from the neighboring bar."

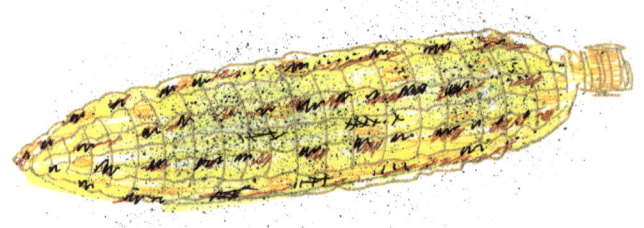

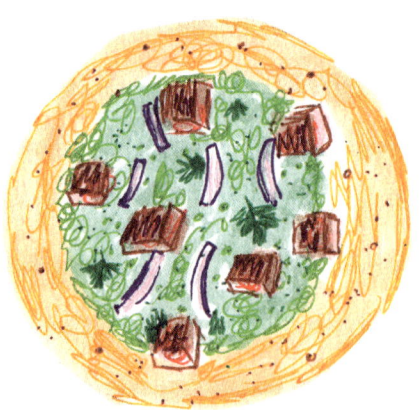

Red Hook Lobster Pound

This lobster vendor maintains an active presence at Smorgasburg, where it was among the very first vendors. They also have a seafood-focused food truck called "Big Red." The truck, as it turns out, is not all that red—but the massive lobster rolls they sell (which, to be fair, are also depicted in big red drawings on the truck) certainly are. The Smorgasburg stall and food truck are both extension of the popular restaurant by the same name that first opened in Red Hook, Brooklyn, on Van Brunt Street, in 2009. Though Red Hook Lobster Pound proudly proclaims to be "your Maine hook-up," they also understand that passions run deep about the "right" way to serve a lobster roll. You can certainly get it the Maine way—typically served cold, with mayo, and on a hot dog bun. But husband-and-wife owners Ralph Gorham and Susan Povich won't begrudge you if you'd prefer it Connecticut style, served warm with butter.

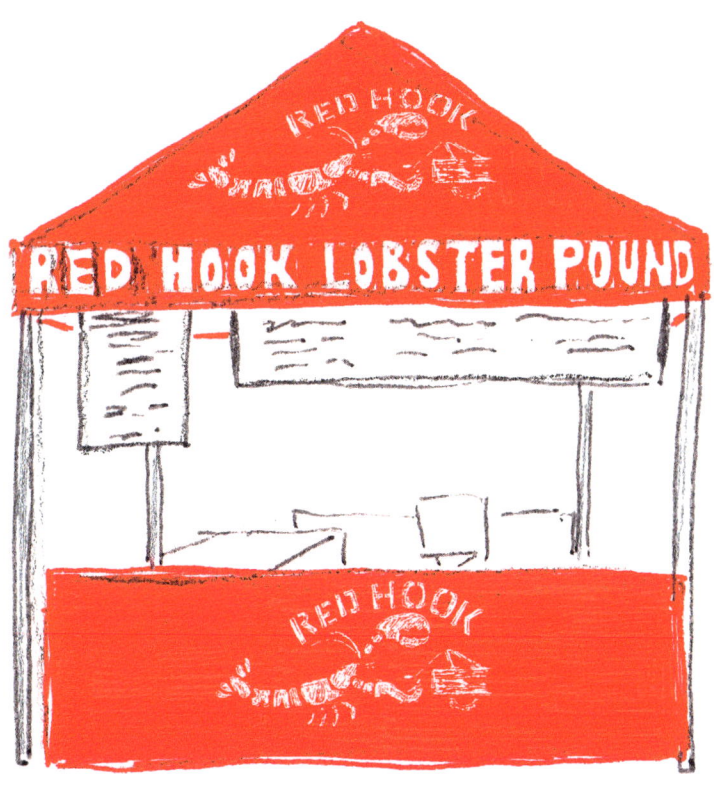

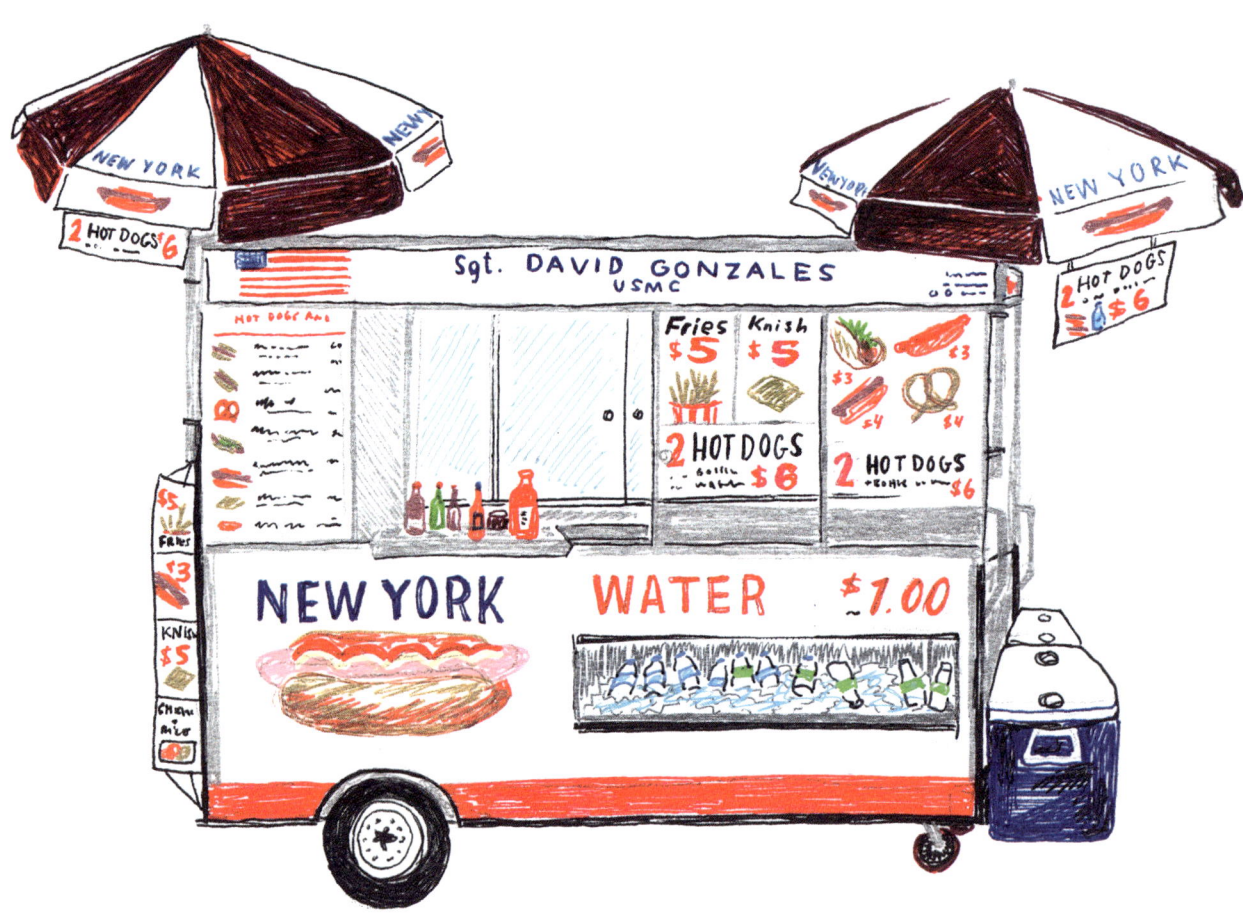

New York Hot Dog King

————

In a city chockablock with hot dog vendors, Dan Rossi, owner of New York Hot Dog King, is likely the most legendary.

Since 2007 Dan has been slinging his dogs outside the Metropolitan Museum of Art, but his fame stems not just from selling near one of the city's best-known cultural institutions. He also has a long, storied history as an advocate for the rights of street vendors, particularly veterans like himself, in New York City.

In 1990 Dan's hot dog cart company was the largest in New York, holding 499 street vending permits across the city. A year later, however, his luck turned. As part of his effort to "clean up" Midtown Manhattan, then-Mayor Rudy Giuliani pushed through legislation that restricted street vendors from operating near cultural institutions and high-profile areas. The state then passed legislation limiting the number of permits street vendors could hold to just one.

Overnight Dan was reduced to a single vending permit, which he eventually used to sell his dogs outside of the Met, in defiance of the new laws. As a result, he faced near daily harassment by the police. Every time officers told him to move, he would—but only by about ten feet each time. "I figured if they kept bothering me, I'd just keep moving toward the center," he told the online magazine *New York Said* in 2024.

Finally, in 2013, a New York Supreme Court judge ruled that veterans were, in fact, allowed to sell food outside of the museum, freeing Dan to legally sell hot dogs in his preferred location. However, the ruling opened competition from other vendors, leading him to sleep in his van almost every night of the week to protect his prized location. "My home is in front of the Met," he said in an interview with the *New York Post* in 2024. "I'm doing what I have to do. I could leave the spot and go do something else, but then I lose. And I can't lose, I can't let these people win over me."

Xiang Mini Cake

Well before he operated one of the most popular food carts in Manhattan's Chinatown, Xiang Situ—who first came to the United States in 1991—was a diamond setter for over ten years. But as the jewelry-manufacturing business started to dwindle in the neighborhood, Xiang found himself looking for work. At first the entrepreneur began cooking and selling food from his native Hong Kong just as a way to make ends meet and support his family. His "mini cakes"—griddled dough balls topped with chocolate, condensed milk, or caramel—proved such a hit, however, that he decided to turn food into his full-time gig.

Xiang has situated his food cart on the corner of Canal and Mott Streets since 2010. His mini cakes (which go by many names, including egg waffles, egg puffs, or eggettes) have become a staple of the downtown lunchtime crowd, as well as a must-try destination for foodies in the know.

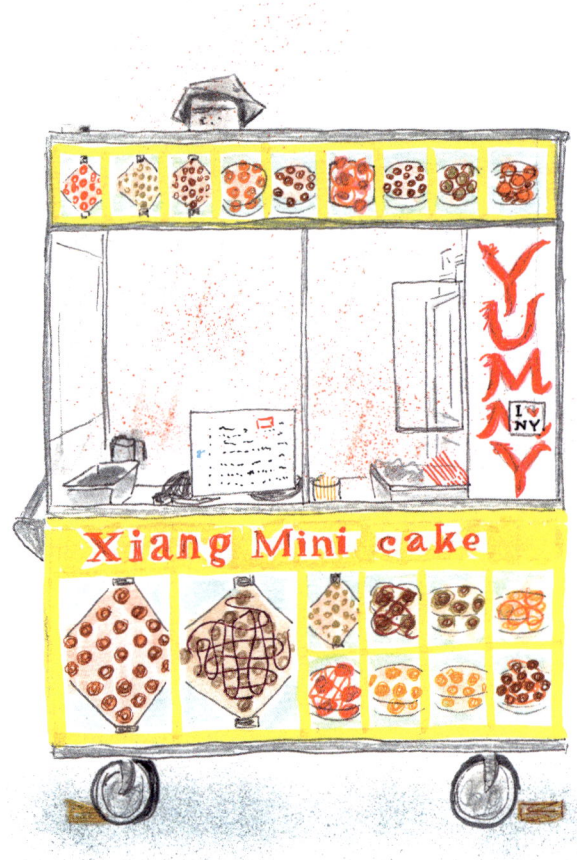

Cesar's Empanadas

This food truck has a few Brooklyn locations—one is typically parked on Hanson Place, just outside the Atlantic Terminal, an extremely busy commuter hub. Others include spots at the corner of Washington Park and Dekalb Avenue in Fort Greene and outside the Apple Store in Williamsburg. Cesar's offers a wide array of Latin American fare, like tacos, as well as typical North American grub, including cheeseburgers. True to its name, however, the empanadas are by far the favorite here. One online reviewer said she can't go near Barclays Center without "jonesing" for them.

The empanadas have traditional fillings, such as beef, chicken, and spinach with cheese, but Cesar's isn't afraid to experiment with the format—past creations have included pizza-inspired and mashed-potato varieties. The business counts Alicia Keys, Jimmy Kimmel, and Guillermo Rodriguez as customers (the latter once visited the truck dressed like a fairy princess for a *Jimmy Kimmel Live!* segment).

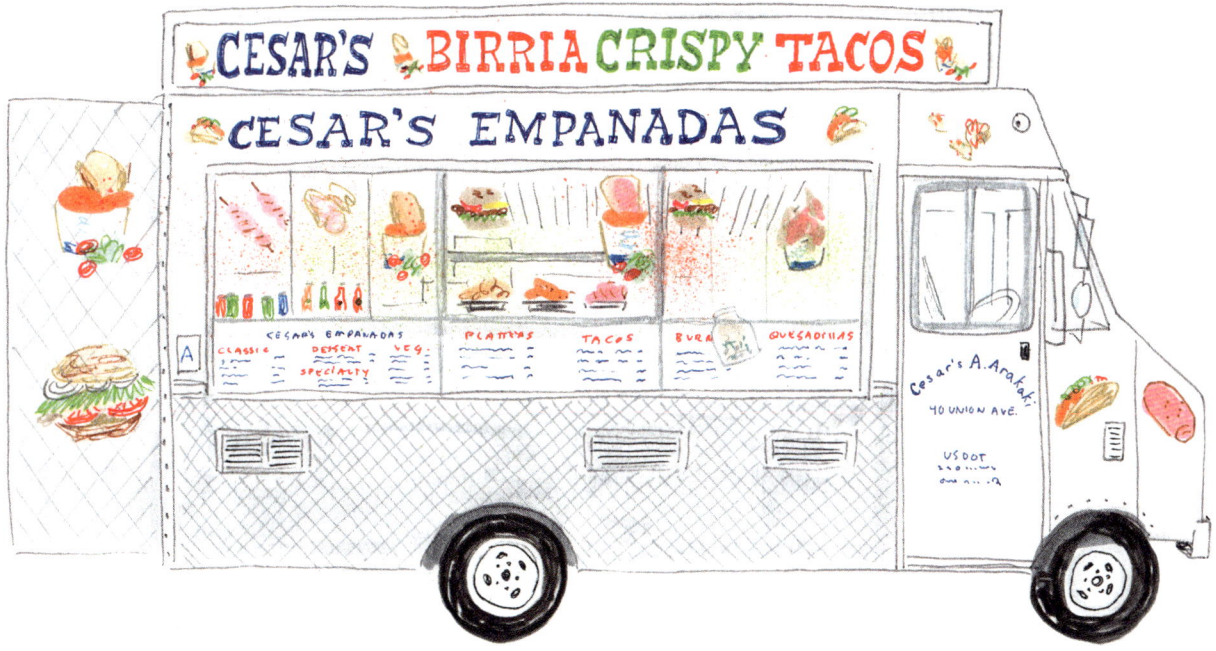

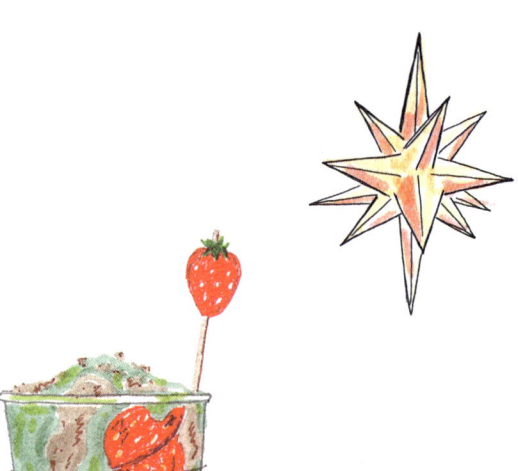
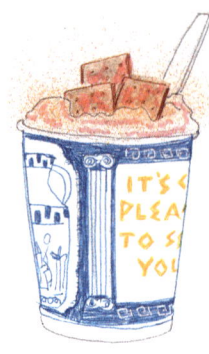
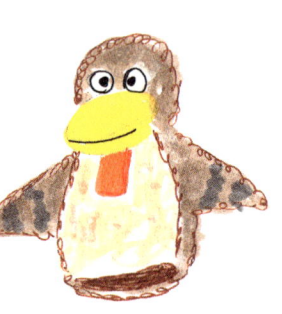
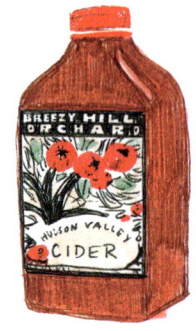

Winter Holiday Markets

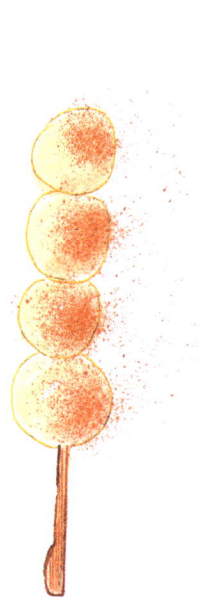
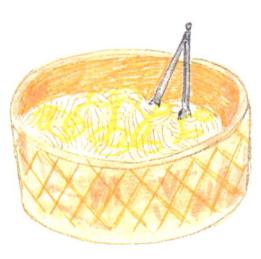
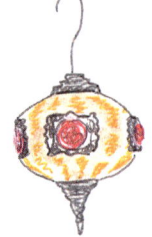
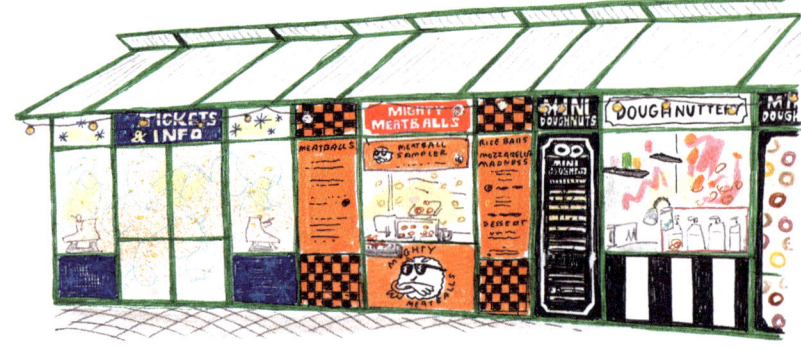

Every winter, during the holiday season, several of New York's prime squares and parks transform from busy commuter areas into markets crammed full of stalls, with vendors selling artisanal crafts, food items, and other gifts.

They spring to life for just a few months each year but have come to be beloved by tourists (and reviled by harried locals accustomed to using these squares as shortcuts). Two of the most popular markets in the city are the Union Square Holiday Market and Winter Village at Bryant Park, both in Manhattan.

The Union Square Holiday Market, the original and arguably best-known of its kind in the city, started in 1993. Modeled after the traditional outdoor "Christkindlmarkts" in Europe, today the market's 185 different vendors offer a dizzying array of handmade items, jewelry, clothing, and treats. Some trek here just for a chance to sample the Liquid S'more from Rubyzaar Baked, a hot chocolate drink served with a toasted marshmallow rim and topped with graham crackers.

First held in 2022, Winter Village at Bryant Park includes over 170 vendors spread throughout the park in custom-designed "jewel box" kiosks. Here, the vendor Strawberro is a standout, known best for their Dubai chocolate dessert made with strawberries, melted Belgian chocolate, chopped pistachios, and kataifi pastry. (To get your hands on one, it's best to visit the stall early in the season. In recent years the dessert has gained viral fame online, leading to wait times of up to two hours during peak periods.)

Plenty of local, lesser-known outdoor holiday markets also pop up all around the city come November. For example, the people behind the Hester Street Fair, an outdoor market started in downtown Manhattan in 2010, operate a holiday-themed version of their venture featuring many independent designers and artists. Since 2016 I AM caribBEING, an organization dedicated to showcasing Caribbean culture and art in New York, also sets up a holiday market with stalls for artists and vendors on Nostrand Avenue in Brooklyn.

Mister Softee

You will hear this vendor before you see it, and—it doesn't matter your age—your Pavlovian response upon noticing its iconic music-box jingle will give you the impulse to run straight into the streets of New York in search of the Mister Softee truck you know is nearby.

Brothers James and William Conway launched the ice cream brand in Philadelphia in 1956, moving its headquarters a few years later to Runnemede, New Jersey. From its humble beginnings, the company quickly grew to include around two thousand Mister Softee trucks in thirty-eight states during its peak in the 1960s.

Due to increased competition, fewer trucks roam the streets today, but the company still boasts over three hundred in New York and Long Island, as well as three hundred fifty franchise dealers across eighteen states.

At times the ubiquitous Mister Softee truck has been a victim of its own success. The company continually finds itself in legal battles with rogue operators in New York, copycat vendors that mimic its trademarked look and song. In 2013, for instance, one of the business's former franchisees left the company to start his own venture, which he called Master Softee.

Mister Softee has faced its share of criticism too. Some street vendor proponents maintain the franchised ice cream brand has siphoned off business from smaller, locally based vendors throughout the city for decades. Other NYC residents are less pleased than their kids to hear the omnipresent jingle—which, in case you were curious, is based on Arthur Pryor's 1905 composition "The Whistler and His Dog" in E-flat major (though the version most trucks play bumps the key up to a more cheerful E). In 2005, to address this issue, then-Mayor Michael Bloomberg brokered a deal with the company. Today the trucks can only play their jingle while in transit, allowing residents to hear the other serene sounds of the city, like incessant car horns and jack hammering at construction sites, much more clearly.

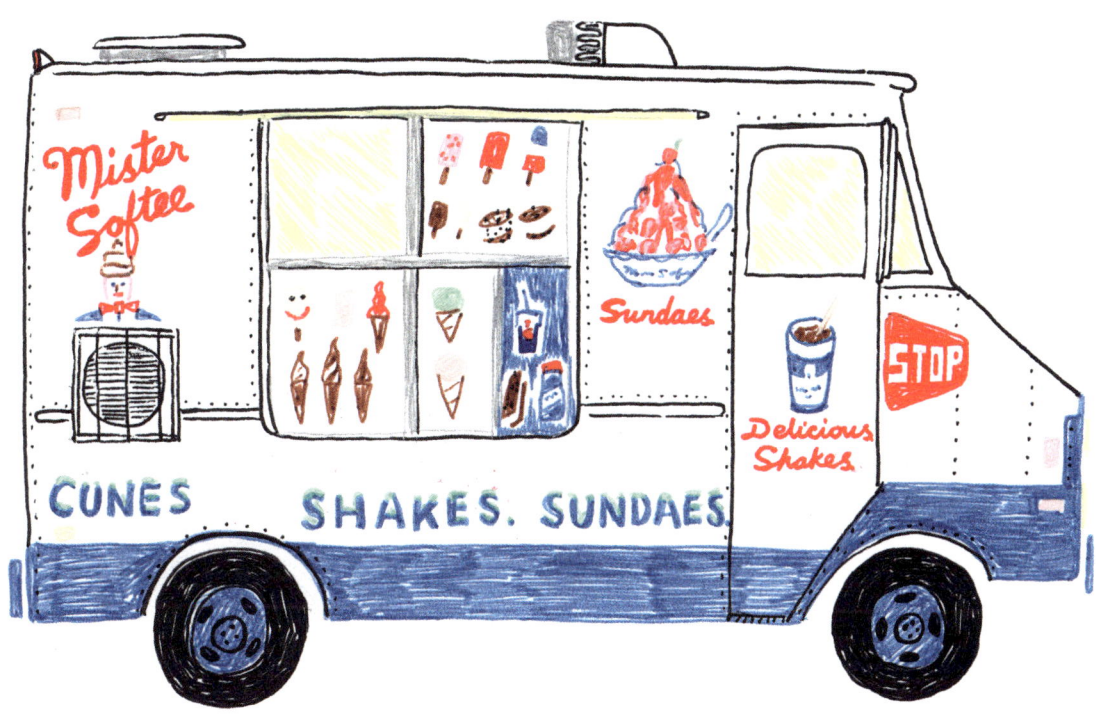

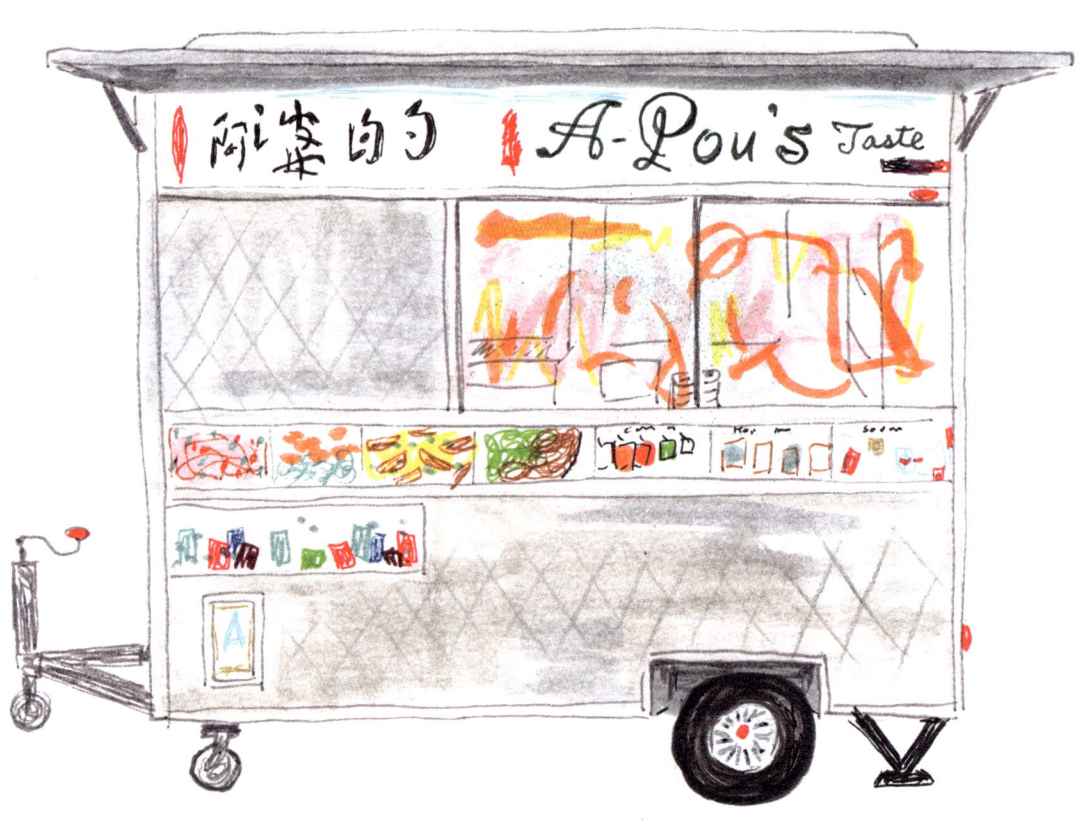

A-Pou's Taste

Yeh Chi Yao, who also goes by Doris, started dreaming of opening a food cart after she moved from Taiwan to New York in 1981. In those days, while walking around Midtown Manhattan, "all you could see were only hot dogs, pizza, peanuts—these three," she recalled in a 2024 video made for *Eater*. "I said, 'Gee, it's very boring!'" She swore then that if she ever got a chance to show New Yorkers what Taiwanese street food tastes like, she'd seize it.

Nearly three decades later, after a career mostly spent in the garment industry, she made good on her word. After seeing an advertisement for a food cart in the newspaper, she contacted the owner—a young man who questioned whether she had the strength necessary to operate it. "You don't know my power," she told him at the time. "Don't judge me." All these years later, the original street cart owner, who calls Doris "big sister," still stops by to see how right she was.

Doris finally started her potsticker cart in 2009, naming it after her grandmother (*a pou* translates to "old lady").

Most often she positioned it somewhere in Manhattan's East Village, and over the years the business gained steam—no doubt aided by the savory-smelling steam used to prepare her potstickers, which are filled with pork, beef, chicken, or vegetables, and then fried. "I call these Chinese Viagra," Doris joked in the *Eater* video while holding up a handful of chives. "There are a lot of vitamins in there."

Though best known for her potstickers, Doris also sells lo mein (what she describes as "Chinese spaghetti") and some soups at her cart. In 2017 she expanded her offerings much further at a new restaurant with the same name, located on Grand Street in Brooklyn's Bushwick neighborhood. Here, in addition to her famous potstickers, Doris cooks up a more robust menu of Taiwanese, Chinese, and pan-Asian options. Though she spends most of her time at the restaurant these days, her original street cart operation is still going strong, selling around a thousand potstickers each day.

INDEX AND VENDOR INFORMATION

INDEX AND VENDOR INFORMATION

BIOGRAPHIES

Joel Holland is an internationally recognized illustrator and hand-letterer living in Manhattan. He can sometimes be found with a hot dog from the Hot Dog King outside the Met, or perhaps buying hard pretzels or vodka sauce in Union Square's Greenmarket. Oh, and beignets on Saturdays. His illustrations have appeared in *The New York Times*, *New York* magazine, and *The New Yorker*, as well as on many book covers and advertisements around the world. He is the author of *NYC Storefronts*, *London Shopfronts*, *Brooklyn Storefronts*, and *Paris Shopfronts*, all published by Prestel.

David Dodge is a freelance writer living in New York City who covers travel, LGBTQ stuff, health and wellness, politics, culture, and more. He is a frequent contributor to *The New York Times* and has had work appear in outlets including *Travel + Leisure*, *Condé Nast Traveler*, *Newsweek*, *USA Today*, and more. His previous books include *NYC Storefronts* and *Brooklyn Storefronts* (both with Joel), as well as *Sassy Planet* and *Category Is: Cocktails!*—all published by Prestel.

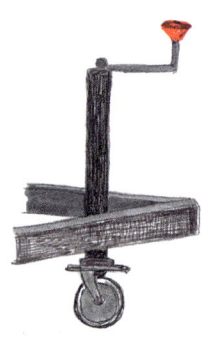

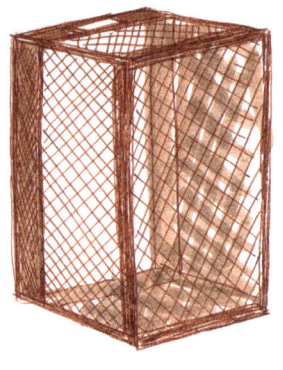

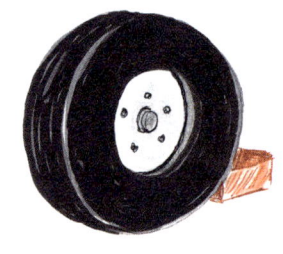

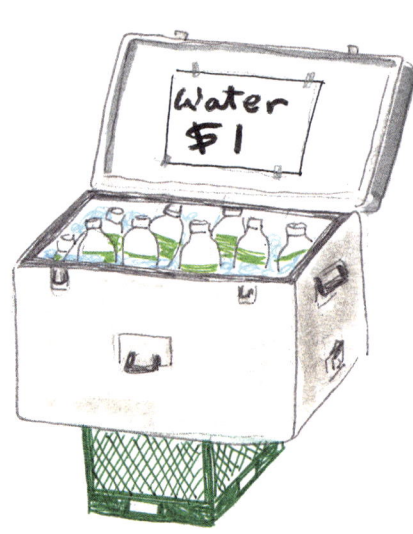

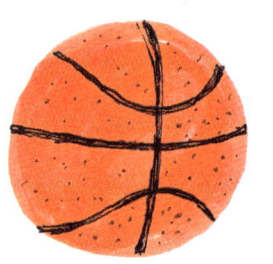

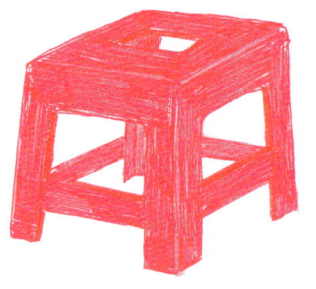

ACKNOWLEDGMENTS

~

JOEL HOLLAND

My deepest gratitude to my family—Ploy, Ella, and Nina. Thank you. I love our life. Thank you to my parents, Blaine and Judy Holland. And to my brother, Stan, and his wife, Sarah, and their sons, Ian and Lars.

I love our team. A special thank you to my editor, Ali Gitlow, for your insight and guidance; to writer David Dodge, for capturing incredible details and giving emotion to each piece; to Alex Stikeleather, designer, who once again made magic; and to Michael Ferut, copyeditor, for your keen eye and attention to detail. I'm so grateful.

Thank you to all of the hustlers working long hours, even in uncomfortable climates and situations, to make a buck—and to make New York the place that it is. Please know you color our city and lives with a unique and invaluable energy.

Thanks to all of you who provided tips from neighborhoods in NYC far and wide, as well as your stories and experiences with so many of these workers.

THANK YOU!

DAVID DODGE

First and foremost, I want to thank the over twenty-three thousand street vendors in New York who play such a vital role in keeping our streets so vibrant—and who give me good reason to walk in this city whenever possible. It was such a treat to learn more about the people behind some of my favorite mobile businesses and food trucks while writing this book. This includes Eugenia, who works with Lani's Farm at the Union Square Greenmarket, who sold me my first-ever carnivorous plant, and Chus, my local fruit-stand guy, whose limes are always far juicer and riper than those at the Whole Foods he sells in front of (sorry, Jeff Bezos).

There are so many street vendors in this book I wouldn't have stumbled across were it not for suggestions made by friends and acquaintances online. There are too many to name here, but thank you to everyone who submitted ideas, introduced us to unique businesses, and helped ensure this book includes vendors from all across the city.

Thank you, of course, to Joel Holland for allowing me to give voice to his beautiful drawings, yet again, in our third book. A million thanks as well to our co-collaborator and editor, Ali Gitlow, for the opportunity to work on another project together—and for your patience and attention to detail as we worked to get the text just right. Thanks to Ali and Michael Ferut for your careful and thorough copyedits. The words are always stronger, in the end, thanks to your work. Thanks as well to Alex Stikeleather, who designed and laid out the book beautifully.

Editorial direction: Ali Gitlow
Copyediting and proofreading: Michael Ferut
Design and typesetting: Alex Stikeleather
Production: Luisa Klose
Separations: Reproline Mediateam, Munich
Printing and binding: DZS GRAFIK, d.o.o., Ljubljana

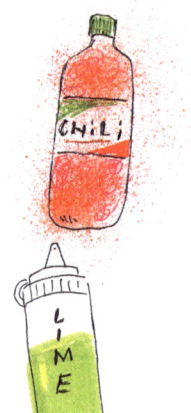

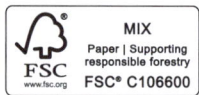

MIX
Paper | Supporting
responsible forestry
FSC® C106600
FSC www.fsc.org

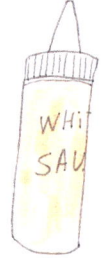

Penguin Random House Verlagsgruppe FSC® N001967

Printed in Slovenia
ISBN 978-3-7913-9372-8
www.prestel.com

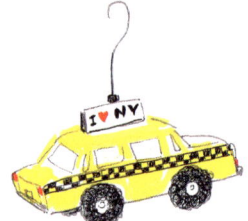

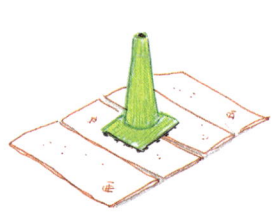

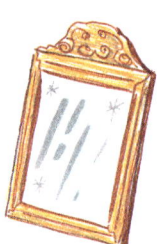

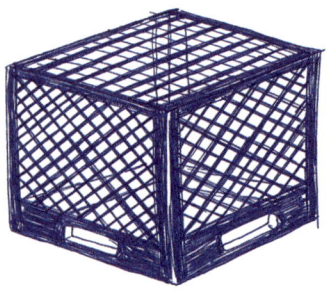

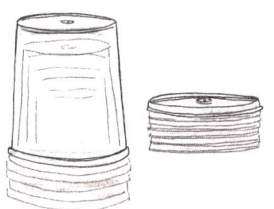

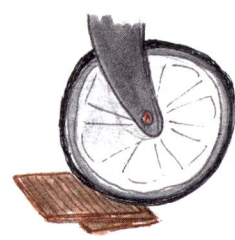